SUPERCHARGED GAS COUPES

Remembering the "Sixties"

Don Montgomery
636 Morro Hills Road
Fallbrook, CA 92028

DEDICATION

To all those who raced or enjoyed the Supercharged Gas Coupes. They all participated in a special portion of drag racing history.

TABLE OF CONTENTS

THE BIG FOUR
"The Big Four" was the name the drag racing newspapers used to refer to the touring A/GS racers K. S. Pittman, John Mazmanian, George Montgomery and Stone-Woods-Cook. Four-car, round robin match races were run at strips in the Midwest, East and South. Later Junior Thompson picked up in John Mazmanian's place and then even later Bob Balogh, followed by Steve Korney, filled the Stone-Woods-Cook spot. The "Big Four" were the first Supercharged Gas Coupe competitors to actually earn a living at drag racing. They got the most publicity, most race dates, and most money of any of the blown gassers for several years.
(Photos courtesy of Ray Tognarelli, Barbara Hamilton Advey, and Charles Strutt)

INTRODUCTION

Drag racing is a difficult subject to cover properly in a single book. The reason is that drag racing includes such a wide spectrum of cars, people and activities it would probably take many books to do justice to the subject. This book is about only one segment of drag racing, the Supercharged Gas Coupes.

The Supercharged Gassers of the 1960's have a special place in the history of drag racing. They were the fastest stock bodied cars in drag racing in the early 1960's. A combination of personalities, publicity and exciting racing elevated the blown gassers to great heights in popularity. Although the racing took place almost thirty years ago, drag racing enthusiasts still remember the cars run by George Montgomery, Stone-Woods-Cook, K. S. Pittman, Big John Mazmanian and many other Supercharged Gas competitors.

The Supercharged Gas class competition began in the 1960 season. The NHRA had decided that a few gas coupe class competitors, by using superchargers, had left their unblown competition "in the dust". In the past the equality between blown and unblown engines had been maintained by an engine displacement or car weight handicap on the supercharged cars. But here for the first time the rules had been written to remove the fastest cars from the popular gas coupe classes and put them in their own classes. It would be three more years before the rules would separate supercharged cars from their unblown competition in the other classes.

The early years of the Supercharged Gas Coupe classes saw many competitors try the "blower route". In fact the classes became popular with numerous entries. Progress was rapid while the guys struggled to get their supercharged horsepower applied to the ground through inadequate tires. One portion of the progress was an almost universal switch to the prewar Willys coupes. But perhaps one of the most important accomplishments the Supercharged Gas Coupe racers made was popularizing the use of the automatic transmission. The racing versions of the early 1950's Hydramatic played a major part in the rapid improvements in performance for the blown coupes and helped open the door to future transmission developments.

Publicity was the most important ingredient in the blown gassers successes of the mid 1960's. The great performances of Stone-Woods-Cook, John Mazmanian, George Montgomery and K. S. Pittman and others made headlines. But the challenges, charges, claims, bragging and sponsor's ads made even bigger headlines. The Supercharged Gas Coupes quickly reached new highs in popularity.

However the number of competitors was beginning to decline. One of the reasons was the increasing costs, especially with the changes to smaller foreign cars and mostly professionally built chassis. Engine developments were also increasing the costs. Another reason for the decline in the blown gassers was the general decline in the number of "hot car" (Roadsters, Altereds, Dragsters) entries in drag racing, while at the same time the number of Stock Class entries were increasing.

In spite of the decline in numbers, the racing was getting better. And in spite of efforts to keep them out, the little foreign cars invaded the Supercharged Gas Coupes. Anglias and Austins quickly put most of the Willys into the background. The exciting, unpredictable and excellent racing by the blown coupes had made them feature performers in match races and show programs. However even though the racing was better than ever, the majority of drag racing's publicity was concentrating on the Funny Cars which had become the fastest stock bodied cars.

The late 1960's were probably the best times for Supercharged Gasser racing. The competition had narrowed down to mostly serious blown gasser racers. The shows and match racing recorded many excellent and exciting races. Competition was strong and racing was often. The new cars were technically advanced and naturally it cost even more to race. And a few racers were successfully making a living running the blown gassers. Some publicity was devoted to the Supercharged Gas Coupes but it was not like it was back in the 1963 to 1966 period.

By 1970 many of the new blown gas cars looked suspiciously like Funny Cars. Naturally the racers had taken advantage of the rapid chassis developments in the Funny Car technology and then used a late model car body such as a Camaro, Barracuda, Mustang, Opel GT or Corvette. Unfortunately the spectators had difficulty telling an AA/GS car from an AA/FC, especially when some of the AA/GS cars ran in Funny Car races.

Although the Supercharged Gas Coupe classes were already fading away the official "term limit" legislation came when the NHRA, in 1970, set up the Professional group (Funny Cars, Fuel Dragsters, Pro Stock) to be the growth direction for the business of drag racing. The blown gassers were left in the Sports racing category.

The next five years saw the number of Supercharged Gassers continually decline as racers moved on to other classes, many to the Professional classes, or retired from drag racing. A few racers continued to compete to the end of CC/GS in 1970, AA/GS in 1973, and BB/GS (renamed AA/GS) in 1975.

The Supercharged Gas Coupe classes had a rich and exciting history. It is full of great performances, controversies, exciting racing and interesting technical improvements. But the important part was all the guys who had both good and bad days, spent money, got a technical education, made friends, had some fun and accomplishments and perhaps those "few moments of glory".

I have tried to mention most of the Supercharged Gas Coupe racers. Unfortunately many of them never, or at least rarely, saw their names in the drag racing newspapers or magazines. This is especially true for the later years as the newspaper reports concentrated on the Professional racing, shows or match races. Some of the racers only ran a blown car for a short time leaving almost no "trace". So I hope that those that were missed will understand that I just could not find anything on them.

In the early days of the classes a large disparity in speeds and E.T.'s existed among the competitors. There were many variations in car, engine and transmission combinations at that time. I have mentioned some of the best speeds and times then. By the late 1960's competition had become so strong that most of the competitors were recording similar speeds and E.T.'s. Part of the reason was that so many competitors were running the same basic combinations. So in the later years I have pointed out the ranges of performances and also the class records.

Throughout this book the classes discussed have been the NHRA classes. Most drag strips used the NHRA classifications. However many of the photos show class letters such as A/MG (AHRA) or A/GB (an independent drag strip). Although many A/GS cars (NHRA) could run B/MG (in AHRA meets) this book will consider only the NHRA classifications so as not to create additional confusion about what class the competitor raced.

So here is the history of the Supercharged Gas Coupes of the 1960's.

Photo courtesy of Jack Coonrod. Photo by Peter Sukalac.

- ACKNOWLEDGEMENTS -

Several years ago I had the pleasure of doing some magazine articles about the gassers in 1960's drag racing. It was fun researching the events, performances and people involved twenty to thirty years ago. The review of newspapers, magazines and photos also helped me clarify my own memories.

This book came about in spite of my "better judgement". That is, I always felt that drag racing was too large and diversified for a book to find enough interested buyers. This book tells the history of only one segment of drag racing, and I hope that readers will find this history interesting. I enjoyed this project - it was great to talk to the racers and hear from racing enthusiasts, and challenging to take all the stories I heard and put them into the correct time periods and clear up some fuzzy or incorrect details from our up to thirty year old memories. It was also fun to do because I enjoy history and I was part of this segment of racing.

Tom Chambliss is due the credit for encouraging me to do this book. After reading my other hot rod books he took the time to encourage me to do this book. He then proceeded to call many racers to get information and photos. He also personally gathered and supplied most of the Northern California info and photos. Tom was involved with the Supercharged Gassers as a chassis builder. He built the chassis for numerous Supercharged Gassers in the Northern California area and even drove either during shakedown testing or competition.

Many racers were kind enough to loan their photographs or albums. In addition, a number of drag racing enthusiasts have loaned photos of the cars from the "good old days" of the blown gassers. I have used both the snapshots, taken by spectators or racers, and photos taken by the strip photographers. In all cases I have credited the photographer (if known) and/or the owner of the photo.

I have greatly appreciated all the help given to me in gathering the data and photos for this book. Thanks are especially extended to:

Gene Adams	Leo Duchaine	Ed Middlebrook
Barbara Advey	Gary Dyer	George Montgomery
Joe Airoso	John Edwards	Gary Newton
Dave Anderson	Eddie Flora	Ron Nunes
Brad Anderson	Paul Frost	Norm Paddack
Joe Andulic	Bruce Gonzales	Don Palfreyman
Ron Arcangeli	Harry Hall	Bob Panella
Wayne Arteaga	Curt Hamilton	Kevin Perry
Bob Balogh	Don Hampton	Billie Petty
Mike Bamber	Mike Hanlon	K. S. Pittman
Mike Bognod	Ernie Hashim	Steve Plueger
Ron Burch	Skip Hess	Bob Plumer
Jim Butler	Vern Hicks	Sherm Porter
Art Carr	Bob Ida	Don Prieto
Greg Castelli	Steve Korney	Phil Quinto
John Chambliss	Mike Kuhl	Terry Rose
Tom Chambliss	Dan Lau	Bob Spar
Erik Chaputa	Anthony Leone	Jeff Storck
Rocky Childs	Don Long	Bob Stroup
Doug Cook	Burt Looney	Charles Strutt
Jack Coonrod	Phil Lukens	Junior Thompson
Len Cottrell	Jim Mack	Ray Tognarelli
Jeg Coughlin	Gary Mallicoat	Don Toia
Dean Court	Ross Martin	Verne Tomlinson
Pat Dakin	Terry McHardy	Tom Willford
Jim Davis	Claudie Meador	Steve Woods
Larry Dixon	Ken Menz	

A special note of appreciation for my wife Claire who spent more than twenty years driving the push car for our race cars (with no retirement benefits) and now had to relive it as she helped get this book together.

By 1959 the Gas Coupe classes were being dominated by supercharged cars. This 1959 NHRA Nationals photo shows two of the fastest Eastern A/G Supercharged Coupes and leaders in the move to Willys in the Gas classes. The '33 Willys (No. 269 A/G) was George Montgomery's (Ohio). He won the class and Little Eliminator at the Nationals with a Cadillac engine and La Salle transmission power train. The Willys' time of 124.65 mph became the initial record for the new A/GS class in 1960. The '40 Willys (No. 264 A/G) in the far lane was Pennsylvania's Jack Kulp. It was Olds powered and it had hit speeds in the 125 mph area. Note the popularity of Moon disc (hubcaps) on the wheels. (Photo courtesy of George Montgomery)

SUPERCHARGED CLASSES - HOW AND WHY

In 1960 the National Hot Rod Association (NHRA) took the unusual action of setting up special classes just to remove a very small number of racers from the traditional dual purpose hot rod classes. The new classes were for gas coupe competitors using superchargers. The unusual fact is that while the gas coupes with blowers were separated from unsupercharged coupes no such separation was made in the other classes. That is interesting because by 1959 the number of supercharged engines in drag racing was skyrocketing. However most of them were in dragsters, modified coupes or roadsters. Only small numbers of fast blown gas coupes were competing in 1959.

Drag racers in the 1950's had been very slow to apply the existing supercharger technology to their racing engines. Superchargers had indeed proven themselves years before. Almost 40 years earlier engine designers like Harry Miller and the Duesenberg Bros. had shown the advantages of supercharging. As an example, Harry Miller's little blown 91 cubic inch, 8 cylinder, engine produced over 200 HP, 2 plus HP/Cu.In., in the late 1920's. Supercharged engines were the money winners in Indianapolis style racing. In Europe the 1930's Grand Prix races were absolutely dominated by the blown creations built by Mercedes-Benz, Auto Union, Maserati and Alfa-Romeo. And most hot rodders, and especially the Air Force veterans of World War II, were familiar with the use of superchargers on all the high performance aircraft. It is obvious that the information about the advantages of supercharging was readily available to all interested drag racers.

There were some supercharged efforts at the dry lakes meets of the 1930's and 1940's. Hot rodders like Bill and Tom Spalding, Don Blair, Barney Navarro, Jack Engle and the Morimoto Bros. experimented with centrifugal or Roots (positive displacement) blowers. In spite of the fact that blowers helped set records the combination of the classification rules against superchargers, the costs and the technical problems kept most hot rodders from adding a blower to their engine.

The Lakes rules generally required that supercharged cars move up a class. That could mean a blown 250 cubic inch engine would compete against a naturally aspirated 350 cubic inch engine. It was not easy to compensate for that handicap in straightaway racing.

The technical problems were even greater with only a limited selection of superchargers, manifolds and drive setups available. The first widely distributed blower was the McCulloch centrifugal, V-belt driven unit built from 1936 to 1940 for the Ford-Mercury flatheads. They offered improved performance but with only 2 to 4 psi boost they did not really meet racing requirements. In the 1950's an Italian made

Roots blower, Italmeccanica (later S.C.O.T.), was produced. It gave good performance (6 psi) and was used for racing. The best part was that manifolds and V-belt drives were made for Ford flatheads, Olds and Cadillac engines. Then in the 1950's McCulloch produced a new centrifugal blower for automotive use. It was even sold on new cars built by Studebaker and Ford. The blower put out about 5 to 7 psi and even had a two speed arrangement to improve the low speed performance.

The most readily available superchargers were the positive displacement (Roots) units found on General Motors diesel engines. War surplus dealers had lots of them. Three sizes were available, the 3-71, the 4-71 and the then considered huge 6-71. But fabrication and machine work was required to adapt a "Gimmy" blower because there were almost no manifolds or drive kits available until the mid 1950's.

Early efforts generally used the small 3-71 blower or the larger 4-71 units. Remember that most of the 1940's hot rodders had engines of only 220 to 300 cubic inches; a 296 cubic inch Merc was considered to be a BIG engine. Thus the smaller blowers were more than adequate. The experiences of the 1940's and early 1950's supercharger enthusiasts ranged from record breaking performances to destroyed engines. The extra strain from 10 to 15 psi boost, and combustion detonation, often resulted in burned pistons, blown head gaskets or trashed bearings. But if the combination was right the blown engine ran unbelievably great.

The early 1950's saw record Lakes blown performances by competitors like Tom Beatty, Tom Cobbs and Harold Osborn. But perhaps the performances of Bruce Crower and "Big" Bill Edwards at the 1954 Bonneville meet really helped hot rodders notice supercharging. Bruce's stock-bodied Hudson sedan used a 4-71 blown Chrysler to record 157.34 mph while the big '53 Ford pickup run by Bill Edwards used a GMC blown Cad engine to hit 151.00 mph.

Serious supercharged drag racing efforts really accelerated in 1955. As might be expected it started in the dragster classes. The top speed of 149.25 mph in 1955 was recorded by Calvin Rice using Doug Hartell's front blower, Chrysler. But Art Chrisman's unblown Chrysler also recorded the 149.25 mph speed and unblown dragsters were winning most of the races. Early in 1956 Ernie Hashim's blown Chrysler dragster set a world's record at 153.91 mph and then bumped it to 155.20 mph in July. At the NHRA Nationals Ken Lindley's blown Chrysler recorded a world record breaking speed of 159.01 mph.

By late 1956 lots of drag racers were on the blower bandwagon. Just a few of them were Jack Hart-Dawson Hadley, Tony Nancy, Tom Sparks, Jim Cassedy, Todd

Rawleigh, John Wolf-Bud Fox, Teresa-Cerneka, Waterworth-Morris, Don Montgomery and Art Chrisman-Frank Cannon. One new blower enthusiast in late 1956 is of particular interest to the history of the blown gas coupes. Howard Johansen mounted a reworked McCulloch centrifugal supercharger on the Chevy V-8 in his personal '55 Bel Air and used a Howard cam (naturally) to set a Santa Ana strip record at 110.71 mph.

Although the dragsters of Ernie Hashim, Calvin Rice, Todd Rawleigh and Ken Lindley were turning speeds near or over the records by January of 1957 they were not dominating drag racing. Most of the meets were being won by the unblown dragsters whose tuners had learned to use the chemical supercharger (Nitromethane). Blower technology was still in the learning stage of combinations of blower pressures, compression ratios, cam timings and the fuel supply. Most competitors were also going down the weakest part, breakage path - blown head gaskets to burned pistons to destroyed bearings to broken cranks, etc.

Drag racers were stunned in early 1957 when many strip managers and the NHRA decided to ban fuel (alcohol and nitro) and offer only gas classes. Suddenly the chemical supercharger was gone (history records that it really never left). The best gas dragsters at that time were recording times in the 135 to 140 mph area. Most of the fuel dragsters switched back to gas, but not all of them. Competitors like Don Garlits continued to develop their fuel dragsters and reap such great publicity that the NHRA eventually had to "unban" the exciting nitro fueled dragsters.

While the former "fuel mixing" dragster owners were working out engine tuning combinations for gasoline, the blower guys were breaking the records. Since most of the blown engines had been depending on boost pressure more that nitromethane, the switch back to gas did not seem to hurt them as much as it hurt the unblown cars. In the first four months Calvin Rice moved the record to 142 mph and then Ken Lindley pushed it up to 146.07 mph. Both dragsters had front mounted 6-71 blown Chrysler engines. Although the supercharged cars were recording the best top speeds, the lowest E.T.'s and race victories were still predominately going to the unblown competitors.

The most important effect of the fuel ban was to encourage the development of supercharging technology. All out efforts to increase horsepower by many different racers produced impressive results. One result was that virtually every top dragster soon was "sporting" a blower.

The dragster builders were not the only guys who saw the potential of a supercharger. By the summer of 1957 a few of the street class coupes and sedans were clocking fast times using "blown" engines. The Glen Ward-Carl Taylor (So. Calif.) '34 Ford (Cad) had recorded 118.11 mph in A/G while Gene Adams' (So.

Calif.) '50 Olds hit a B/G time of 112.77 mph. The Eddie and Junior Thompson (So.Calif.) '41 Studebaker (Chevy) also ran B/G at 108.57 mph. George Montgomery (Ohio) '34 Ford (Cad) set records at the A.T.A.A. Nationals with a top A/G time of 115.38 mph. Around the country racers were experimenting with GMC, Latham, McCulloch and SCOT blowers on all types of cars. Johnny Lovelean (Texas) had a '32 Ford with a Latham blown Buick (A/G - 108.43 mph) and George Woolever (Oklahoma) dropped a 4-71 boosted Chrysler in his big and heavy 1941 Lincoln Continental to record a good 100.67 mph speed.

By the end of 1957 perhaps several hundred competitors at the drags all over the country were using supercharged engines. Most of them were street model coupes, sedans or sports cars using the readily available McCulloch centrifugal blower. Latham axial blowers were also used on some of the Gas Coupe class competitors cars while the competition class cars, Dragsters and Roadsters, were generally using the GMC diesel blowers. Most of the top performing gas coupes were also using GMC blowers, producing boost pressures from 12 to 15 psi. The majority of the McCulloch and Latham blowers were putting out about 7 psi although a few competitors were able to get up into the 10 psi area by modifying the McCulloch unit. Since horsepower and boost pressure were almost directly related it is easy to see why the GMC blowers became the standard drag racing blower. Naturally as the engines grew in displacement, the interest in the 4-71 blower lagged and virtually everyone switched to the larger 6-71 supercharger.

Although probably more than 99% of the supercharged gas class competitors used the GMC series Roots blowers, or improved versions, the contribution of the McCulloch, and the Latham, superchargers should be acknowledged. These units were designed to improve street performance and hopefully to gain broad acceptance by the motoring public. They were not designed for racing. The McCulloch centrifugal supercharger was introduced in 1953 with installation kits to fit most of the popular Detroit cars and trucks. Studebaker and Kaiser installed them on their more expensive cars in an effort to keep up with the rest of the industry. Remember the late 1950's were marked by an all-out horsepower race. That horsepower race even encouraged Ford to buy especially designed McCulloch superchargers for installation on their optional 300 hp engines in 1957. And by no mere coincidence blown Ford stock cars did exceedingly well in the NASCAR and USAC stock car races.

Many performance enthusiasts purchased a McCulloch supercharger to get better performance. McCulloch said that the blower, which was limited to 5 psi boost, would give a 33% horsepower increase. No doubt most of guys were happy to get a quick 33% gain, but after racing around town and at the local drag strip some of them wanted even better performance. It was obvious that more boost pressure could offer better performance. More rpm would accomplish this. It didn't take long for racers to figure out modifications such as locking the pulley in the high blower ratio. Now instead of the McCulloch limit of 30,000 rpm the superchargers were getting an impeller speed of almost 50,000 rpm. Failure rates were high and McCulloch's reputation suffered because the blower was not designed to be worked that hard.

Even though McCulloch blowers were not used on most of Supercharged Coupes of the 1960's, they should get some of the credit for popularizing supercharging of drag racing engines. Many drag racers had an early education to supercharging with a McCulloch blower. Just a few of them were Eddie and Junior Thompson, Howard Johansen, Art Chrisman-Frank Cannon, George Montgomery, Jim Cassedy, Bill Waddill and Hayden Proffit-Gary DuBach; not to mention the guys who raced against McCulloch blown cars. And - what happened to McCulloch? Robert McCulloch went on to found Lake Havasu City (with the London Bridge) while the supercharger's name became Paxton, and it is still in production today, almost 40 years later.

Gas Coupe and Sedan classes had an exciting year in 1958 and blown cars created most of it. Although rules varied from strip to strip most of the blown cars were running A/G or B/G. Probably the first shocker to Southern California A/G competitors was the Glen

Ward-Carl Taylor new '35 Willys (Cad) which hit a best of 123.90 mph at the beginning of summer. George Montgomery's '34 Ford (Cad) recorded a best of 126.40 mph at the A.T.A.A. Nationals while Jack Kulp (Pennsylvania) showed Eastern drag racers what a blower can do with his '39 Willys (Olds) at 123.00 mph. Eddie and Junior Thompson now had their own McCulloch blown Chevy for their Studebaker and were soon hitting B/G times around 108 mph. Doug Cook (So. Calif.) joined the B/G competition by joining his '37 Chevy with Howard Johansen's blown Chevy engine (108.17 mph). Doug also drove the Al Hirshfield-Howard Johansen's '40 Studebaker sedan (Bln-Chevy) to speeds of 112 mph and the '40 Willys of J.W. Richter and Cook (111 mph). All three Howard built B/G cars had 4-71 blown Chevys. One of the fastest B/G cars in 1958 was the big '50 Olds coupe run by Dick Harryman, John Edwards and K.S. Pittman. A blown Olds engine pushed the big car to a 116.73 mph clocking. Dick Harryman, with the Harryman, Frank and Brown dragster, had broken the world's gas top speed record with a run of 157.61 mph earlier in 1958. Other Southern California gas coupe competitors with supercharged engines included Hayden Profitt-Gary DuBach (McCulloch blown B/G '37 Chevy), the Roach-Torgeson A/G Model A sedan (Olds) and the '57 Chevy (McCulloch blown) run by Gordon Funk.

The first cam grinders "ad war" occurred in 1958. The participants were the Howard, Iskenderian and Engle cam firms. It did not get the publicity the mid-

Glen Ward and Carl Taylor, from Southern California, could be considered the founders of the blown Willys gassers in the Southern California area. After setting the 1957 NHRA A/G record with a '34 Ford coupe the 402" blown Cadillac engine was hidden under the hood of this stock appearing 1935 Willys. By the fourth weekend (11-10-57) the Willys had set strip records of 123.28 mph and 12.00 sec. Later in 1958 the Willys was sold to C.J. Hart. Both C.J. and his wife Peggy blasted down their own Santa Ana drag strip (as shown in this photo) in the blown gasser. Peggy recorded a 127.62 mph time with it in 1959.
(Photo courtesy of Jerry Hart)

This neat maroon street rod was the first record holder in the C/GS class. Doug Cook (So. Calif.) teamed with Howard Johansen (Howards Cams) to win the 1959 NHRA Nationals with a speed of 105.88 mph. When the new Supercharged Gas Coupe classes were set up in 1960 the winning A/G, B/G and C/G records were transferred to A/GS, B/GS and C/GS because all three classes had been won by blown cars. Doug raced his '37 Chevy at both the Lakes (147 mph) and Drags in addition to driving various Willys' and Studebakers for Howard. (Photo courtesy of Doug Cook)

1960's ad war received but it did set the stage for it. After the Thompson Bros. went from Howard to Iskenderian and Doug Cook switched to Howard, the two cam grinders took turns proclaiming their guy was faster and the other guy afraid to race. Naturally Jack Engle was not reluctant to advertise the performances of the Harryman-Edwards-Pittman Olds. Drag strip managers like C. J. Hart and Mickey Thompson were quick to offer a $50 Savings Bond award in B/G to take advantage of the interest. The results of these B/G meets naturally led to more ads. When C/G competitors asked for a $50 Bond meet the result was the Doug Cook and the Thompson Bros. cars, weighted into C/G, racing for the $50 Bond (worth $37.50 in cash). When it came to cash prizes in those gas classes it appeared that unblown cars need not apply. Incidently the "ad war" was carried out in the issues of Drag News, the only drag racing, bi-weekly newspaper then with national coverage.

Unlike 1957 when the few Supercharged Gas Coupes showed record potential, 1958 saw the future domination of the gas coupe classes by supercharged engines. The top blown A/G competitors were running 120-126 mph, while the 9.0 lbs/cubic inch, or more, blown B/G cars were hitting solid 108 to 116 mph speeds. In general, unblown cars were running about 8-15 mph slower than the top blown cars.

The publicity the gas coupes had received in 1958 was almost immediately converted into new competition. New cars and names appeared in the faster classes. But if it didn't have a blower, forget it.

The 1959 season got a BIG send off in January when the new K.S. Pittman, Ron Scrima, Gene Adams and John Edwards '41 Willys coupe recorded an A/G time of 124.19 mph. Pat O'Brien and John Holthaus debuted a dual McCulloch blown, Chrysler powered '41 Willys with A/G speeds to 121 mph. Other Southern California B/G competitors turning good gas coupe speeds were Doug Cook-Jerry Johansen ('40 Studebaker - Chevy), the Thompson Bros. ('41 Studebaker - Chevy), Stol-Lawrence (Chevy) and the Tim Woods-Dick Harryman '42 Studebaker with Olds power. Visiting B/G racers to Southern Cal strips included Jimmy Nix' (Oklahoma) '40 Ford sedan - Chevy and Arlen Vanke (Ohio). Good performances were being recorded all over the country. Texas had the Curt Carroll Olds powered A/G Model A coupe, the Evans-McCary-Roberts blown Olds and Phil Parker's '40 Willys (Chevy) A/G coupe (built by the Dragmaster crew).

The Hix Bros. A/G Olds from Kansas, Oklahoma's Jim Love with his A/G Chrysler powered '34 Ford pickup, Jim and Wayne Burt (A/G - Oklahoma) and Mike Marinoff's C/G '55 Chevy (Latham blown Chevy) from Wisconsin were all recording excellent speeds in their areas.

Back in the East the Hammer-Czerniak '32 Ford A/G sedan (Olds) and Vern Rowley's B/G Chevy were winning in New Jersey. North Carolina had a strong A/G competitor in Wayne Shepard (Olds). Maryland's Wilton Zaiser exceeded 120 mph in A/G with a supercharged Olds engine as did A/G competitor Ed Jepsen in New Jersey. Jack Kulp's '41 Willys A/G was perhaps Pennsylvania's fastest gas coupe and Ohio's George Montgomery A/G (Willys-Cad) recorded apparently the fastest gas coupe time in 1959 at 132.65 mph. Wisconsin also had a 120.00 mph speed recorded by the A/G coupe of Ruso Michalek while Michigan's Bill Waddill had a fast A/G Henry J with two McCulloch's on a Chrysler.

In Northern California Al Del Porto was going over 120 mph with his A/G '41 Willys pickup (Chevy) as was the Bruce Kaiser '35 Willys coupe (Chrysler). Another top Northern Cal A/G '40 Willys was the Richter-Masters (Olds) which hit 127 mph.

Southern California gained many new blown cars while the existing cars played "musical" classes. Howard and Doug Cook jumped between B/G and C/G as did the Thompson Bros. The Pittman-Edwards Willys ran three classes - A/G, B/G and C/G. Some of the new entries included: Ed Weddle, Mike Nichols, and John Peters - B/G and C/G Willys sedan (Chevy); Joe Pisano's D/G '55 Chevy (his Bonneville racer), Dan Brechtel's A/G Willys (formerly Ward-Taylor), Verlon Gaines' A/G (Cad), Jim Dunn's A/G Henry J (Chevy) and Don Montgomery's '41 Willys (Chrysler).

Naturally these were only some of the many blown gas coupes running in 1959, but the point is that the gas classes from A to D were being dominated by blown cars. The top A/G cars were recording speeds of 125 to 132 mph while the B/G and C/G competitors were in the 115 to 120 mph area. The major events generally were won by supercharged cars including those owned by George Montgomery (A/G), Doug Cook (C/G), Ed Coughlin (D/G) at the NHRA Nationals and Jim Butler (A/G) and Billings-White (B/G) at the AHRA Nationals.

As 1959 came to a close the problem of superchargers on gas coupes came to a head. Did George Montgomery or K. S. Pittman have a problem? No! The problem was the 90% of the gas class racers were hopelessly outclassed by the blown cars and remember that in 1959 the gas class cars were supposed to be street driven cars. All legal items were required. In addition, they had to start, race and return to the pits without push cars. Most of the competitors indeed had street type coupes with a "full race" engine. The weekly local drag meet usually had fairly equal competition in the A/G, B/G and C/G classes. But equality disappeared when a blown car signed in. So the local strips found that the 90% of their gas class customers were complaining about the 10%. So when the subject came up at the 1960 rules committee meeting, the strip representatives were quick to ask for rule changes to solve the supercharger problem in the Gas Coupe and Sedan classes.

Hot Rod Magazine published an article by Bob Pendergast, right after the NHRA Nationals, that basically said that the big news at the Nationals was superchargers. It said that some competitors had even designated certain classes as "Blower" classes.

"Blower" classes were classes where unblown cars were not competitive. The article said that "Blower" classes happen because the weight breaks were too close to compensate for the added horsepower. Was the NHRA aware of this situation? The answer is Yes; remember that the then Editor of Hot Rod Magazine, who approved the magazine article, was NHRA chief Wally Parks.

The 1960 NHRA rules committee made three major recommended changes to the Gas Coupe/Sedan rules. They were:

1. Return the class to "Dual purpose street machines". That meant the cars had to have all street legal equipment - lights, mufflers, upholstery and etc. No push cars would be allowed.

2. New automatic transmission gas coupe classes were formed.

3. Supercharged Gas Coupes would advance a class, as previously required, but would also have an additional weight penalty.

When the 1960 NHRA Official Drag Rules were published the dual purpose rule and the automatic transmission classes rule were there but the supercharged engine rule had been changed. Instead of continuing the method of handicapping blown cars with added weight, the final rules put the supercharged cars into separate classes and thus returned the gas coupe classes (A/G, B/G, etc.) to the unblown cars. The three new classes were named A/Gas Supercharged, B/Gas Supercharged and C/Gas Supercharged. Interestingly the only supercharged cars with their own classes were the gas coupes. All other classes including Dragsters, Altereds and Street Roadsters continued the practice of advancing a class as a handicap.

So what happened to the supercharged rules between the rules committee meeting and the final rules? It is probable that the top NHRA management in Los Angeles made the change. The rules committee was composed of NHRA Divisional representatives and NHRA sanctioned drag strip representatives. In 1959 the NHRA listed 74 sanctioned drag strips, located from California to Maine. But many of the major strips did not use NHRA sanction. Strips at Union Grove (Wisc.), Cordova (Ill.), Great Bend (Kansas), Minneapolis Dragways (Minn.), Alton (Ill.), and Lancaster (Penn.) were just a few of the major strips not running under NHRA sanction. And in California none of the major strips ran under the NHRA banner. Every week Supercharged Gas Coupes were blowing away unblown competitors at Lions (Long Beach), San Gabriel, San Fernando, Bakersfield, Riverside, Half Moon Bay, Fremont or Cotati drag strips. None of these were NHRA sanctioned. What this meant was that the rules committee did not have the input from the strips where most of the supercharged coupes were running. This was where top NHRA management was able to help solve the problem. Los Angeles was the NHRA's

Although Gene Adams (So. Calif.) had many dragster successes, his 1950 Olds 88 is probably the best remembered of all of his race cars. After Gene added a V-belt driven 4-71 blower to the Olds engine the "88" set the Santa Ana record up to 112.77 mph (8-4-57) and the NHRA B/G record at 111.24 mph. Note that Gene's 1957 record was faster than the initial B/GS 1960 record based on the 1959 B/G winning speed (109.89 mph). One photo shows Gene with Ron Scrima (who later built many gasser chassis - Exhibition Engineering) and Gary Adams at the NHRA Nationals. Gene's Olds is shown racing the Hamilton-Alexander '37 Chevy (352" Chrysler power) at Santa Ana. Although the Chevy was about 800 lbs. lighter both cars were in the HO (heavy coupe, overhead valve) class. The Chevy was a previous class record holder.
(Photos courtesy of Gene Adams)

home town and the NHRA leaders were well aware of local developments. After dominating the NHRA Nationals the blown cars were going faster and becoming more numerous. The decision was made in Los Angeles to separate the blown cars into their own classes. The initials for the three Supercharged Gas Coupe classes were A/GS, B/GS and C/GS. The weight per cubic inch of engine displacement breaks were set at:

A = 0 - 8.59; B = 8.60 - 10.59 and C = 10.60 and up.

Even though a large number of drag strips did not run NHRA classes the idea of Supercharged Gas Coupe classes seemed to be well accepted. Perhaps it was because the supercharged classes appeared to be racers classes as compared to the Gas Coupe classes where 95% of the competitors were hopped-up street coupes. In fact many strips ran "hot-cars", including Supercharged Gas Coupes, in separate lines from the Gas Coupes and Stock Cars. Generally the hot-cars got preferential treatment. Naturally there were fewer blown gas coupes than there were regular Gas class competitors. But virtually all the supercharged efforts were "full-race" efforts. And in fact many names that appear in the history of the Supercharged Gas Coupes will also be found in the records of other classes like Pro-Stock, Funny Car and Dragsters in later years, or still today. In addition many of the guys have made their living in the racing industry.

So in 1960 the NHRA set up Supercharged Gas Coupe classes because a few guys were going too fast.

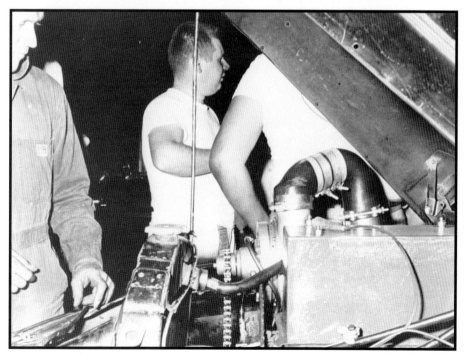

The first B/GS class record holder was this '41 Studebaker raced by Eddie and Junior Thompson (So. Calif.). It was the 1959 NHRA Nationals B/G winning time of 109.89 mph that was the initial B/GS record. Eddie bought the Studebaker on Howard Johansen's suggestion and the brothers raced in B/G using a McCulloch blown Chevy built by Howard. Later they built their own McCulloch blown Chevy with Iskenderian's help. Studebaker Champions, like this one, were briefly popular. Although the Thompson Bros., Tim Woods and Al Hirshfield-Jerry Johansen had successes with the Studebakers it was only a matter of time before they all had switched to Willys coupes. Note the single row, roller chain drive on the McCulloch blower. (Photos courtesy of Junior Thompson)

The K. S. Pittman-John Edwards '41 Willys was a legal street coupe in 1959. It had no lettering and only a small B&M decal on the windwing. It also had white-wall tires; yes there were white-wall M & H slicks. The Pittman-Edwards team made Southern California Gas Coupe competitors take notice when they used a Gene Adams engine to hit 124.19 mph and 12.05 sec. in A/G class (1-18-59). After that smaller 305" and 327" Olds engines were used to compete in B/G with speeds up to 120 mph. (Photo courtesy of Junior Thompson)

Most of the gassers in 1960 were like this '38 Chevy owned by Jim Walls (Missouri). Jim had put his blown Chevy engine into a basically stock Chevy sedan to go racing. The money went into the engine; the car was cheap. That is it was cheap until parts started breaking (axles, transmissions, etc.) or handling problems surfaced. This is the way most guys got into drag racing. Incidently Jim built his own blower chain drive. (Photos courtesy of Wayne Arteaga)

The first A/G record holder was George Montgomery's '33 Willys. When the record was set the Willys looked as it appeared in the photo on Page 10. In 1960 it looked like this photo at the Thompson Raceway (Ohio). Note that the entire car has been raised by 9 to 10 inches. The stock parallel spring suspension in the front had been replaced with "coil over" springs. Also "Mag" wheels were used to mount the M & H slicks. Almost all the top gasser competitors engaged in a height race beginning about 1960. The object was to raise the center of gravity of the car in an effort to increase traction. Although traction was improved, safety concerns about these "top heavy" gassers careening down the strips resulted in height limit rules. Later, as tires and chassis improved, the cars were moved closer to the ground. (Photo courtesy of George Montgomery - Photo by Candid Classics)

THE FIRST YEARS

- 1 9 6 0 -

Competition in the Supercharged Gas Coupe classes started developing slowly in early 1960. The limited amount of competition was due to the small quantity of Supercharged Gas Coupes around and the limited number of strips running NHRA rules. Both of these items were soon changed. In 1960 the NHRA embarked on an aggressive expansion program that included regional championship and record meets and a national points championship program. Both the number of NHRA sanctioned drag strips and the number of major drag meets were expanded. These major national and regional events naturally attracted the attention of the most active competitors including some who jumped into the new Supercharged Gas Coupe classes. The NHRA started these new programs in April, 1960.

But even with the new NHRA programs, Supercharged Gas Coupe competition was still scarce. It was not because there were not any fast cars, because there were. The problem was there were rarely two Supercharged Gas Coupes in the same class at the same strip and on the same day. And it wasn't just that they were avoiding each other, it was that one might be in Dayton, Ohio, another in Morton, Texas and yet another might be in Los Angeles, California.

The top A/GS performances in the first half of 1960 included those by: George Montgomery (Ohio) 133.13 mph, Curt Carroll (Texas) 131.88 mph, Ollie Olsen (Florida) 131.00 mph, Richter & Masters (No. Calif.) 127.89 mph, Burt Looney (Oklahoma) 127.10 mph, Jim Butler & Weldon Day (Texas) 126.23 mph, Bob Egizi (So. Calif.) 125.69 mph, Roach & Torgeson (So. Calif.) 125.17 mph, Jack Kulp (Pennsylvania) 123.34 mph, and Al MacKenzie (Illinois) 121.62 mph.

Some of the fastest B/GS cars were those entered by: K. S. Pittman & John Edwards (So. Calif.) 124.82 mph, Wilton Zaiser (Maryland) 122.61 mph, Doug Cook-Howard Cams (So. Calif.) 121.85 mph, Palmer Lazarus (Illinois) 121.62 mph, Mike Marinoff (Wisconsin) 120.81 mph, Junior Thompson (So. Calif.) 120.48 mph, Gasmaster (So. Calif.) 120.70 mph, Don Montgomery (So. Calif.) 119.52 mph, Dennis Baca (No. Calif.) 119.52 mph, Mickey Hart & Gary Cox (Ohio) 119.04 mph, Dick Harryman & Tim Woods (So. Calif.) 118.42 mph and Gene Vian (Oklahoma) 118.00 mph.

Top speeds in the C/GS class included cars run by: K. S. Pittman & John Edwards (So. Calif.) 125.00 mph, Doug Cook & Howard Cams (So. Calif.) 119.78 mph, Junior Thompson (So. Calif.) 118.80 mph, Jack Bayer & Frank Freitas (So. Calif.) 118.11 mph, Mike Marinoff (Wisconsin) 115.83 mph, Ed Weddle-Mike Nichols-

John Peters (So. Calif.) 115.23 mph, Interstate Sandblasting (So. Calif.) 114.21 mph, Glen Lawson (So. Calif.) 115.00 mph, Bill's Garage (So. Calif.) 113.94 mph, Sam Gellner (Ohio) 113.63 mph, Frank Billings & Don White (Kansas) 110.15 mph, Ron Vito (Washington D.C.) 109.75 mph and Jim Anderson (Penn.) 109.75 mph.

It is impossible to really compare the elapsed times (E.T.) because the different strips varied greatly, probably due to both the quality of the timers and the traction of the track starting area. For example the top A/GS cars recorded E.T.'s from 10.86 to 12.60 seconds with some cars recording E.T.'s varying up to 1.0 seconds from strip to strip. The best of the C/GS cars were recording E.T.'s from 11.01 to 12.46 seconds. It must be noted that some of the quick times and fast speeds recorded by B/GS and C/GS cars may have been made running at a local strip where no verification of the car weight was made. The best way to get an accurate picture of the E.T.'s that Supercharged Gas Coupes were achieving is to review the NHRA records. In July of 1960 the E.T. records were 11.67 sec. (A/GS), 11.51 sec. (B/GS) and 12.08 sec. (C/GS). Remember that these records were set only during record sessions and were not necessarily the quickest times for those, or other cars. But the times show the E.T. range the quicker cars were actually running.

Drag racers always knew that gearing and traction were prime ingredients for successful E.T. times. But "knowing" and "having" can be two separate things. Gearing was a major problem. Most of the Olds, Cad, Chrysler or other large engine cars used the 1937-39 Cadillac three-speed manual transmission, while Chevy engine cars usually had a three- or four-speed Chevy transmission or an early Ford transmission. Automatic transmissions were just beginning to be successfully used in supercharged cars in 1960. The problem was that the combination of low gear and too much horsepower produced a lot of tire spin, especially on the A/GS cars. One solution was to do as the faster competition classes were doing, start in second gear. This might solve the tire spin problem but the engine could bog down or the acceleration might be too slow. The four-speed hydro had similar traction problems but the smooth application of power seemed to work better than the manual transmissions.

Actually the critical point of the problem was traction. There were two parts to the traction problem but the most important was the "slicks" (tires with a flat no-tread surface). Prior to 1959 the only slicks available were recaps using passenger car or racing tire casings. Some of the best known recap slick builders were Inglewood, Moxley, A-1 and Bruce's. When

M&H released all new racing slicks in 1959 a big improvement in traction was recorded especially by the top fuel dragsters. The widest treads in 1960 were about 9" wide. The heavy rubber layers on the edges and the casing shape dictated a design inflation pressure in the 30 psi area. Remember these tires were bias-ply tires, not radials, so the casings were very rigid. The result was a tire footprint only about 4" long and about 9" wide. The traction was the best ever seen but absolutely nothing like today's tires.

The other component of the traction problem was the static and transferred weight on the rear wheels. Interestingly the lowest class cars, with heavy weights in the rear, to make class, came up with the best combinations as evidenced by their more consistent performances. It was not uncommon for C/GS competitors to be recording E.T.'s very close to the A/GS times at a particular meet even when going 5 - 8 mph slower. Then on another day and another drag strip the same A/GS cars would be as much as one second quicker than the C/GS cars. It is easy to see the problem when the static weight on the rear wheels is compared. The typical A/GS Willys had about 1300 lbs. static weight on the rear wheels while an equivalent C/GS Willys would have about 1800 to 1900 lbs. The difference was weight added in the rear to make the 10.6 lbs/cu.in. regulations. So the combination of perhaps 20% less horsepower and 40 - 50% better traction helped the C/GS cars hit more consistent E.T.'s.

Starting in 1959 the competitors worked to reduce tire spin by increasing the weight transfer. It was accomplished by raising the car's center of gravity (C.G.). Very quickly some of the A/GS cars were jacked up in the air with re-arched springs or spacer blocks like many of the 1980's 4-WD trucks. Questions of poor handling by these jacked up coupes eventually resulted in an NHRA rule limiting the engine crank pulley centerline to 24 inches above the ground. This forced some of the cars to be pulled down; Jr. Thompson recalls that he was able to meet the rule by installing smaller front tires.

"Getting a bite" was the main focus for the efforts of the 1960's Supercharged Gas competitors, as it would continue to be for all drag racers. But the technology then was still in an infant stage. Tire development, which has been responsible for perhaps the major portion of the advances in drag racing, was just beginning. The concepts of working chassis design was essentially not existent. So there was plenty of room for improvement.

The Union Grove (Wisc.) drag-strip was one of the first to organize match race programs for Supercharged Gas Coupes. Local favorite, Mike Marinoff, had a fast '55 Chevy C/GS while in nearby Chicago, Palmer Lazarus was running his '56 Chevy C/GS coupe. By the end of the 1960 season Union Grove had offered several Marinoff-Lazarus match races to the fans.

Unlike the rest of the country where the competitors were spread out, the California area had a number of blown coupes. But there were also a bunch of drag strips; four to eight running in Southern California alone. So in spite of a relative wealth of Supercharged Gas Coupes it was rare when two or more showed up in the same class. The result of this situation was relatively little competition pressure to improve. The only real measurement of performance was racing other class cars and reading about how the other guys were doing in Drag News or National Dragster.

The publicity war waged by the Supercharged Gassers from 1963 to 1967 really had its start in the summer of 1960. One of the major catalysts in the ad war was Howard Johansen of Howard Cams. He didn't start the ad war, but his personal racing helped escalate it. Most speed equipment manufacturers had been racers, but stopped racing to concentrate on business. In addition many manufacturers did not feel comfortable racing against their customers. But Howard just enjoyed racing. In addition to his twin engine dragster, which would become the 1961 NHRA World Champion, Howard was actively racing B/GS and C/GS cars with several racers including Eddie and Junior Thompson, Doug Cook and Al Hirshfield. Howard's cam grinding competitors, Ed Iskenderian and Jack Engle, competed by encouraging, sponsoring and helping their Supercharged Gas Coupe guys. Naturally it was important to advise the world, via an ad in Drag News, when Doug Cook (Howard Cams), Pittman-Edwards (Engle Cams) or Junior Thompson (Iskenderian Cams) had a good day. So the initial Supercharged Gas Coupe ads that would later escalate into an ad war appeared in the mid-1960's. The ads generally lauded the performances of cars using their products and occasionally complained that the other guys were afraid to race. Interestingly the majority of the ads were about the B/GS and C/GS competition and not the faster A/GS class cars.

The interest in the Supercharged Gas Coupes apparently encouraged the American Hot Rod Assn. (AHRA), under President Don Garlits, to quickly add classes for the Supercharged Gas Coupes, A/MC, B/MC and C/MC. Actually the classes included unblown engine gassers with modified firewalls too, but the Supercharged Coupes owned the classes.

The 1960 NHRA Nationals at Detroit were won by three of the best performing Willys in the country. George Montgomery's Cad powered '33 Willys won A/GS, while Willy Zaiser's '41 Willys (Olds powered) was the B/GS victor. The Doug Cook-Howard Johansen '41 Willys coupe used a Chevy engine to win C/GS after the K. S. Pittman-John Edwards '41 Willys had set the best speed and E.T. (120.40 mph, 11.85 sec.). Just one week earlier, at Alton, Illinois, George Montgomery had pushed his Willys to a 136.56 mph at 10.86 sec. clocking.

As 1960 wound down the action shifted to the West Coast as winter came to the East. Performances were improving and new cars were making their appearances. The Pittman-Edwards Willys was running A/GS, B/GS and C/GS with speeds up to 128.40 mph (11.09 sec.) while the Cook-Howard Willys ran both B/GS and C/GS, recording a top of 123.95 mph (11.36 sec.). Willys fever had grabbed Jr. Thompson and his new B/GS Willys with a Chevy engine set a time of 126.05 mph (11.37 sec). This was promptly heralded in Isky's ad. Another new B/GS Willys appeared when former C/GS campaigner Bob Balogh pulled the blown Chev engine from his '49 Chevy sedan and installed it in the Mallicoat Bros.' Willys (122.98 mph, 11.89 sec.). Some of the other best performing cars were: Al MacKenzie (A/GS), Roach-Torgeson (A/GS), Dan Brechtel (A/GS), Joe and Lee Airoso (B/GS), Dale Emery (A/GS), Burt Looney (A/GS), Jim Clinton (B/GS), Jim Butler (A/GS), John Myroniak (B/GS), Richter-Masters (A/GS), Pat Stewart (B/GS), Interstate Sandblasting (C/GS), Mike Marinoff (C/GS), Palmer Lazarus (C/GS), Jameson-McClellan (C/GS), Pete Johnson (C/GS), George Chorman (C/GS), Glenn Lawson-Jack Bayer-Frank Frietas (C/GS), Charles James (C/GS) and Sam Gellner (C/GS).

The final NHRA records in 1960 were A/GS - 131.57 mph (George Montgomery) and 11.40 sec. (Jim Butler-Weldon Day); B/GS - 125.87 mph and 11.51 sec. (Wilton Zaiser) and C/GS - 120.16 mph (Doug Cook-Howard Johansen) and 11.84 sec. (Junior Thompson).

Perhaps the most important item about the first season of Supercharged Gas Coupe competition was the crowd appeal. The "super" coupes were the fastest full-sized cars in drag racing. They looked like they could be driven home and indeed had lights, mufflers and windshield wipers. The supercharged engines sounded louder and sharper than those in other stock bodied coupes or sedans. But most importantly the racing was exciting and unpredictable with traction problems ranging from wheelspin to wheelstands. And they were faster than the other stock looking coupes and sedans. Remember that all the fast A/GS, B/GS and C/GS cars were going from 110 to 135 mph. The fastest stock cars were the Super Stock (S/S) class Ford, Chevys and Pontiacs that were recording 100 to 102 mph times. The cars in the unblown gas classes were turning speeds 10 to 20 mph slower than the equivalent supercharged cars. So the combination of crowd appeal, good tight competition, and lots of publicity made the first year of competition a success for the Supercharged Gas Coupe classes.

At the time that the Supercharged Gas Coupe classes were set up there were three distinct groups of cars running in the classes.

1. The first was the full size street coupes or sedans. The majority of these were '55 to '57 Chevys with a few '49 to '50 Olds or '50's Fords. Most of these were cars that the owners had progressed from almost stock to "full race" as they became caught up in drag racing. Because of their heavy weight most of this group of cars competed in C/GS class. There were exceptions where a very large Olds, Cadillac or Chrysler engine was used. This usually moved the car into B/GS.

2. The second group was the lightweight, early model street coupes and sedans. Early Ford and Chevy models (1930-1940) were always popular for street and drag racers. One of the best things about them was that they were light. Stock early V-8 Ford coupes weighed in the 2450 to 2700 lbs. area while the 1950's Chevys, Fords and Olds were approximately 1000 lbs. heavier. The early, mostly Ford, coupes and sedans had been the hot rodders favorites, so it was only natural to update them with a modern V-8. By the late 1950's the majority of the top gas coupes were 1930 to 1934 Fords with Cad, Olds, Chrysler or Chevy V-8 engines under the hood. The majority of these would fit into the A/GS or B/GS classes.

3. The third group was unique in that the cars in this group had never been built as street hot rods; in fact hot rodders had previously ignored them. The cars in this group were strictly built for racing. The group was composed of Willys and Henry J coupes or sedans. The stock Willys weighed only 2000 to 2200 lbs. while the Henry J models weighed about 2400 lbs. One important difference for the racer was that a Willys required a complete new and stronger drive train while a '55 Chevy could be progressively modified. Thus Willys were basically built for racing only even though they did have all the necessities the rules required. Thus

Burt Looney (Okla.) used a 460" Olds engine to blast a 127.10 mph speed (5-20-60) with his '40 Willys. Ed Iskenderian highlighted Burt's Willys in ads about Burt's performances from Texas to California. After setting the first A/GS E.T. record at 12.02 sec. he had to recapture it two months later with a 11.67 sec. clocking. The Willys used a La Salle transmission and tried a double disc clutch. Burt apparently had the usual traction problems with low gear so he generally ran in second and high gears only. This Willys was one of the first to raise the front end way up to gain traction. The photo was taken at Pomona on Burt's visit to Southern California, where he easily beat the author's B/GS Willys. (Photo courtesy of Junior Thompson)

The Studebaker battles in B/GS and C/GS by the Thompson Bros. and Doug Cook-Howard Johansen were terminated when they both switched to Willys. The Willys in the background of this photo was the orange colored '41 built by Howard and Doug. The B/GS class racer, with a Howard chain blower drive on a 317" Chevy engine, debuted in August, 1960. It was called the "Howard 8 cycle" car. Why "8 cycle"? Because Ed Iskenderian's big ad campaign was promoting his new "5 cycle" cams. Naturally "8 cycle" had to be better than "5 cycle" even if everyone knows that the engines operated on only 4 cycles. The Willys usually ran in C/GS where the competition was said to be the toughest, but did record a 125.62 mph speed running in the B/GS class. (Photo courtesy of Doug Cook)

they could be built for either A/GS, B/GS or C/GS class by adjusting the weight and engine displacement. Adjust perhaps is not the correct word when it is considered that a typical 1960's style Willys Supercharged Gas Coupe would weigh about 2700 lbs. But at the drag-strip those lightweight Willys would often tip the scales at as much as 3600 to 3800 lbs. The added weight was used to meet the class limits (and improve traction). After the handful of Willys' running in 1958 recorded excellent performances the result was a 1960 Willys stampede. It seemed like everyone was building a Willys. In fact within a few years it appeared that every Willys left was on the drag-strips.

The most popular Supercharged Gas Coupe engines in 1960 were those from Chevrolet and Oldsmobile. Almost every C/GS and most of the B/GS cars had Chevys in them. The racers were building Chevy engines in displacements ranging from 265 to 339 cubic inches. Remember that the biggest stock small block Chevy in 1960 was the 283. The top Chevys appear to have been running with about 470 hp (Howard said that his 317 cu.in., 4-71 blown engine was hitting 520 hp on his dyno in 1961). Judging by the performances the 470 hp figure seems about right in 1960. But if you wanted to go really fast with a Supercharged Gas Coupe the "conventional wisdom" said to use an Olds engine. Most of the fastest Gas Dragsters and Supercharged A/GS Gas Coupes were using Olds engines. "Conventional wisdom" also said that the Chrysler was great for

fuel but gas ran better in a wedge chamber like the Olds, Chevys and Cads. Naturally the excellent performances of the Olds engine cars in the 1958 to 1960 period did nothing to disprove that theory. Displacements from 306 to 460 cu.in. were being used. George Montgomery and several others ran the Olds' bigger brother, the Cadillac engine. The Olds and Cad engines appear to have been pumping out around 450 to 575 hp depending on the engine displacement.

Although the Olds engine weighed over 100 lbs. more than a Chevy the displacement could be over 100 cu.in. more. Therefore the Olds, or Cads, were a natural for A/GS where competitors like Burt Looney and George Montgomery used about 460 cu.in. engines. The Pittman-Edwards's Olds powered Willys had the distinction of running all three classes, A/GS, B/GS and C/GS by changing engines. When the Pittman-Edwards Willys first blasted to a 124 mph time the 407 cu.in. engine in it was borrowed from Gene Adams (1959). After that 306 and 327 cu.in. Olds engines were campaigned. The smaller engines allowed the Willys to run in the lower classes where it was very competitive as evidenced by the C/GS times at the 1960 Nationals.

There were some good performances by other engines in the supercharged classes. Chryslers powered some of the fastest A/GS and B/GS cars and Jim Butler was proving that a 430 cu.in. Ford could be a winner also. But in general the headlines in 1960 were made by Cadillac,

Olds and Chevy powered supercharged coupes.

The results of the first year of A/GS, B/GS and C/GS competition were increasing spectator interest in the Supercharged Gas Coupes and a rush to build Willys coupes. Partially due to the increasing interest the cars being built for the supercharged classes were not just hopped up street-hot rods; they were race cars.

- 1 9 6 1 -

Only a few rule changes for the Supercharged Coupe classes were made by the NHRA for the 1961 season. In addition to the engine 24" height rule previously mentioned, the changes included a minimum of 4.0 lbs./cu.in. (weight to engine displacement) in the A/GS class, a minimum wheelbase of 92 inches (up from 86 inches) and clearly stating that all gas coupes and sedans had to use a body made by an American auto manufacturer. However, in mid-season the NHRA modified the American car only rule to allow some foreign cars in the Gas Coupe and Sedan classes. An interesting ruling from NHRA race coordinator Jack Hart required superchargers to be mechanically driven by the engine being supercharged. This ruling, obviously meant to eliminate the auxiliary engine driven blower, effectively banned turbochargers. Naturally this interpretation was later modified.

The NHRA Supercharged Gas Coupe records established in 1960 were retired. The reasons given included the new minimum weight break requirement in the A/GS class and the engine height limit. There was no way to check the 1960 record cars to insure that they met the new rules, so 1961 started out with an empty record list.

The initial 1961 records were set at the first NHRA Winter-nationals held at Pomona (the real "first" NHRA Winternationals was in Florida - 1960) in February. The new record holders were the Pisano Bros. (A/GS), Fred Stone-Tim Woods (B/GS) and K. S. Pittman-John Edwards (C/GS). An interesting item is that K. S. Pittman drove both the Pittman-Edwards C/GS Willys and the brand new Stone-Woods owned similar B/GS Willys.

The 1961 season saw most of the top A/GS cars recording times in the high 120 mph bracket. Several competitors pushed over the 130 mph mark including George Montgomery (Ohio) 137.12 mph, Chuck Finders (So. Calif.) 132.45 mph, Stone-Woods (So. Calif.) 132.15 mph, Pittman-Edwards (So. Calif.) 136.77 mph and Jack Kulp (Penn.) 130.45 mph. Other strong A/GS competitors included the Pisano Bros. (So. Calif.) 129.50 mph, Butler-Day (Texas) 129.12 mph, Gordon Selkirk (Illinois) 128.94 mph, Otis Brewer (So. Calif.) 127.11 mph, Doug Cook-Howard's (So. Calif.) 126.76 mph, Al Del Porto (No. Calif.) 126.50 mph, Balogh-Mallicoat Bros. (So. Calif.) 125.87 mph, the Burt Bros. (Okla.) 125.17 mph, Dale Emery (No. Calif.) 123.45 mph and Arley Langlo (So. Calif.)

123.33 mph.

There were many good B/GS performances in 1961. Some of them were by Jr. Thompson (So.Calif.) 131.96 mph, Jim Clinton (Ohio) 129.68 mph, Stone-Woods (So.Calif.) 134.12 mph, Pittman-Edwards (So. Calif.) 129.30 mph, Mike Marinoff (Wisc.) 127.66 mph, Doug Cook-Howard's (So.Calif.) 125.62 mph, Ray Moore (Ohio) 121.45 mph, Bob Balogh-Mallicoat Bros. (So.Calif.) 120.00 mph, Willy Zaiser (Maryland) 120.00 mph and Roger Latampa (Ohio) 120.00 mph.

Perhaps the most competitive Supercharged Coupe class was C/GS. Good C/GS speeds were posted by Pittman-Edwards (So.Calif.) 127.11 mph, Moody-Jones (Indiana) 126.76 mph, Doug Cook-Howard's (So.Calif.) 123.45 mph, Bob Balogh-Mallicoat Bros. (So.Calif.) 123.78 mph, Palmer Lazarus (Illinois) 123.82 mph, Porter-Stearns (So. Calif.) 120.96 mph, the Airoso Bros. (No. Calif.) 120.00 mph, Chuck James (So. Calif.) 120.00 mph and Rocky Childs (So. Calif.) 119.89 mph.

The 1961 NHRA Nationals winners were George Montgomery - A/GS, Ray Moore - B/GS and Pittman-Edwards - C/GS.

A quick review of the fastest times shows that many of the cars were competing in two or three classes. The other side of that coin is that there was no way to tell if the class speeds recorded were with legally weighted cars for that class.

Before everyone is accused of cheating, consider that most of the cars were racing weekly at local drag strips and only several times a year at big NHRA events. Practically everyone ran legal weight for the class eliminations against similar A/GS, B/GS or C/GS competitors. Class winners then moved on into the local Little, Middle or Top Eliminator brackets where racing against Dragsters, Roadsters, Altereds or other Gas Coupes was heads-up. That is there was no handicap system. So if a B/GS Willys is racing a Dragster for Top Eliminator (it happened on several occasions) why not take weight out if it would help. Remember that the Top, Middle or Little Eliminator awards were not given to a class. Test runs before eliminations were also made occasionally at different weights to determine what combinations worked. And don't forget that a fast run could be good for the ego and public relations. The results printed in Drag News and National Dragster usually just mentioned the name, class and times. There was no explanation that a certain speed was obtained while running several hundred pounds light. So actually the guys were not cheating, it was that there was no way to be sure that a certain class time was legal at the local strips.

The structure of the NHRA National and Regional meets was such that the class limitations were closely checked. So the most representative idea of the legal performances of the Supercharged Gas Coupes would be the 1961 NHRA class records. The final 1961 records, and they were final because the NHRA erased them for the 1962 season, were held by George Montgomery (A/GS - 131.77 mph, 10.83 sec.), Stone-Woods-Cook (B/GS - 128.57 mph, 10.99 sec.) and Pittman-Edwards (C/GS - 126.22 mph, 11.28 sec.).

Perhaps due to more competition, the gains in the B/GS and C/GS classes seemed to be greater than the A/GS gains in 1961. Most of the top B/GS and C/GS cars were Willys. The most successful B/GS combination was to use a big engine with weight in the rear to make class and add traction. As an example, Stone-Woods-Cook's '41 Willys was listed as running a 425 cu. in. Olds engine and a staggering 3800 pounds total weight. The C/GS cars generally used 300 to 340 cu. in. Chevys or Olds engines and vehicle weights around 3100 to 3600 pounds. The weight of a Willys with all the equipment except added weight could be in the 2500 to 2800 pounds area depending on the engine, transmission and rear end types used. All this added weight (usually behind the rear tires) was great for traction. And almost all the fastest cars had switched to the four speed Hydramatics. All of the Supercharged Gas Coupes, and especially the weighted B/GS and C/GS cars, were improving both their E.T.'s and their consistency. And in fact many B/GS and C/GS cars could, and did, compete in the A/GS class.

Drag racing fans were becoming even more excited about the Supercharged Gas Coupes. They were recording times 15 to 20 mph faster than the other full size cars. And the ad war was really escalating. For example in December a quarter page ad, signed by the Stone-Woods-Cook team, appeared in Drag News. It accused the other competitors of refusing to race and challenging them to race at the 1962 Winternationals. It even offered to bet $200 on a race (2 of 3) of the B/GS Stone-Woods-Cook Willys against the "certain A/GS Willys from Ohio which claims to be the Worlds fastest A Gas car". It was great hype. So 1961 was a good year for the Supercharged Gas Coupes, and it would get better.

- 1962 -

The NHRA rule changes for 1962 were evidence that drag racing had finally accepted the gas coupe/sedan competitors to be serious racers. In the 1950's the gas classes had been set up to get street racing off the streets. The rules had evolved over the years to separate out race oriented competitors. Drag strip managers had reacted to the complaints of the numerous street coupe and sedan owners. The then new gas coupe classes were set up with restrictions to keep out modified, "gutted" or fuel burning race cars. Remember the majority of the customers (spelled "income") for the drag strips were the "hot" street coupes and sedans. Although the rules changed at various drag strips throughout the 1950's, the premise remained to

keep classes to get street racers off the street and encourage them to race at the drag strips.

The NHRA rules for 1962 indicated the beginning of a new direction in drag racing's approach to the gas coupe classes. The rules requiring full street operating equipment were deleted. No longer were mufflers, windshield wipers, generators, horns, emergency brakes or even license plates and registration required. The required roll-up windows could now be replaced by screwed in place plexiglass. The rule changes were small but it is obvious that 1962 was the beginning of the major changes to come in the gas coupe/sedan classes. The gas coupes were being accepted as real race cars.

The most obvious rule changes for 1962 were the weight breaks. The new A/GS class breaks were set at 5.0 to 8.99 Lbs/cu.in., from 4.00 to 8.59 Lbs/cu.in. The B/GS class figures became 9.00 to 12.59 Lbs/cu.in. (was 8.60 to 10.59 Lbs/cu.in.) and C/GS became 12.60 Lbs/cu.in. and up. The new weight breaks appear to be meant to control the minimum weight of the A/GS cars, probably due to concern for safety. But actually a 4.00 Lbs/cu.in. break was lower than even the light weight Willys could obtain then. So the A/GS change did not actually affect the 1962 competitors. The B/GS and C/GS increases were perhaps meant to improve competition by reducing the number of competitors that could run the same car in two, or all three, classes. It particularly gave the heavy big cars (Chevy, Olds, Fords etc.) a better opportunity to compete in the new 20% heavier C/GS class. Naturally the rule changes dictated that the speed records be retired again.

The A/GS records at the completion of the 1962 season were 140.84 mph and 10.25 sec. set by Stone-Woods-Cook. Previous 1962 record setters were Hirshfield-Finders, Pittman-Edwards-Cizar, and Eddie Schartman. Note that even though the minimum weight break had been increased by 25% in 1962, the 1962 speed and E.T. records were significantly improved. One example of the reasons for the performance improvement is to review the activities of the Stone-Woods-Cook team. After starting the season running B/GS the team moved into A/GS with a big engine. Late in the year the team debuted a new '41 Willys, named Swindler A. It was much lighter than the Swindler II car. Starting in October, Tim Woods, Fred Stone and Doug Cook ran every weekend at the Long Beach, Pomona or San Gabriel drag strips. Their Willys was the first A/GS car to run consistently under 10 seconds, with a 1962 best of 9.79 seconds. Each week they topped 140 mph; their best speed was 142.85 mph. It is not hard to get the impression that the team's success was due to a real dedicated effort.

But Tim Woods' team was not the only A/GS competitor that was hard at work. Some other outstanding A/GS competitors included Jim Clinton (Ohio) 139.75 mph, 10.47 sec.; Hirshfield-Finders (So.Calif.)

139.44 mph, 10.11 sec.; Brewer-May (So.Calif.) 137.19 mph, 11.52 sec.; Pittman-Edwards (So.Calif.) 140.62 mph, 10.21 sec.; Ed Schartman (Ohio) 137.61 mph, 10.79 sec.; George Montgomery (Ohio) 134.32 mph; Selkirk-Bork (Illinois) 134.28 mph, 10.99 sec.; Lewis-Harry (Washington) 130.82 mph, 11.99 sec.; and the Charioteers-Laskey (New Mexico) 134.73 mph, 10.61 sec.

The 1962 NHRA B/GS record setters were Stone-Woods-Cook, the Airoso Bros., Thompson-Cornelius-Pisano and Mike Marinoff. Mike's final 1962 numbers were 129.68 mph, 11.03 sec. Some of the top B/GS performances were by Mike Marinoff (Wisc.) 132.35 mph, 10.82 sec.; Thompson-Cornelius-Pisano (So.Calif.) 132.84 mph, 10.71 sec.; Stone-Woods-Cook (So.Calif.) 129.87 mph, 11.15 sec.; Larry Dixon (So.Calif.) 128.75 mph, 11.15 sec.; Jack Merkel (New York) 126.58 mph, 11.42 sec.; Pittman-Edwards (So.Calif.) 126.22 mph, 10.98 sec.; Mallicoat Bros.-Balogh (So.Calif.) 126.05 mph, 11.26 sec.; Hill-Zartman (Penn.) 127.11 mph, 11.12 sec.; Gary Dyer (Illinois) 126.76 mph, 11.33 sec.; Finders-Watson-Casper (So.Calif.) 124.82 mph, 11.07 sec.; and Frank Bash (Penn) 124.31 mph, 11.56 sec.

Perhaps the most evenly matched class was C/GS. Moody and Jones held the record for the entire last half of 1962. Their final records were 115.08 mph and 12.05 sec. Top 1962 performances included those by Moody-Jones (Indiana) 124.65 mph, 11.85 sec.; Pittman-Edwards (So.Calif.) 120.96 mph, 11.62 sec.; Palmer Lazarus (Illinois) 122.44 mph, 12.05 sec.; D.

Anderson (No.Cal.) 120.00 mph; Pat Stewart (No.-Calif.) 116.70 mph, 12.11 sec.; Charles James (So.Calif.) 116.58 mph, 11.99 sec.; Tom Montalbano (Illinois) 116.12 mph, 12.57 sec.; Thomason-Pagniano (Ohio) 115.58 mph, 12.14 sec.; Garry Newton (So.Calif.) 115.38 mph; and the Brown Bros. (Arizona) 114.42 mph, 12.30 sec.

The 1962 NHRA Nationals class winners were: A/GS - Stone-Woods-Cook, B/GS - Mike Marinoff and C/GS - Moody-Jones. It is interesting to note that the existing record holders each won their class at the Nationals. With all the potential things that can happen in drag racing, the victories by the three record holders was an unusual occurrence.

Although the supercharged gassers had made significant performance improvements in 1962, it was a relatively quiet year for A/GS, B/GS and C/GS cars. The manufacturers ads in Drag News and National Dragster only occasionally mentioned the Supercharged Gas Coupes. The three most mentioned competitors were Stone-Woods-Cook (A/GS), Junior Thompson (B/GS) and Mike Marinoff (B/GS). Although there were only a relatively few Supercharged Gas Coupes running, the ranks were increasing and new names were being added to the Supercharged Gas competitors list. But still most local meets rarely had more than one car in a Supercharged Gas Coupe class.

By 1962 the Supercharged Gas Coupe classes could have been renamed the "Willys" classes. All the top cars were Willys, except the very strong C/GS '37

Joe Pisano and his brothers Carmen, Frankie and Tony have been a part of drag racing with their businesses (Venolia, Wedge Engineering, J.P. Engines) and many race cars. This beautiful maroon '29 Ford coupe was their A/GS entry to the 1961 NHRA Winternationals. They won the class at 121.52 mph and also set the first 1961 A/GS records with times of 118.40 mph and 11.98 sec. The Model A had Chevy power. Joe Pisano's engines later ran in Junior Thompson's Willys and in the Bones-Dubach Willys. After that the Pisanos moved up into the Fuel Altered and Funny Car classes. (Photo courtesy of Junior Thompson)

Chevy run by Moody-Jones. Interestingly most of the fastest Willys were the larger '37 to '42 models, not the smaller '33 to '36 models. There appears to be no special reason for the popularity of the later Willys model. But they were more available and only about 100 lbs. heavier than the earlier '33 to '36 models (2146 to 2034 lbs.). Also perhaps hot rodders felt that the later styling was less ugly than the early styling. Incidently the introduction of fiberglass front body components in 1962 soon made almost all the '37 to '42 Willys look like the 1941 models. The early model Willys ('33 - '36) eventually all became 1933 models with the change to fiberglass front ends.

Although the Olds engine was still the King, other engines were increasing the pressure on them. The Cadillac engined Willys of George Montgomery and Al MacKenzie were very competitive as was the big wedge Dodge engined Willys run by Hirshfield-Finders. But the most interesting trend was the strong performances of light weight small block Chevy powered cars. The Chevy engined Willys' of Mike Marinoff, Eddie Schartman, Jim Clinton, Hill-Zartman, Jack Merkel, Jr. Thompson, Balogh-Mallicoat Bros., Palmer Lazarus and the Chevy of Moody-Jones were proving that the little Chevy had the ability to compete with the "big boys". Although a number of competitors were using the Chrysler Hemi ('51 to '58), the feeling was still that the Hemi ran great on fuel but gas ran better in a wedge chamber.

Perhaps the most important item that resulted in improved performance in 1962 was traction. And tires were the main ingredient. The new 10.00-16, M & H Racemasters, became the biggest drag racing tires available. Now the tire spinning antics of the high powered supercharged cars could be controlled a little better. The majority of competitors were now using the four-speed Hydramatic (Olds '53-'56 type) transmissions pioneered by B&M. The stall speed of the fluid coupling (not a torque converter) resulted in a relatively smooth application of power to the tires on the initial launching from the starting line. This helped make wheel-spin a little more controllable than with the sharp jolt of the clutch, manual transmission combination. But it must be noted that C/GS teams often used the clutch, manual transmission combination successfully on cars that did not have the traction problems of the more powerful cars.

The most important benefit of the improvement in traction was consistency. In the earlier days of classes, the fastest cars would record E.T.'s varying as much as one second from week to week. But by the end of 1962 most of the top cars were repeating within .2 to .3 of a second every week and at different tracks. Also the performances improved for the cars that had lots of power, as evidenced by the speeds they recorded, but poor traction, as measured by their E.T.'s. The new tires and transmissions not only improved the E.T.'s

and speeds, they actually set the stage for the next step forward, which was to be the application of more horsepower. The cars were ready for bigger and more highly developed engines.

- 1 9 6 3 -

The Supercharged Gasser rules for 1963 remained essentially the same as the 1962 rules. The only classification change was to increase the minimum weight again, setting the A/GS minimum at 6.0 lbs./cu.in. (from 5.0 lbs./cu.in.). This change actually had little effect on most of the existing A/GS cars but was an important factor in controlling the designs of the new race car style A/GS gassers to come. What it did do was effectively limit the engine displacement of the very light early ('33-'36) Willys that could be made ready to race as light as 2200 pounds. The 6.0 lbs./cu.in. requirement now limited those cars to an engine displacement of about 366 cu. in.. Perhaps this new requirement was the major influence in George Montgomery's decision to discard the big Cadillac engine and install a smaller Chevy in his newly rebuilt '33 Willys.

The reason for the rule change had to be a concern for safety. The A/GS cars had broken the 140 mph mark. They were the fastest stock bodied cars in drag racing. But they also were raised up high and had traction problems resulting in some unpredictable antics off the starting line and at speed. The weight limit would hopefully eliminate reduction of weight at the expense of safety.

The 1963 rules did have a change that did not apply to the supercharged cars but would greatly effect them in the future. The new rules allowed 1948 to 1953 English Fords (Anglias) to run the gas classes even though they did not meet the minimum wheelbase requirements. The rules did limit them to small-block Chevy engines, or equivalent, and specifically stated that no superchargers would be allowed.

Gas class competitors, who had seen a complete revolution from 1960 to 1962 with the Willys gassers, were about to see more revolutionary progress. The light, short wheelbase Willys had become the winners in most of the gas classes. Since racers were always looking for a way to get ahead of their competition, a few racers appeared with the little Anglias, usually with small engines. These often ran in the lower gas classes and at local drag strips. The 1963 decision to legalize the gas class Anglias was facing the reality that these cars were already running at local drag strips. The decision was not popular with many gas class racers who saw it as a fundamental change from the full-sized street style hot rod to small, foreign bodied racers. The result was that the gas classes would soon become the Anglia races. It was progress but what if the Anglias had not been approved and the gas classes had remained full sized cars. Would the gassers have enjoyed more popularity such as NASCAR maintains by racing full sized American cars? Naturally the supercharger rule ban meant that the A/GS, B/GS and C/GS classes were not effected. But, then again, rules seem to be made to be broken.

The NHRA records in A/GS set by Stone-Woods-Cook in July of 1962 were not broken until the 1963 Nationals when George Montgomery's new Willys-Chevy combination reset the E.T. record to 10.04 sec. The 1962 speed record of 140.84 mph was not broken at any NHRA record event. Actually competition in A/GS was a little thin in 1963. Stone-Woods-Cook were continuing to record strong performances with a best of 9.92 sec - 142.89 mph. George Montgomery debuted his newly rebuilt Willys-Chevy combination in August in time to win the NHRA Nationals and record times of 10.04 sec. and 140.62 mph. Other fast A/GS times were recorded by Otis Brewer (So. Calif.) at 10.97 sec and 142.40 mph; Richard Beesley (So. Calif.) at 11.23 sec., 141.06 mph; K. S. Pittman (So. Calif.) - 10.29 sec., 138.00 mph; Jim Clinton (Ohio) 11.25 sec., 136 mph; Gordon Selkirk-Saul Bork (Illinois) 10.30 sec., 138.63 mph; Ray Lollar (Oklahoma) 10.32 sec., 138.81 mph; Al MacKenzie (Illinois) 11.12 sec., 128.57 mph; Don Langford (So. Calif.) 11.71 sec., 128.20 mph; and Phil Walker (So. Calif.) 11.28 sec., 128.84 mph.

In contrast to the relatively quiet A/GS scene the competition was fierce in the B/GS class. The final 1963 records showed a modest increase in speed to 131.77 mph, by Jack Merkel, from 129.68 mph in 1962. The E.T. record was significantly dropped to 10.60 sec. (from 11.03 sec.) by the Stone-Woods-Cook team. For most of the year the Stone-Woods-Cook name was on both the A/GS and B/GS NHRA records. Unlike many competitors who ran their only car in a different class on occasion, the S-W-C team ran their new car in A/GS and their older car in B/GS.

The best running B/GS competitors were improving their performances, including Stone-Woods-Cook (So. Calif.) 10.34 sec., 134.12 mph; Junior Thompson (So. Calif.) 10.60 sec., 129.22 mph; K. S. Pittman (So. Calif.) 10.28 sec., 130.90 mph; Mike Marinoff (Wisc.) 10.82 sec., 134.55 mph; Jack Merkel (New York) 10.65 sec., 132.00 mph; Charley Hill (Penn.) 10.88 sec., 129.68 mph; and Finders-Watson-Caspers (So. Calif.) 10.68 sec., 124.84 mph. New or improved B/GS performances were also recorded by the entries of Big John Mazmanian (So. Calif.) 10.40 sec., 136.98 mph; Tom Grove (No. Calif.) in the Melrose Missile, a '63 Plymouth AFX with a 6-71 blower at 11.04 sec., 129.31 mph; John Dunlap (Ohio) 11.68 sec., 126.76 mph; Gene Ciambella (So. Calif.) 10.60 sec., 129.65 mph; Seevers-Wiesner-Owens (Colorado) 10.75 sec., 131.57 mph; Dean Brown (Texas) 11.56 sec., 127.88 mph; The Porsche Bros. (So. Calif.) 11.56 sec., 125.84 mph; Coy Martin (No. Calif.) 11.32 sec., 125.35 mph; and Nunes-Frank (No. Calif.) 11.42 sec. 125.64 mph.

The C/GS class E.T. record fell to Tarantola-Cruciata (New York) at 11.74 sec., down from 12.05 sec. at the beginning of the year. The Brown Bros. (Arizona) blasted the speed record up to 124.37 mph, 9 mph faster than the 1962 record.

The top C/GS competitors in 1963 included Tarantola-Cruciata (New York) 11.74 sec., 129.13 mph; the Brown Bros. (Arizona) 12.08 sec., 126.05 mph; Moody-Jones (Indiana) 11.70 sec., 128.64 mph; Palmer Lazarus (Illinois) 11.11 sec., 126.76 mph; Larry Dixon (So. Calif.) 12.40 sec., 120.32 mph; John Dunlap (Ohio) 12.31 sec., 120.80 mph and Chuck James (So. Calif.) 11.43 sec., 118.26 mph.

Things were starting to jump in the supercharged classes in 1963. Big John Mazmanian and Bones Balogh put their supercharged Corvette sports car aside and debuted a beautiful red B/GS Willys coupe with Chevy power. As mentioned before Stone-Woods-Cook were running both A/GS and B/GS Willys with Doug Cook or Chuck Finders driving. George Montgomery returned with probably the most "hi-tech" supercharged car, his renovated Willys with a Chevy small-block engine. Unfortunately Mike Marinoff's very fast B/GS Willys had been written off when it flipped in the lights, so Mike joined the Dragster class racers. Vince Tarantola's performances were probably from the only four-door Willys sedan to appear in the NHRA Supercharged Gas Coupe records.

The winners at the NHRA Nationals were George Montgomery (A/GS), Jack Merkel (B/GS) and Moody-Jones (C/GS). The NHRA newspaper, National Dragster, reported that the Montgomery vs. Stone-Woods-Cook A/GS runoff was one of the most exciting races of the meet. Drag News reported that the supercharged class runoffs were the biggest action in the gas coupe ranks. They commented that "all the favorites got waxed". Overall the best racing in 1963 came in the B/GS competition. Unlike previous years local strips sometimes found from two to six B/GS cars in the pits, especially if some cash was offered to the winner. California had drag strips like Long Beach, San Gabriel, Vaca Valley, Fremont, Kingdom, Bakersfield and Pomona running races with the B/GS cars of Stone-Woods-Cook, Jr. Thompson, C&O - Gene Ciambella, Big John Mazmanian, the Mallicoat Bros., the Airoso Bros., K. S. Pittman, Coy Martin, Ron Nunes plus some of the other area cars.

The supercharged cars in 1963 continued to be Willys, with a few Fords or Chevys mostly in the C/GS class. The same engine combinations were used; mostly Olds and Chevys. Virtually everyone had a four-speed Hydramatic transmission. The traction improvements from the new 10" and 10.5" wide M&H and Firestone slicks were apparently the major reason for the lower and more consistent E.T.'s. That was particularly evident in the quicker B/GS times.

The 1963 Supercharged Gasser season was what should be considered as normal until August; then the publicity war started. From the end of August to the end of the year almost every issue of Drag News had an ad promoting "our" guy and challenging "their" guy. The major players were Iskenderian Cams with Big John Mazmanian, George Montgomery and the Mallicoat Bros., against Engle Cams with Stone-Woods-Cook. After a particularly strong challenge of the Mallicoat Bros. B/GS car by Engle's Stone-Woods-Cook ad, the famous "Pebble-Pulp-Chef" reference to Stone-Woods-Cook appeared in Isky's ad. And Isky's ad that appeared just before the NHRA Nationals stating that he hoped the Big A/GS gassers would not be afraid to show up to race George Montgomery certainly helped make the Montgomery vs. Stone-Woods-Cook race one of the most exciting races at the Nationals. Ads about their supercharged guys were also run by the B&M and Cal-Hydro transmission firms.

So 1963 ended with George Montgomery showing A/GS competitors that smaller and lighter worked too; Stone-Woods-Cook running a team of two cars; Jr. Thompson discarding his Chevy for a bigger Olds engine; and some very strong performances around the country by competitors like Vince Tarantola, Dale Moody-Sam Jones, Jack Merkel, Glen and Charlie Brown and Seevers-Wiesner-Owens.

Some of the other Supercharged Gas Coupe competitors in the 1960 to 1963 period were:

Ray Alley (So. Calif.)	Ron Lapinski (Ill.)	Al Anso (Ohio)
Martin-Hightower (Okla.)	Avila Bros. (No.Calif.)	Don McIntosh (Colo.)
Mike Bamber (So.Calif.)	Don Merryfield (Wash.)	Braskett-Skinner (So.Calif.)
Ray Moore (Ohio)	C. Brent (So.Calif.)	Jim Morris (Tex.)
Wayne Calvert (Tex.)	W. Morrison (Ind.)	Andy Cameron (Ill.)
Calvin Moyer (Penn.)	Carroll-Flanders (So.Calif.)	Larry Nail (Kansas)
Cavalieri-Spaulding (No.Calif.)	Walt Nothaft (Wash.)	F. Coleman (Indiana)
Bill Novothy (Ohio)	Bill Crow (Wash.)	Procure-Grundy (Okla.)
Dave Doogan (Ill.)	John Render (Ohio)	Dick Doyle (Conn.)
Warren Reynolds (Okla.)	Ed Edwards (Kentucky)	Pete Robinson (Georgia)
Evans Bros. (Mo.)	Ed Rosa (So.Calif.)	Fernandez-Purves (No.Calif.)
Mike Schmitz (Mich.)	Angelo Greco (Conn.)	Jim Selkirk (Ill.)
Whit Harvey (New Mex.)	Fred Simon (Tex.)	Tom Jandt (So.Calif.)
Howard Stitch (Tex.)	P. Jeatzer (Wash.)	Dennis Toll (Ohio)
A. Jetton (Tex.)	Verdi-Odie (Mich.)	Johnson Bros. (Tex.)
Bill Waddill (Mich.)	Keikiak-Fiske (Penn.)	Charley Young (Arizona)
Don Langford (So.Calif.)	Al Zerbarini (Conn.)	

The C/GS class winner at the 1961 NHRA Nationals at Indianapolis was the Willys of K. S. Pittman and John Edwards (So. Calif.). Note that it had a full steel stock body and all the street equipment including windshield wipers, mufflers and lights. The team had a good year in 1961. They set and held the NHRA C/GS records for the entire year (126.22 mph and 11.28 sec.). This Willys made many trips down the drag strips. (Photo courtesy of Wayne Arteaga)

Al Hirshfield and Chuck Finders (So. Calif.) built this neat little blue (formerly called "Candy Apple Dirt" by one reporter) 1935 Willys for the 1962 season. Success came quickly with a Winternationals victory in A/GS and then the NHRA A/GS records (132.93 mph and 10.87 sec.). This Willys was one of the very few blown gassers that used a Dodge wedge-head engine. Certainly the 482" engine was one of the biggest in the gasser ranks. The transmission was a B&M Hydro and the injectors were from Scott. Al Hirshfield on occasion had teamed with Howard Johansen so it was natural that the engine used a Howard cam, rods and stroked crankshaft. The photo was taken at Inyokern when the Willys set the A/GS record (5-20-62). (Photo courtesy of Bob Balogh)

Perhaps in an effort to keep up with the competition both Junior Thompson and the Howard Johansen-Doug Cook team abandoned Studebaker and built Willys coupes at the same time (Aug. 1960). This is Junior Thompson's Chevy powered '41 Willys (Doug Cook's is on Page 24). It is pictured at Inyokern (11-20-60) where it set the NHRA C/GS record at 11.84 sec. Junior ran it in both B/GS and C/GS classes in 1960 and performed well enough to have protests on the engine registered by competitors on several occasions. The Willys' best B/GS time in 1960 was 126.05 mph. Note that this Willys and most of the others had no names, ads or decals on them. Most of the racers didn't fully consider the publicity aspect and in fact putting a racer's name on the car was like "bragging" or similar to wearing a big name tag all the time. (Photo courtesy of Junior Thompson)

Model A coupes were not very popular in the Supercharged Gas Coupe classes but there were several fast ones running. Gordon Selkirk (Illinois) put a blown 394" Olds in his '30 Ford coupe and hit A/GS speeds as high as 128.94 mph. Note the popular Moon disc hubcaps and "toy" headlights. Gordon soon switched to a 1935 Willys coupe. With partner Saul Bork he campaigned several different supercharged gassers. The metallic blue coupe is pictured here in 1961.
(Photo courtesy of Ray Tognarelli)

Ron Nunes (No. Calif.) began racing in the Supercharged Gas Coupe classes in 1960 with this '32 3-window Ford coupe. The blown Olds engine had a chain driven 6-71 blower and dual four-barrel carburetors. Ron teamed with Bob Joaquin and Pat Stewart to run the coupe to a best of 124.50 mph and 11.42 sec. (1961). It used a B&M Hydro. The coupe usually ran at the nearby Fremont drag strip in either B/GS or A/GS (Fremont called them A/GB and B/GB). A few years later Ron Nunes joined the Willys ranks with a record setting '41 coupe.
(Photo courtesy of Ron Nunes)

After his Studebaker Champion was destroyed in a towing accident Tim Woods decided to go the Willys route. Tim enlisted the aid of K. S. Pittman and John Edwards to build his new Swindler II. The light blue '41 Willys, complete with a custom two-bar grill, used a big 425" Olds engine and a lot of weight to compete in the B/GS class. The Fred Stone-Tim Woods Willys owned the NHRA B/GS records for the entire 1961 season with the final numbers of 128.57 mph and 10.99 sec. The results of the 1961 NHRA Winternationals printed in the drag racing papers were interesting because they showed that the Pittman-Edwards team had won both the B/GS and C/GS classes. Actually the Pittman-Edwards Willys had won the C/GS trophy but the B/GS winner was the Stone-Woods Willys with K. S. Pittman at the wheel.
(Photos courtesy of Junior Thompson)

George Montgomery replaced his '34 Ford coupe with this Willys in 1959. Like most of the Willys this one was found at a junk yard. Weighing only about 2200 lbs. and powered by a big Cadillac engine, George quickly hit speeds over 130 mph. These 1961 photos show the take-off and the engine (Union Grove, Wisc.-July 1961) and the car in the pits at the Nationals (1961). Note that the front suspension now uses high arched parallel springs and "Mag" wheels all the way around. George's very neat work can be seen, especially in the engine photo. Not only was the Willys a winner on the drag strip, but George also won car show awards with it. One interesting item is that George was able to make the old 1948 Ford "Banjo" style rear end hold up under stress of the blown Cadillac engine.
(Photos courtesy of Wayne Arteaga and Ray Tognarelli)

The street driven hot rods in the late 1950's were often early Fords with Olds, Cad or Chevy engines. This red, '34 coupe had a Chevy engine, a 6-71 blower and a Weiand six carburetor manifold. In 1960, John Dunlap (Ohio) ran this car in the B/GS class recording times in the 111 mph area. Here was another example of the popularity of Moon discs in 1960. Barbara Hamilton, who later campaigned her own C/GS class Willys, made her first supercharged gasser run in John's coupe. (Photo courtesy of Barbara Hamilton Advey)

Other than early Ford coupes the most popular gassers were the '55 to '57 Chevys. Probably most were mainly fast street cars rather than race cars. This Chevy was Bill Fitzgerald's (Missouri). Bill's Chevy was just one of the fast '55 - '57 Chevys in the Midwest like Mike Marinoff's and Palmer Lazarus'. Bill's Chevy used two gears (second and high) in his manual transmission while many of the other Chevy racers used "four-speed boxes". He also had Moon discs. (Photo courtesy of Wayne Arteaga)

Anthony Leone and Harvey Walter (Louisiana) ran this bright yellow '55 Chevy in the C/GS class (1960). It had a 352" engine with a 4-71 blower. The engine was built by friends and dragster racers "Q-Ball" Wales and Paul Candies. Later the blower was replaced by injectors and the car campaigned as a C/Gasser. Eventually the Chevy was sold and Tony started to build an A/G '40 Willys. (Photo courtesy of Anthony Leone)

Gary, Bob and Chic Dyer (Illinois) had a red '33 Ford coupe with a blown 327 Chevy engine. On the Ford I-beam axle was written "Strickly Business". The brothers ran the car for about two years. The race photo shows the Dyer Bros. racing the B/GS Willys of Jim Selkirk at the World Series of Drag Racing (Cordova, Ill.). Gary moved on to drag racing fame running the Mr. Norm Dodge, one of the early Funny Cars. And today Gary Dyer is the owner of Dyer Machine Service producing superchargers for racing or street use. In 1962 the coupe was clocked at 126.76 mph. (Photos courtesy of Wayne Arteaga & Ray Tognarelli)

Probably the most famous Midwest C/GS Chevys in 1960 were Mike Marinoff's (No. 21 C/G) and Palmer Lazarus' (No. 411 C/GS). Mike's Wisconsin based '55 Chevy, 3800 lbs., started with a Latham supercharger before graduating to a 6-71 blower. Palmer's (Illinois) '56 Bel Air had a 4-71 blown 292" Chevy engine and a four-speed trans. Both cars hit 121 mph and E.T.'s in the 11.75 sec. area. They were quickly featured in match races at strips like Union Grove (Wisc.) and Oswego (Ill.). After Ed Iskenderian featured Mike Marinoff in his ads stating that Mike would "race anyone, anytime", Howard replied in his ad that "Marinoff wouldn't race Doug Cook". Both Marinoff and Lazarus replaced their Chevys with Willys' and continued to record very good performances. (Photos courtesy of Wayne Arteaga)

The fastest Supercharged Gas Coupe at the 1960 AHRA Nationals (Alton, Ill.) was this neat maroon '38 Willys. Mike Kuhl (standing) and Ralph Heine (in car) had one of the few Buick (364") powered blown gassers. That Buick powered the Willys to an excellent 132.74 mph AHRA A/GS record. The Missouri based Willys ran two gears (second and high) with a La Salle transmission. Mike raced four different '38 to '41 Willys in the 1959 to 1962 period including the Plymouth (413" wedge) powered '41, shown at a St. Louis car show. After moving to Southern California in 1962 Mike dropped out of drag racing only to return in 1966. For eight years Mike Kuhl made his living running his Top Fuel Dragsters. Today Mike's company, Mike Kuhl Enterprises, manufactures racing superchargers and other parts. (Photos courtesy of Mike Kuhl -Car Show photo by Robert Hegge)

The J & J Muffler Willys was the 1961 team effort by the Mallicoat twins (Jerry and Gary) and Bob "Bones" Balogh (So. Calif.). The car was the Mallicoats' while the blown 283" Chevy engine was built and owned by Bones. Although the car was usually run in the C/GS class on occasions it ran in A/GS or B/GS. The best times were 126.52 mph and 11.04 sec. (C/GS). In 1962 Mallicoats split away from Bones and the J & J sponsorship so they could race on their own. Their own 283" Chevy, a new stronger rear axle and a 600 lb. weight hidden in the empty gas tank put the twins car solidly in the C/GS class. But in 1963 they moved up to B/GS with a 327" Chevy and blasted to a 130.92 mph and 10.59 sec. clocking while winning a big $1000 B/GS meet at Lions.

(Photos courtesy of Bob Balogh, John Hellmuth and Barbara Advey)

Another fast Willys from Oklahoma was this '41 Willys campaigned by Ray Lollar. It used an Olds engine and a B&M Hydro to record speeds up to 138 mph. Note that Ray's Willys was set with a low stance at a time when most of the blown gassers were set high. This photo was at Alton, Ill. (Photo courtesy of Mike Kuhl)

Very few 1950's Fords competed in the supercharged classes. George Chorman (Ohio) achieved good 115 mph speeds (1960) with this '52 Ford in C/GS. But the engine wasn't a Ford, it was a Chevy. By 1962 George had purchased a stock '37 Willys to replace the Ford. But he then decided to join the Marines and the Willys was sold to Barbara Hamilton ($250). It was completed by her to run in the C/GS class. (Photo courtesy of Barbara Advey - Photo by Candid Classics)

Wayne Arteaga (Missouri) had this '33 Ford coupe for 1960 Supercharged Gas Coupe competition. It had an Olds engine with a chain driven blower (Wayne advised that the chain was very noisy). The transmission was from a big prewar Buick. The La Salle and Buick transmissions were equally strong. The coupe's appearance was set off with white wall slicks and Moon discs. The engine photo shows Wayne (left) and his future brother-in-law Paul Wessel with the chain disconnected. The light coupe ran in A/GS with speeds near 115 mph and in B/GS before Wayne bought a Willys. (Photos courtesy of Wayne Arteaga; Photos by Eldon Arteaga and Larry Bouldin)

There were lots of '55 - '57 Chevys in the C/GS class in 1961. This one was run by Tom Montalbano (Illinois). Note that at Oswego (Ill.) the class initials were C/GB - "B" for blown was used instead of "S" for supercharged. Many strips, including Oswego, were using their own classification rules in the early 1960's. Tom's Chevy hit speeds in the 116 mph area. In this photo the car still had a steel front end. It also had an interesting solution to the question of where to place the header outlets. (Photo courtesy of Ray Tognarelli)

The Brown Bros., Glen and Charlie, ran this neat metallic red '41 Willys in C/GS class at both AHRA and NHRA strips. Their home strip at Phoenix, Arizona was an AHRA strip in 1962. The Willys usually used a 283" engine. The brothers captured the NHRA C/GS speed record with a time of 124.37 mph at the 1963 Winternationals. The racing weight of the Willys was over 3500 lbs. The best times for the car early in 1963 were 126.05 mph and 12.25 sec. At AHRA strips it ran in DMG class which was about the same as C/GS. The car was soon retired when the Brown's joined the Dragster ranks. (Photos courtesy of Bob Balogh and Ray Tognarelli)

Probably the most successful early Chevy supercharged gasser was the '37 coupe raced by Dale Moody and Sam Jones (Indiana). In addition to winning the C/GS class at the NHRA Nationals, the gold colored coupe set National records in 1962 and 1963. After initially using a four-speed manual transmission the team changed to a B&M Hydro. Their E.T. record of 11.99 sec. in 1963 was the first record under 12 sec. set in C/GS under the 12.6 lbs./cu.in. rules. The coupe hit speeds up in the 128 mph area and successfully competed with the onslaught of Willys at that time. (Photo courtesy of Barbara Advey)

Gordon Selkirk, with partner Saul Bork (Illinois), joined the Willys ranks when the Olds engine from Gordon's Model A (Page 32) was shoe-horned into a '35 Willys coupe. The A/GS class coupe quickly was one of the fastest Midwest blown gassers with speeds in the 134 mph area. In 1965 Gordon duplicated the actions of K. S. Pittman, Stone-Woods-Cook and others by putting the Olds engine in the garage and placing a 430" Chrysler into the 2640 lb. coupe. The blue coupe responded with 140 mph times. When the late model cars came in during the late 1960's Gordon switched to a Camaro. (Photos courtesy of Wayne Arteaga and Mike Kuhl)

Ohio claimed to be the home of the gas coupes and this maroon '33 Willys was an example of why the claim was a legitimate one. And in fact perhaps Dayton could have claimed to be the capitol of Ohio's gassers with two of the fastest A/GS class cars in the country; George Montgomery and Jim Clinton. The photo shows Jim Clinton's '33 Willys at the 1962 NHRA Nationals. After recording some of the fastest B/GS times in 1961, Jim moved up to A/GS with this '33 Willys. His 139.75 mph in 1962 was perhaps the fastest A/GS time in the country. In early 1963 the car was put up for sale and Jim dropped out of the Supercharged Gas Coupe competition. (Photo courtesy of Ray Tognarelli)

The forerunner for the small foreign mini-car invasion of the Supercharged Gas Coupe classes was this four-door French Simca built by Jack Kulp (Penna.). It was originally built with a blown Olds engine to run in the A/GS class. But apparently it was a case of "too soon" because foreign cars were still unwanted in the blown gas coupe classes. This photo shows the little blue Simca in 1961 after the engine had been switched to a 283" Chevy to run in the B/GS class. Jack didn't continue to race this car because his interest had by then turned to dragsters. The nice thing about this car is that it was probably difficult to tell that it had a blown Chevy under the hood. It would have been a terror on the streets. (Photo courtesy of Ray Tognarelli)

Although this very nice '37 Chevy looked like a nice street rod. It was actually a very fast C/GS class race car. Rocky Childs (So. Calif.) was the owner-builder. The appearance was set off with polished wheels and whitewall tires. Rocky's Chevy hit speeds up to 119 mph at the nearby San Fernando drag strip in 1961. Cal Auto made their first fiberglass front ends for the '37-'38 Chevys for Rocky's car (and Don Noel's). After 1961 Rocky dropped out of Supercharged Gas Coupe competition. Today Rocky Childs' firm, Childs and Albert, manufactures racing engine components. (Photo courtesy of Rocky Childs)

Here is an example of how high the cars were being set in an effort to get traction. By 1963 George Montgomery could be certain that his tires wouldn't rub against the fenders (10" - 12" clearance). This photo at Cordova, Ill. shows how the soft top in the early model cars ballooned up at speed. Air flow caused a low pressure area to be formed over the top. (Photo courtesy of Wayne Arteaga)

At the 1963 NHRA Nationals everyone was talking about the West Coast B/GS gassers including Big John Mazmanian and K. S. Pittman. But when the meet was over the winner was the '39 Willys run by Jack Merkel (New York). His winning times of 130.05 mph and 10.95 sec. were achieved using a 368" Chevy hooked to a Vitar Hydro. The not often seen fiberglass '39 Willys Overland front fenders and hood were obtained from Hill-Zartman, who also had competed in the Supercharged Gas classes on occasion.

Although Jack won the Nationals twice he moved up to the A/GS class after being quoted as saying that there was "not enough recognition or publicity and few match races in B/GS". This photo was taken at Alton, Ill.   (Photo courtesy of Mike Kuhl)

Larry Dixon spent most of his drag racing career in dragsters, (Howard Cam Rattler and others), but in 1962 this '41 Willys was his race car. The B/GS Willys had a blown 327" Chevy and B&M Hydro. Although shown here at his local strip, San Fernando, Larry's best times, 128.57 mph and 11.20 sec., were recorded at Lions. After running with the supercharged gassers in 1962 and 1963 Larry moved on to Top Fuel competition. (Photo courtesy of Larry Dixon)

Although K. S. Pittman and John Edwards' red Willys had a fine A/GS time of 140.62 mph, their entry at the 1962 NHRA Nationals was in the B/GS class. Since B&M sponsored both the Pittman-Edwards Willys and the Stone-Woods-Cook Willys it was logical for one (S-W-C) to run A/GS and the other (P-E) to cover the B/GS class. Note changes from the photo on Page 30 taken the previous year. The Willys front fenders and hood were changed to fiberglass (Cal Automotive's first set) and plexiglass windows were installed. The car was raised up in the front and much wider rear slicks were added on "Mag" wheels. The Willys looked like a blown car with the Hilborn scoop protruding out of the hood. The engine was still a blown Olds. This car displayed its versatility in 1962 by winning the C/GS class at the Winternationals and then setting the A/GS record only four months later. (Photo courtesy of Ray Tognarelli)

After K. S. Pittman returned to concentrating on his blown Willys, Tim Woods was without a driver for the 1961 NHRA Nationals. Tim talked to Doug Cook, who he had competed against for several years. After a test run at Lions (8-12-61) the deal was on with Doug. The photo shows the car at the 1961 Nationals lettered as Stone-Woods. Doug Cook's name appears in the credits on the quarter panel. Note in the photo on Page 32 at Bakersfield the Olds engine had a 2-hole Hilborn injector while at the Nationals six months later a larger 4-hole injector had been installed. This car held the B/GS records for the entire 1961 season with the final records of 128.57 mph and 10.99 sec.
(Photo courtesy of Wayne Arteaga)

In 1962 Stone-Woods-Cook's Swindler II moved up to A/GS with the help of a bigger Olds engine. By the latter months of the year Swindler II was up to 142 mph and just under 10 secs. Then in November Doug Cook completed a new lighter Willys for A/GS class. This one was named Swindler A and was said to be "1000 lbs. lighter". Doug, who was by now working full time on the Stone-Woods-Cook car, ran this car every weekend for five weeks to get it dialed in. It hit 140 to 142 mph at each meet. The photos show Swindler A leaving the line at Pomona and Lions. Swindler A was also Olds powered. Swindler II was put back into the B/GS class and on occasions the team raced both cars which kept Doug Cook very busy. (Photos courtesy of Erik Chaputa and Charles Strutt - Photos by Charles Strutt)

46

Next to Willys coupes the other popular body style in the gasser classes was the Willys pickup. The "We Haul Spl." was a 1940 model. It was the B/GS entry belonging to Art Carter and Pee Wee Whitaker (Indiana) and shown here in the pits at the 1962 NHRA Nationals (Indy). The neat little truck was powered by a blown Chevy engine. (Photo courtesy of Ray Tognarelli)

In Southern California within the tough competition in the blown gas classes there was another competition. This was the Sandblasting competition. Interstate Sandblasting ran a Willys with a Chevy engine in the C/GS class and Safeway Sandblasting also ran a C/GS class racer with Ardun power. Interstate's "White Litenin" only competed in the C/GS class in the 1960 to 1961 period, it then moved up to B/GS with Olds power (1962). (Photo courtesy of Junior Thompson)

In 1959 Jack Kulp raced at the NHRA Nationals in A/G class with a '40 Willys coupe (Page 10). In late 1961 the car was back on the strips, including Great Meadows Dragways, shown here, with new owner Harry Hall (Penna.). It had Harry's blown Olds engine in it to compete in the A/GS class. Naturally Jack Kulp supported Harry with technical help. (Photo courtesy of Harry Hall)

This exceptionally neat '39 Willys Overland looks like a nice 1990's street rod but it really was a B/GS class race car in 1963. Wayne Arteaga and John Hellmuth (Missouri) raced this all steel coupe with a blown 371" Olds engine and a Hydro built by Hydromotive. The Olds engine pushed the coupe up to the 139 mph area (1964) before the team switched to a Chrysler. Most rodders did not like the looks of the '39 Willys front end. They were rarely seen on the drag strips because almost every 1937 to 1939 Willys had fiberglass 1940 or 1941 style fenders and hood, or one piece assembly. In spite of how great it looked, Wayne and John had to try and keep up with their competition so the '39 sheet metal did get replaced with '41 style fiberglass. The 1963 race at the Mid-America Raceway was a C/MG (AHRA classes) run-off between Arteaga-Hellmuth and Jim Selkirk (Illinois). (Photos courtesy of Wayne Arteaga and Roger Schoenfeld)

Junior Thompson's (So. Calif.) '41 Willys was one of the major players in the Southern California B/GS competition of the early 1960's. The Willys was built in 1960 and Junior raced it until 1965 when he put it up for sale ($850 less engine and trans). A small block 317" Chevy engine drove the purple coupe to 131 mph in 1961. It also used Joe Pisano's Chevy engine to set NHRA records in 1962. After experiencing too many expensive problems with the Chevys, Junior switched to a 360" Olds engine in 1963. The Olds engine kept the Willys in the 131 mph area. Junior ran almost all the major events in Southern California and Arizona, winning his share of them. (Photos courtesy of Junior Thompson and Charles Strutt)

Late in 1963 the B/GS class was hotly contested by Stone-Woods-Cook, the Mallicoat Bros., Junior Thompson, Nunes-Frank and the Airoso Bros. John Mazmanian could see that the blown gassers were getting opportunities for publicity, match races and money that his blown Corvette couldn't get. So he sold the Corvette and had a Willys built. The chassis work was done at B&M. His 338" Chevy was just right for the B/GS class. The pretty candy red Willys, driven and tuned by Bob "Bones" Balogh debuted in August with a fast 133.60 mph and 10.40 sec. clocking. The photo shows the B/GS '41 Willys in the pits at the NHRA Nationals a month later. "Bones" was in the car and Rich Siroonian is on the other side. The Willys ran a few more meets late in 1963 with a best B/GS time of 136.98 mph. Then "Bones" put a Chrysler in the Willys and Big John Mazmanian was ready to go A/GS racing. (Photo courtesy of Ray Tognarelli)

The B/GS winner at the 1962 NHRA Nationals was Mike Marinoff (Wisc.). Mike had switched to this red Willys from his very fast '55 Chevy (Page 36) and moved up to the B/GS class. In March the Willys came West to the Bakersfield meet where a victory in the B/GS (called BGCCS) class was heralded in Isky's ads. They said that Mike had won undisputed title to the B/GS class. A good year was capped off with NHRA record clockings (129.68 mph, 11.03 sec.) and a best of 132.84 mph. The flip open one-piece hood made engine work much easier. The photos are at the 1962 Nationals and Bakersfield meets. On May 5, 1963 the Willys was destroyed at Oswego, Ill. Mike Marinoff then moved on to the Dragster classes. (Photos courtesy of Wayne Arteaga, Junior Thompson and Ray Tognarelli)

Let's Stop The Hoax

Racing fans are entitled to know the truth. A certain car advertized as the World's Fastest B Gas Supercharged Chevrolet claims 10.63 E.T. at Inyokern. This time is not recognized by N.H.R.A. or the Inyokern Drag Strip. The back up times on this car was 11.38.

Facts; No 1 - We were ready to race said B gas Chevrolet at Inyokern, but said Chevrolet conveniently developed phony trouble and refused to race. No 2 - One week later at San Gabriel this car refused to show up to race and back up the phony E.T. they claim. We were there to race. No 3 - Again on December 3, 61, this B gas Chevrolet pulled into the Pomona Dragstrip and after our car turned a good E.T. he again refused to race.

Fans, we want to know how this B gas Chevrolet can claim these phony E.T.s and still refuse to race our car.

Listen cam grinders — are you going to allow your gas class supercharged cars to continue to offer the same phony car trouble week after week? We are in the sport of racing and want you to tell us and the public whether you are going to allow the following cars to race; No 1 Said B Gas Supercharged Chevrolet hereto referred to; No 2 A certain A gas Willys from Ohio which claims to be the Worlds fastest A gas car.

Challenge to No 2- Your claim is one of a champion. A champion must show that he is champion of all, not just champion of the east coast. We challenge you to a race at the Pomona Nationals in February, 62. We will be glad to pay you $200 if your A Gas car is champion over our B Gas car. Will you pay us $200 if you find that we are the real champions. We will run a B Gas 3600 lb Supercharged 416 Olds car against your 2200 A Gas 440 blown Cad car. Two out of three. Can you prove what you said in your ad of December 7th thru the 10th in the Mickey Thompson Car Show Program? We don't believe that you're game to try. Will you bring your car to the West Coast?

Cam grinders - we want to race your gas coupes and sedans. The racing public is entitled to know who is who. Will your cars be present at the showdown at the Pomona Nationals? Or will you continue to make phony advertizing claims as you have in the past as lastly there is a C Gas car driven by Mac which all the racing fans of Southern California would like to see race, not disappear. Will you let them race?

Fred Stone of the Stone-Woods & Cook Racing Team
B Gas Supercharged Coupe   4329 S. Broadway, Los Angeles 59, Calif.
Signed, Fred Stone

Stone-Woods & Cook B Gas Supercharged Coupe set a new E.T. 1320 Record of 10.61 secs at Pomona on Sunday December 3rd.

'KING OF THE MOUNTAIN'

Probably the most competitive class at any drag strip is the the gas coupe and sedan class. The 'B' Supercharged division has an entry list that contains just about the hottest gas coupes around. Always a top name in this hotly contested division is Doug Cook's Chevy powered Willys. Doug again became 'King of the Mountain' at Long Beach May 27th when he upped the record with a tremendous top end run of 124.48 mph. This blast was backed up with times of 124.30, 124.23 and et's of 11.38, 11.49 and 11.41.

Theres no secret to Dougs brute horsepower and envious consistency ... the power for this 3500 lb Willys comes from a 317" bln Chevy that utilizes the best equipment available ... HOWARD Aluminum rods, HOWARD supercharger drive kit, and the revolutionary HOWARD adjustable Roller Tappet Cam.

HOWARD'S RACING CAMS

10122 S. Main St. PH. PL 5-1168
Los Angeles 3, Calif.

Howard Cams Ad
DRAG NEWS — 6-3-61

Stone-Woods-Cook Ad
DRAG NEWS — 12-16-61

52

53

Drag strip promoters were happy to schedule the name A/GS cars because their match races drew good spectator crowds. This was Detroit's Motor City Dragway in August, 1965. The racers were K. S. Pittman and Doug Cook in the black Stone-Woods-Cook Willys, both from the Southern California area. These cars were very similarly built - Engle equipped Chrysler engines, B&M Hydros and Cal Automotive fiberglass. Doug Cook won the two out of three match races with best times of 148.02 mph and 9.84 sec. Both K. S. and Doug had become full time racers and toured throughout the Midwest, East and South for most of the year. (Photo courtesy of Doug Cook)

The Great Gasser Wars

- 1 9 6 4 -

Although the Supercharged Gas Coupe classes had a good year in 1963, the 1964 season was even better. In fact 1964 was the first of what might be called the "glory" years of the Supercharged Gas Coupe classes. And many of the things that came about in 1964 had a major effect on the classes and on drag racing as a whole, both at the time and in the future. Incidentally the 1964 NHRA rules remained essentially the same as used the previous year, so there were no surprises there. The first big shock wave came in January when John Mazmanian had his driver, Bob Balogh, build a Chrysler for his formerly B/GS Willys. Remember, as previously stated, it was common knowledge that Chrysler Hemi's did not run as well on gas as the wedge chambered Olds and Chevys. Fresh off the dyno the 467" Chrysler quickly rocketed Big John's Willys to 150 mph clockings while breaking under the 10.0 second mark. Any question about the effect of John Mazmanian's Chrysler power plant on the A/GS class was soon answered when both the Stone-Woods-Cook and K. S. Pittman cars appeared with their "if you can't beat them, join them" Chrysler Hemi's.

In March, 1964 an issue of Drag News included a statement that said that B&M was putting a Chrysler in the Stone-Woods-Cook entry because they didn't feel that the Olds engines would go any faster. What did B&M have to do with it? Lots - B&M (Bob and Don Spar) were among the biggest supporters of the Supercharged Gas Coupes and with good reason. Their work in 1959 and 1960 with Dick Harryman, K. S. Pittman-John Edwards and others had developed the Hydro-Stick (Hydramatic) transmission to become the dominant transmission in the higher powered gas classes. This success was probably the major building block that resulted in the very successful B&M manufacturing firm operating today. Both the Stone-Woods-Cook cars and the Pittman-Edwards car were effectively B&M factory cars, continually testing their transmissions. But in addition to supplying transmissions, B&M had their own Ron Scrima redesign and rebuild the rear suspensions and Cal Auto (Curt Hamilton) design and build lightweight fiberglass body components. The publicity B&M received from the performances of the Stone-Woods-Cook cars and the Pittman-Edwards Willys was great. And as other supercharged competitors like John Mazmanian and the Mallicoat Bros. did well, B&M also helped many of them. Since the Supercharged Gas Coupes were B&M's most important advertisement, B&M became an important decision-maker and contributor to the A, B and C Supercharged Gas Coupe competition.

How successful was the Chrysler hemi engine in the Supercharged Gas Coupe classes? Within a few years most of the fastest competitors were running the 1954 - 1958 Chrysler Hemi's. The Oldsmobile basically disappeared while continuing development of the Chevys and the new big block Chevys allowed them to remain competitive. So the Supercharged Gas Coupes began to seriously swing to Chryslers in 1964. It must be noted that by 1964 the Top Gas Dragster competitors had already discovered the Chrysler Hemi's and the fuel guys had known about the Hemi all the time.

On the West Coast the action was very hot at the early meets. The John Mazmanian vs. Stone-Woods-Cook competition became one of the top topics of interest. Big John won at the big UDRA race at Lions on February 2, 1964. An important item here is that both cars were paid to race. That was not often done at the major Southern California strips prior to 1964. Usually money was awarded winners of brackets or specific classes at that time. That was the situation for all classes except some Dragsters and a very few Superstock competitors. Stone-Woods-Cook won at the NHRA Winternationals two weeks later at 10.03 sec., 142.85 mph. However Big John displayed what a Chrysler could do with a 9.99 sec., 149.00 mph clocking.

In addition to the switch to Chryslers, 1964 saw other competitors making major changes. Chuck Finders joined with Stone-Woods-Cook to run the "Dark Horse", an Olds powered '33 Willys painted "Stone-Woods-Cook Blue". Excellent times of 9.83 sec. and 144.69 mph were recorded. Then a few months later Chuck Finders reappeared with the now red '33 Willys, 389" Chevy power and the lettering on the door said Altizer-Finders-Kibler. This combination hit a quick 9.76 sec. and 146.57 mph. In the meantime K. S. Pittman had parked the '41 Willys and built a '33 Willys with a hemi Chrysler under the hood. A quick 9.70 sec., 146.81 mph showed that Pittman's move was a good one. Pittman's new Willys went on to set the final 1964 NHRA A/GS records. Bob "Bones" Balogh joined with Gary Dubach to build a beautiful red Chevy powered '33 Willys, debuting with a 10.50 sec., 142.18 mph time. The New York team of Sanzo-Pellicane-Siedlecki hit a good 143.00 mph and 9.99 sec. with their '41 Willys pickup while in Illinois the Selkirk-Borg '35 Willys, Olds powered, was recording times of 10.33 sec., 144.00 mph. By the end of the year Stone-Woods-Cook with Chrysler power recorded a terrific 9.57 sec., 149.25 mph run. As for George Montgomery, his Chevy powered Willys recorded speeds of up to 144 mph but did not get the headlines that the cars running in the 150 mph area were getting. But when the chips were down his 9.95 sec. E.T. was good enough to win the NHRA Nationals, beating Stone-Woods-Cook in the process.

Although the A/GS cars were getting most of the publicity ink, the B/GS competitors were very busy. Jack Merkel (New York) continued to perform well including setting the NHRA B/GS records at 10.42 sec. and 135.13 mph. The Mallicoat Bros. (So. Calif.) recorded times of 10.38 sec. and 133.72 mph while Junior Thompson (So. Calif.) was hitting 10.64 sec. and 130.81 mph clockings. The Stone-Woods-Cook "Swindler B" was one of the quickest at 10.33 sec. and 134.96 mph. Two of the fastest Willys pickups were Bob Panella's (No. Calif.), at 10.36 sec. and 133.78 mph, and the MGM-Ciambella (So. Calif.) car at 10.61 sec. and 133.35 mph. Other B/GS competitors recording top performances were Arteaga-Hellmuth (Missouri) 11.18 sec., 131.30 mph; Jim Selkirk (Illinois) 11.41 sec., 130.78 mph; Coy Martin (No. Calif.) 11.10 sec., 132.11 mph; Szabo-Basty (Pennsylvania) 10.83 sec., 130.00 mph; the Airoso Bros. (No. Calif.) 10.81 sec., 128.96 mph and Scott Hammack (So. Calif.) 11.03 sec., 128.57 mph.

The activity in C/GS seemed to be fading somewhat perhaps due to the great amounts of publicity given the A/GS class and to a lesser extent the B/GS class. The Tarantola-Cruciata (New York) Willys sedan set the only NHRA C/GS record set in 1964 with a 11.62 sec. blast. Palmer Lazarus (Illinois) recorded a 11.14 sec., 131.00 mph time with his '41 Willys coupe while the Leibham-Strine (Texas) entry hit 11.73 sec. and 121.45 mph. Other top C/GS cars included the Levy-McLorn (So. Calif.) '55 Chevy sedan 11.37 sec., 122.57 mph; Mitchell-Yabsley (So. Calif.) 11.93 sec., 119.12 mph; and Don Toia (Arizona) 12.30 sec., 118.00 mph.

Although mostly unnoticed by drag racing enthusiasts, the performance of the Herrara and Sons C/GS Anglia was a view of the future. But wait a second, the NHRA rules stated that Anglias were not legal to run in the Supercharged class. That is true but Long Beach (Lions) and Fontana were not NHRA sanctioned drag strips and thus not bound by the NHRA restrictions. The Anglia only ran supercharged for a short time, but it was turning record speeds. In the near future other Anglias would come into the Supercharged Gas Coupe classes in numbers that would eventually lead to rule changes (1968) after almost four years of controversy. Although the Herrara and Sons C/GS Anglia was not accepted under the NHRA rules, it did show the way of the future that would eventually sweep aside the Willys and larger cars in the Supercharged Gas Coupe classes.

The publicity war that escalated in late 1963 continued in the early part of 1964. The major players were Stone-Woods-Cook (Engle) and John Mazmanian (Iskenderian). Ads as large as one-half page in Drag News included challenges, name calling and bragging meant to incite interest. In addition to the ads Drag News columnists Terry Cook and Bob Ramsey were reporting "hot scoop" information on both Eastern and Western Supercharged Gas Coupe competitors. What was the result of this publicity? The real result was that drag strips realized that the top A/GS cars could draw spectators. This translated into paid bookings. Thus 1964 can be considered the year the Supercharged Gas Coupes joined the ranks of the small but growing professional drag racers.

Match racing was where the money was for the newly professional drag racers. And most of the match racing was in the Midwest and East. This was probably because the major West Coast strips could just put some money up and be buried with Dragsters, Stockers, Altereds and Gassers. So they did not need to pay cars to appear; although this was not true for a few big names like Don Garlits. Drag strips in the other areas quickly found that a match race between two or more well known cars increased the gate more than enough to cover the costs. The result was opportunities for the Supercharged Gas Coupes to earn some money. Some of the Western cars that toured in 1964 were John Mazmanian (A/GS), Stone-Woods-Cook (A/GS), K.S. Pittman (A/GS) and the Mallicoat Bros. (B/GS). Perhaps the biggest tour was the trip to England by George Montgomery (A/GS) and K. S. Pittman (A/GS) for the six race English Dragfest. So for the first time the Supercharged Gas Coupe racers had a chance to earn some money.

The match races were the best payoffs available to the drag racers then. It was not like it is today with large amounts of money in the NHRA events. In fact the NHRA had only a few major events then and the winnings were mostly merchandise awards and trophies. But winning the NHRA Winternationals and Nationals was important for the publicity value and the resulting good match race bookings. The 1964 travels of the Supercharged Gas Coupes also created much interest and exposed the exciting blown gasser racing to many parts of the country. The result was better payoffs.

The A/GS cars had broken past the 150 mph mark and under the 10 second time in 1964 and were still considered the fastest big, stock bodied cars on the drag strips. The racing was exciting, unpredictable and the cars were really LOUD. The publicity hype was in high gear and some of the guys were earning some money. The competition was fierce and the performances getting better and better. It appeared that the "sun was shining" on the Supercharged Gas Coupe guys.

But, things were happening in the Stock Car ranks that would soon affect the blown gassers. The Superstock wars waged by racers like Don Nicholson, Dave Strickler, Arlen Vanke and many others had produced E.T.'s in the 11.5 sec. area and speeds up to around 125 mph. Mercury, Plymouth, Pontiac and Chevrolet were competing on somewhat equal terms. Then Chrysler came up with a pair of exhibition cars meant to win publicity. They were Dodge Chargers

Perhaps one of the most important events in the history of the Supercharged Gas Coupes was the debut of John Mazmanian's Chrysler powered '41 Willys. It was important for several reasons. One reason was the stampede to using Chrysler engines after John's Willys used 824 dyno tested horsepower to blast to 150 mph. Perhaps the most important item was the rivalry between John and Tim Woods. While most gas class racers were what you could call "little guys" who did their own work and drove their racers, John and Tim were successful businessmen who paid to have their race cars prepared and run. Drag racing enthusiasts enjoyed the competition between the two "big guys". That rivalry spurred on by John and Tim created one of the greatest publicity boons that drag racing had ever seen. It not only helped John and Tim, it helped all the blown gas coupe competitors. The photos show the candy red Willys as it appeared early in 1964 at Lions and Pomona, the 467" Chrysler engine and Bob "Bones" Balogh (the engine builder and driver). (Photos courtesy of Bob Balogh, Junior Thompson and the author. Photo at Lions by Charles Strutt).

with superchargers which the NHRA put in a special exhibition class they called S/FX. Chrysler then proceeded to tour the country with their 140 mph "Stockers". Well, it is easy to see that Chrysler just waved a red flag at everyone. So very quickly supercharged stockers like Arnie Beswick's GTO appeared and speeds climbed. The crowds loved them. Then Jack Chrisman, with years of Fuel and Gas Dragster experience, showed what happens when a Stocker runs a blower on fuel - 156 mph. This was the beginnings of the Funny Car development. And never again could the Supercharged Gas Coupes claim to be the fastest big stock bodied cars on the strips.

- 1 9 6 5 -

Although 1965 turned out to be a successful year for the Supercharged Gas Coupe classes, important developments were happening in drag racing that would cause major changes. It was not fully appreciated at the time, but what was in progress was that drag racing was turning professional. The leaders in the rush into professional status were the Factory Stock racers. The developments in the experimental Factory Stock competition in 1965 were nothing short of mind-boggling and confusing. Together with the Top Fuel Dragsters, the Factory Stockers and their offspring - the Funny Car - stole virtually all of the drag racing publicity.

The NHRA Supercharged Gas Coupe rules for the second year remained virtually unchanged. The only actual change was the C/GS weight break which was moved to 12.0 Lbs./cu.in. (from 12.6), probably to make an even step from the A to B to C classes (6.0, 9.0, 12.0). The new rules now clearly stated that foreign coupes and sedans qualified in the gas classes if they met the 92 inch minimum wheelbase requirement. The rules also continued to note that Anglias would run the gas classes with small blocks but were NOT allowed to run in the Supercharged Gas Coupe classes. An item added this year was a ban on fiberglass bodies in all the gas coupe classes. However, fiberglass components - doors, hoods, fenders, etc. - were acceptable.

Supercharged Gasser competition was very hot during the winter months on the West Coast. K. S. Pittman's '33 Willys won A/GS at both the NHRA and AHRA Winternationals (9.87 sec., 145.86 mph) while Stone-Woods-Cook won at Bakersfield (9.71 sec., 148.51 mph). Good A/GS performances by Hamberis-Mitchell (145.40 mph), Bones-Dubach (10.10 sec., 143.00 mph) and Altizer-Finders-Kibler (145.16 mph) were obtained using the early '33 style Willys. Other fast A/GS competitors included Warren-Miller-Warren (10.17 sec., 142.00 mph) and Big John Mazmanian (9.95 sec., 148.86 mph).

New technology was highlighted at the NHRA Winternationals when the Mallicoat Bros. used turbochargers to win the B/GS title (10.65 sec., 135.55

mph). Other top B/GS competitors in early 1965 included Kirby-Foster (10.25 sec., 137.50 mph), Coy Martin (10.88 sec., 132.75 mph), the Airoso Bros. (10.40 sec., 134.12 mph), MGM-Ciambella (10.24 sec., 138.08 mph) and the Stone-Woods-Cook "Swindler B" (10.44 sec., 133.54 mph).

From the shadow of Chrysler and Chevy engines an old Ford flathead, with assist from Ardun heads, stepped up to win C/GS at the NHRA Winternationals when Bones Balogh drove Chuck James' Willys to victory at 11.92 sec., 116.12 mph. Other C/GS cars recording good runs in the winter of '65 were Levy-McLorn (11.62 sec., 122.44 mph) and Cliff Dysart (11.60 sec.).

Activity picked up in the spring as the Eastern drag strips started their seasons and it continued into November. Some West Coast teams like K. S. Pittman, Stone-Woods-Cook and Big John Mazmanian found enough bookings to allow extended touring in the Eastern half of the country. Naturally the guys like George Montgomery, Jack Merkel, Eddie Sanzo and Gordon Selkirk were happy to see the West Coast guys and earn some money racing them. It is important to note that most bookings were for A/GS cars. Promoters had very little interest in the slower B/GS or C/GS cars unless a particularly interesting car or rivalry was involved.

By the end of the season some very good performances had been recorded. John Mazmanian captured the NHRA A/GS records with a strong 9.71 sec. and 152.28 mph performance. The crowd at the NHRA Nationals saw an exciting A/GS show when Stone-Woods-Cook captured the trophy over strong competition including George Montgomery, Jack Merkel, Eddie Sanzo and John Mazmanian. Doug Cook's best National's times were 9.53 sec. and 152.54 mph. Perhaps the fastest A/GS speed in 1965 was a 157.78 mph clocking by Stone-Woods-Cook at Rockford, Ill. The switch to a Chrysler engine yielded good times for Bones-Dubach-Pisano's '33 Willys (9.98 sec., 150.25 mph) and the MGM pickup (9.85 sec., 151.51 mph). In addition the A/GS Willys of Coonrod-Harry, George Montgomery, Eddie Sanzo, Selkirk-Bork and Jack Merkel were all well into the 140 to 145 mph area. New A/GS cars coming out late in the year included Junior Thompson's Chevy powered '51 Austin (10.19 sec., 140.00 mph) and the Dempsey Bros. turbocharged wedge Dodge powered '41 Willys pickup (10.20 sec., 146.00 mph). The most noteworthy new A/GS cars were the Anglias of Shores-Hess, Gene Altizer and Delling-Janisch at the end of the year. But wait a minute - Anglias were not legal in A/GS. So why was were they allowed to run illegal cars? The answer is that they ran at drag strips which were not using NHRA sanction or rules. So although most didn't fully realize it then the Willys would soon be losing their grip on the Supercharged Gas Coupe classes, just as the '32 to '40 Fords had about five years before.

The Anglia question became a major topic of discussion among the Supercharged Gas Coupe competitors for the next two years. In the early days of the classes, an Anglia appeared to be too small to be classified with the full sized cars, predominately '55 Chevys or early Fords or Willys. Thus the NHRA rules were basically written to exclude the little cars by saying "American only" and 92" minimum wheelbase. A few years later it was decided to allow foreign bodied cars in and actually accept Anglias in the gas classes. This happened because there were already so many Anglias running around the country. NHRA did not have the predominant control of drag racing then as they do now. The NHRA was only then in the process of expanding their National meets from two events (Winternationals and Nationals) to include the Springnationals, Summernationals and World Finals. Thus the majority of cars were built to meet the requirements of their local strips and as mentioned before many strips had their own rules, or AHRA, or NASCAR rules (yes, NASCAR was sanctioning drag racing then). In many areas the Anglias were running in the gas classes. So the NHRA accepted them for the gas classes as long as they had small block engines and no superchargers. The interesting point of the rule was that similar size Austins and Prefects (4-door Anglias) actually met the 92" minimum wheelbase and thus were legal Supercharged Gas class cars. The contro-versy continued on but was basically buried under an avalanche of new Anglias in both A/GS and B/GS. Incidently the advantages of building an Anglia or Austin were not just the small size or the neat appearance. The real advantages were weight placement and weight transfer during acceleration, which could result in quicker E.T.'s. By the time the rules were changed in 1968 to legalize all the by then blown, big block Anglias that were running, the racers were already starting to consider switching to newer cars. Looking back at this controversy it is easy to understand that it was just a continuing development of the car and chassis designs and thus "no big deal". In 1965 and 1966 it was a big deal to many of the racers, especially those whose cars effectively became obsolete. However progress marched on and now years later there are still some drag racing enthusiasts who maintain that the influx of Anglias in the Supercharged Gas Coupe classes took the cars away from those that the spectators identified with and thus lost much crowd appeal.

Back in B/GS the sky caved in for those who wanted to run the NHRA Eliminator brackets. The NHRA brackets dialed-in on the class record. So it was tough on anyone if his class E.T. record was set low. And that is exactly what happened when Ron Nunes "bombed" the B/GS E.T. record by .48 seconds with a 9.94 sec. run, backed up by a 9.90 sec. run. It is interesting to note that Ron's '41 Willys was powered by (what many guys

One of Northern California's best known blown gassers was the '40 Willys built and run by the Airoso Bros., Joe and Lee. Built in 1960 with a De Soto Hemi engine and a La Salle transmission, the Root Beer colored, B/GS coupe set the initial 1962 NHRA E.T. record (12.01 sec.). In 1965 the color was changed to blue and a Chrysler engine, with the B&M Hydro attached, filled the spot under the hood. It is pictured at Bakersfield, towing in the pits, where the Willys was the B/GS class winner in 1965. They won over the Stone-Woods-Cook B car in the final race. The Airoso's recorded times up to 136.87 mph and E.T.'s down to 10.24 sec. that year. (Photo courtesy of Sherm Porter)

The "Kamakazi Koup" was campaigned in the Northwest by Jack Coonrod and Wayne Harry (Oregon). The '33 Willys coupe was a replacement for the early Willys pickup the team had run before. The pickup apparently had some handling problems. In 1965 the A/GS "Koup" hit 145.86 mph using a stroked 392 Chrysler engine and a B&M Hydro. Jack continued to race and improve the Willys after Wayne decided to drop out of drag racing, eventually joining the touring pro blown gassers in the East. (Photo courtesy of Jack Coonrod - Photo by Jagelski-Fertello)

felt was obsolete) an Olds engine. Ron's great performance made it very hard on B/GS racers racing the NHRA events. It became such a problem that the NHRA "retired" his record in 1967. The B/GS speed record was also set at the same meet by the Mallicoat Bros. at 136.36 mph. That October meet at Half Moon Bay (No. Calif.) was noteworthy as both the 1965 A/GS and B/GS records were set then. The NHRA Nationals B/GS winner was Billy Holt (10.61 sec., 131.96 mph). Good B/GS performances included those by Coy Martin (10.09 sec., 138.84 mph), the Airoso Bros. with a Chrysler replacing their DeSoto (10.24 sec., 138.67 mph), Palmer Lazarus (11.08 sec., 134.38 mph) and John Edwards (11.06 sec., 136.5 mph).

The NHRA C/GS record was nudged down from 11.62 sec. to 11.52 sec. in three steps by Levy-McLorn, Leibham-Strine and finally Tarantola-Cruciata. Vinnie Tarantola's Willys sedan also took the NHRA National's C/GS trophy home with a final run of 11.45 sec. and 121.45 mph. Competition in C/GS included the above group running in the mid 120 mph area and the cars of Ron Rinauro, the Langlo Bros., George Reese, Cliff Dysart and Straka-Tscaida.

Unlike 1964 the Supercharged Gassers did not benefit from a lot of publicity this year. The reason was because drag racing was changing. Drag racing was being promoted by the strips and the NHRA to be a professional sport. The top draw was the Top Fuel Dragsters. In spite of the fuel ban of a few years previous the Fuel Dragsters had survived and were

going over 200 mph in as low as 7.5 seconds. They smoked the tires, thundered down the strip and had spectator appeal. The drag strips scheduled match races and 8, 16, and even 32 Dragster programs. Most of the publicity from the drags hyped the Dragsters except for special events and competitors.

At first the Experimental Stockers were able to get some publicity but feuds between the manufacturers and the drag racing associations (NHRA, AHRA and NASCAR) were confusing to drag racing enthusiasts. Then the drag racers themselves took control of the situation. While the factory Mustangs, Dodges and Comets were hitting times around 11.0 sec. and near 130 mph, the real publicity thunder was stolen by the guys who didn't worry about the class rules. They built exhibition stockers under the "run what you brung" rules. The crowds loved Jack Chrisman's new Comet, Arnie Beswick's Pontiac, Don Gay's Pontiac, Sox and Martin's Plymouth and Don Nicholson's Comet. Early in the year these injected or blown 1965 "Stockers", many of them running nitro, were into the 10 second area. Progress was quick, spurred on by the excellent money available for match races. New entries included Gary Dyer (former B/GS racer) in Mr. Norm's blown Dodge; Fuel Dragster racer Bob Sullivan (Hemi-Barracuda); Tom McEwen in the Hemi-Cuda built in the B&M shop and Richard Petty, of NASCAR, with his Hemi powered Barracuda. Although the cars were not NHRA legal, they were an instant success with publicity second only to the Top Fuel Dragsters and the best money bookings in drag racing. By the end of 1965 Gary Dyer's Dodge had recorded a 8.68 sec. E.T., Tom McEwen (Hemi-Cuda) ran a 8.88 sec. E.T. and Don Gay's Pontiac GTO had stopped the clocks at 170.45 mph. So 1965 had seen the "Stockers" go 20 to 40 mph faster and over 2 sec. quicker in only one year. And a new name was tagged on these Stockers - FUNNY CARS. Not everyone liked the name but it stuck.

So although the Supercharged Gas Coupe classes had a good year of competition and progress the spotlight had shifted to the new Funny Cars. The Funny Cars were faster, as noisy as a Top Fuel Dragster and commanded more money. Several A/GS competitors including George Montgomery, K. S. Pittman and Stone-Woods-Cook successfully booked match races with Funny Cars. Interestingly the ad for a Tennessee match race between the Stone-Woods-Cook A/GS Willys and Don Gay's S/FX Pontiac said that both cars would be running nitro.

The successes of the Fuel Dragsters and A/FX and S/FX Stockers left only a limited amount of publicity for the Supercharged Gas Coupes. Race results often gave only a mention to the A/GS, B/GS or C/GS competition. A few magazines did feature some of the supercharged cars including George Montgomery, Junior Thompson, K. S. Pittman, John Mazmanian, Jack Merkel, Stone-Woods-Cook, Bones-Dubach-Pisano and Hamberis-Mitchell. But in general the Supercharged Gas Coupe classes were just becoming one of the many competition classes. The two bright spots in a publicity sense were (1) the match races and touring by K. S. Pittman, George Montgomery, Stone-Woods-Cook and a few others and (2) the many interesting and informative articles about the Supercharged Gassers in the new Drag World newspaper. The articles in Drag World were the works of Terry Cook, Ben Brown and Bob Ramsey. Their articles about the happenings in the Supercharged Gasser ranks helped to spur competition (new cars), encourage strips to put up some money and build spectator interest. The results were to be seen in the 1966 season.

- 1 9 6 6 -

Major changes occurred in both the Supercharged Gas Coupe classes and overall drag racing in 1966. The item at the top of everyone's list was money. The results of the previous several years of paying money for "shows" or match races had convinced many drag strip operators that the spectator gate receipts could be improved substantially with good racing programs. So 1966 was the year that most of the larger, and many of the smaller, strips dug into their pocket books to get "shows" to please their spectators. Naturally the biggest drawing cards were the Funny Cars, followed by the Fuel Dragsters. But Funny Car shows were expensive and so were Fuel Dragsters. Thus many

strips found that they could pay some lower class cars much less money and often get a very good show. The Supercharged Gas Coupes fit the requirements well as they made lots of noise, were unpredictable, fast and generally put on a good show for the spectators. So semi-pro drag racing arrived in 1966 for the Supercharged Gas Coupes .

There were two different programs that drag strip promoters used to buy a racing show. The first method was a scheduled match race. Usually a contract was signed with a car owner agreeing to pay a specific amount of money for a certain number of runs or races. The drag strip promotor could then advertise the names of the participants and tell the public what and who they would see. Normally the strips booked two or four cars from the same class or with roughly the same performance. The second type of paid shows was four, eight or sixteen- car elimination programs. Generally the four, eight or sixteen fastest qualifiers ran off eliminations with a fixed payoff for each round loser and the final winner. This program was usually less costly than the match race program but the promoter could not advertise for certain who would be racing or if enough cars would show up.

Match racing was really developed in the Midwest, East and   South. By 1966 many of the strips were scheduling match races almost every week. Many of them had been pleased with the shows put on by K.S. Pittman's, Stone-Woods-Cook's and John Mazmanian's A/GS Willys' the previous year. So the trio once again booked their calendars and as early as April K. S. Pittman was back in Ohio. Stone-Woods-Cook and Big John were close behind. It was an opportunity for New York A/GS competitors like Eddie Sanzo, Jack Merkel and Jim Oddy to get in on the action. But the most eagerly awaited races would be Ohio George Montgomery vs. Stone-Woods-Cook races, and they did race numerous times. George had a good year (he said he was booked solid for 1966 by the end of January). The four-car, round robin shows with the George Montgomery, K. S. Pittman, Stone-Woods-Cook and John Mazmanian A/GS Willys cars, were probably the most publicized of the Supercharged Gas Coupe match races. Incidently these races were all held in the Eastern half of the country.

In Southern California new Austins and Anglias had sprung forth and were recording great performances. Based on the interest, Irwindale and Long Beach both started offering money to four-car A/GS elimination brackets. The initial payoff was $100 to winner, $50 to runnerup and $25 to the first round losers. But with two local strips running at the same time, the brackets didn't always fill at both strips. What was the answer? Easy, Irwindale raised the winner to $125. Actually the almost weekly A/GS money encouraged competition resulting in new cars being built. Irwindale also put on an eight-car A/GS show and Fontana (Ben Christ) tried a 16-car A/GS show. Where most strips around the country were running handicap eliminator brackets, like Super Eliminator and Competition Eliminator, the Southern California strips were having good spectator response from heads-up racing of A/GS coupes, A Fuel Altereds, Junior Fuel Dragsters and Top Fuel Dragsters.

In contrast to previous years the rules became a major topic of conversation in 1966. Actually the only thing that changed in the NHRA rules was the class initials, from A/GS, B/GS and C/GS to AA/G, BB/G and CC/G. This aligned the initials with the other supercharged classes in altereds, dragsters, etc. So the rules didn't change, but the cars DID. So - what happened to the cars?

In late 1965 Shores-Hess and Delling-Janisch converted their A/G Anglias to AA/G and Junior Thompson debuted his Austin. All had small block Chevy engines and showed good promise with below 10 second capability. But then January saw the Kohler Bros.' Anglia record a 9.49 sec. run with a big block Chevy and the MGM team move their Chrysler into an Austin pickup. Junior Thompson switched to a Chrysler and soon the Shores-Hess small block was replaced by a big block Chevy. In only a few months the Kohler Bros., MGM and Shores-Hess machines were cutting 9.20 sec. E.T.'s.

By the time the Eastern drag strips were ready to open for the season, the fierce competition in California had dropped the E.T.'s by almost .5 sec.. As an example, the NHRA record in AA/G was 9.71 sec., but the Kohler Bros. and MGM both hit 9.25 sec. times in April. The competition had also added more cars to the fray. Korney-Montrelli (Anglia-Chrysler), Finders-Bizio ('33 Willys pickup-Chevy), the Dempsey Bros. ('41 Willys pickup-Dodge), Delling-Janisch (Anglia-Chevy), Altizer-Kibler ('33 Willys-Chevy), Herrera and Sons (Anglia-Chevy), Jim Kirby ('41 Willys-Chrysler), Bones-Dubach-Pisano ('33 Willys-Chrysler), Hicks-Galli-Modlin ('40 Willys pickup-Chrysler) and Bill Eisner (ultra light '33 Willys) all helped keep the competition interesting. Before starting their Eastern tours the AA/G cars of K. S. Pittman, Stone-Woods-Cook and John Mazmanian were part of the Southern California competition. The Fontana AA/G show in February ran off fourteen AA/G and one BB/G (the authors'). Other than the Nationals this may have been the biggest gathering of AA/G cars to that date.

Strong competition in almost any endeavor will result in major changes and improvements. This really proved to be true for the AA/G class in 1966. The most important "change" had to be the rules. As stated previously the NHRA rules did not change anything except the class initials. But many AA/G cars did change with little concern for the NHRA rules.

The key to the problem was that the NHRA and AHRA rules for A/GS were slightly different. The main difference was that AHRA allowed the 90" wheelbase Anglias to run while NHRA held to a 92" minimum wheel- base. Another very important variance was the minimum weight/displacement ratio: AHRA - 5.0 lbs./cu.in. vs. NHRA - 6.0 lbs./cu.in.. It is easy to see what rules the competitors used when it is pointed out that the weekly cash payout, AA/G shows were being held at Irwindale and Long Beach, both AHRA sanctioned strips.

The sudden influx of cars in AA/G was the result of some unblown A/G competitors adding superchargers. Some of the reasons to jump into AA/G were to go faster, earn more money and get more publicity. Both the Anglias of Shores-Hess and the Kohler Bros. had been record holding A/G cars. The rush to run small cars, Anglias and Austins, began at the very beginning of 1966 and became a mini stampede as Willys owners replaced their "big" cars with little cars. Interestingly when a racer built his new small car the old car was often sold to a new participant in the Supercharged Gas Coupe classes. This helped increase the number of competitors around the country.

The A/GS situation prompted Terry Cook to comment in his Drag World column (1-7-66) titled "Is The Willys Obsolete" that "in the future the Willys will be a classy street coupe and tow car rather than a race car". His forecast was accurate. Comments from New York's Eddie Sanzo and Jack Merkel reportedly were that they would not race the West Coast cars unless they were NHRA legal. In addition many of the AA/G competitors in California were questioning the legality of some of the cars. But perhaps the feeling of many of the racers was summed up by Junior Thompson in an interview with Drag World (4-15-66) when Junior said "If it is the AHRA tracks that give away the money for A/GS cars, why not build a car to take advantages of the AHRA rules".

In an effort to "stem the tide of confusion and hard feeling" (Terry Cook, Drag World) the UDRA's (United Drag Racers Assn.) Tom McEwen had a meeting with representatives of many AA/G competitors and the NHRA Division 7 officials. After much discussion the group was able to agree on a list of five rules that would apply to NHRA Division 7 competition only. The agreement allowed 5.0 lbs./cu.in. and the elimination of front brakes (many of them had been disconnected anyway). It also allowed big block engines in Anglias and Willys could move the rear wheels forward to a minimum wheelbase of 94". The agreement also said that strips running handicap eliminator brackets would let the AA/G cars dial their own handicaps rather than using the AA/G record - remember some of these cars were running about .5 under the NHRA record. The final stamp of approval from Wally Parks (NHRA) agreed to all except the Willys had to retain the stock 100" wheelbase. So the Southern California guys proved how democracy works, just "grab the ball and run". And guess what, the NHRA rules for the next year (1967) said 5.0 lbs./cu.in. minimum.

Perhaps little noticed under the major controversy afforded the small cars were two technical improvements. The most important was the introduction of the three speed Torqueflite in the Supercharged Gas Coupe classes. Prior to 1966 most of the Supercharged Gassers were using four-speed Hydramatics, originally manufactured for 1950's Oldsmobiles, modified for racing by B&M, HydroMotive, C&O, Vitar and other transmission builders. But from about 1962 the Chrysler Torqueflite transmission had been progressively improved and modified and was successfully used in Plymouth and Dodge Super Stock drag race cars. The leader in redesigning the Torqueflite for racing was Art Carr. His transmissions were in the original S/FX Dodge Chargers and were used by a large percentage of the new Funny Cars. When the Kohler Bros. shattered records early in the year, the public talked about big block Chevys and Anglias, but some of the racers were more interested in the transmission. Instead of the traditional Hydramatic the Kohler Bros. had an Art Carr built Torqueflite. The Torqueflite's torque converter certainly gave a good "launch" off the line. The three gears instead of four eliminated the 1-2 shift of the Hydramatic that often seemed to break the tires loose. So in almost no time the Shores-Hess Anglia had an Art Carr Torqueflite in it and the MGM and Junior Thompson Austins both had Torqueflites built by C&O. And almost everyone

else switched to a Torqueflite. It varied with each car but Torqueflites gave more consistency to E.T.'s and in some cases were up to .2 sec. quicker.

The other technical change that helped the Supercharged Gassers were tires. Once again the Funny Cars had taken the lead on developments, as they had with transmissions. The wide racing slicks in the early 1960's had been designed to run on wide rims with air pressures of 25 psi. Reducing the tire pressure in these tires allowed the center of the tire to pull in - resulting in less traction. But work in 1965, mostly with the Funny Car racers, developed tires that when mounted on narrower rims, 8" instead of 10", achieved excellent traction. In fact, under hard acceleration the wheels seemed to turn in the tire enough to put deep wrinkles in the tire sidewalls. As a result the tires were nicknamed "wrinkle walls". The only drawback was the low 3 - 9 psi tire pressures seemed to yield poor tire stability at high speeds. The Supercharged Gas Coupes benefitted from these new low pressure tire designs as did most drag racers.

The AA/G racers all over the country were also very active this year with strong performances by Paul Frost (Ohio), Jack Merkel (New York), the Lee Bros. (Michigan), Eddie Sanzo (New York), Ron Nunes (No. Calif.), the Baroumes Bros. (Washington), Carter-McGavock (Indiana), Glen Drake (No. Calif.), Jack Coonrod (Oregon), Christoferson-Williams (Wash.), Hamberis-Mitchell (No. Calif.), Jeg Coughlin (Ohio), Ratliff-Carothers (Illinois), Jim Oddy (New York) and Stoltz-Velasquez (Indiana).

In 1965 the Bee Line Auto Willys had the standard A/GS '40 Willys look. It had a fiberglass hood and fenders, a Hilborn 4-port scoop and "Mag" wheels. It was red and except for the lettering it could have been mistaken for K. S. Pittman's coupe. The owner was Al Zerbarini (Conn.). A big 464" Olds engine and a Hydro transmission pushed the Bee Line racer to speeds of 134 mph. The photo was taken at the Dover Dragstrip (N.Y.). (Photo courtesy of Ken Menz)

The NHRA events were won by AA/G regulars George Montgomery (Nationals) and MGM (Winternationals). Jack Merkel and George Montgomery played "catch" with the NHRA records with George keeping them at 9.34 sec. and 155.97 mph. Perhaps the lowest E.T. at a major meet was the 9.04 sec. cut at the AHRA World Championships by the MGM Austin pickup (at 5.0 lbs./cu.in.).

Proof of the new interest was the increased number of advertisements telling about the Supercharged Gassers. About one half of the ads were manufacturers like B&M, Isky, C&O, Crane, Herbert and Hydro-Motive showing the performances of the AA/G cars using their products. The rest of AA/G oriented ads were by competitors like Fred Stone (Stone-Woods-Cook), Shores-Hess or Junior Thompson often challenging other cars, relating their victories or asking for "bookings".

All the excitement and publicity for the AA/G competitors didn't help the BB/G and CC/G competitors, in fact it made them virtually disappear. There were still many fine racers in BB/G and CC/G but very few bookings for match races or shows were available. Most of the strips were beginning to run handicap brackets, like Super Eliminator or Street Eliminator, so there was very little opportunity to race other Supercharged Gas Coupes. Some of the BB/G racers had already moved up to AA/G (Jim Oddy, Jack Merkel) and others went on to dragsters, like Levy-McLorn.

The NHRA Nationals were repeat victories for the 1965 winners with Billy Holt (BB/G) and Vinnie Tarantola (CC/G) taking home the trophies. The NHRA BB/G records in 1966 were not broken while the CC/G records were reset by Tarantola-Cruciata (11.17

sec.) and the Marrs Bros. (126.58 mph). In spite of the limited publicity there were many strong running BB/G and CC/G competitors. A few more of them were Bob Lombardi (New York), Chuck James (So. Calif.), Moody-Jones (Indiana), the Airoso Bros. (No. Calif.), Richard McKinstry (Mass.), Bob Chipper (N. Y.), Barb Hamilton (Ohio) and Pat Steward (No. Calif.).

So the Supercharged Gas Coupe competitors had an exciting season in 1966. The new small cars had virtually taken over and the big block Chevy "Rat Motor" had joined the early Hemi-Chryslers and small block Chevys as the most successful powerplants. In regards to transmissions, everyone already had, or wanted, a Torqueflite transmission. The top cars were recording E.T.'s in the 9.20 to 9.40 sec. area and speeds around 155 mph.

It is important to point out that cars running NHRA events had to meet 6.0 lbs./cu.in., cars at AHRA events could run at 5.0 lbs./cu.in. minimum, and cars running other meets could sometimes run what ever weight they could manage. It is very possible that some of the 1800 to 2000 pound Anglias, Austins and early Willys were running as low as almost 4.2 lbs./cu.in. Remember most local strips didn't check the engine size and at match races no one cared except the other racers. What this means is that many of the times recorded were not made at legal weight. And in fact for match racing some cars ran alcohol, it made them go faster and was easier on the engine. So it is impossible to compare all the times the various Supercharged Gas Coupes recorded. But regardless they went faster and became more popular in 1966.

Some of the other Supercharged Gas Coupe competitors in the 1964 to 1966 period were:

Safeway Sandblasting (So.Cal.)	Phil Castronovo (New York)
Nimphius Bros. (New York)	Thomas Bros. (New Jersey)
Sanford Bros. (Louisiana)	Dondero-Cole (No.Calif.)
Carlton Franks (Mississippi)	Ron Still (Delaware)
Hicks-Wood (Alabama)	Harry Wilson (No.Calif.)
Wouters-Gray (Canada)	Frank Bash (Pennsylvania)
Lamar Bobo (Georgia)	Larry Nails (Missouri)
Dean Brown (Texas)	Nick Mayer (Pennsylvania)
Bob Harrington (Arizona)	Al MacKenzie (Illinois)
Mel McGinnis (Pennsylvania)	Bob Roper (Arkansas)
Lemma Bros.-Hence (New Jersey)	Arteaga-Hellmuth (Missouri)
Hank Wilko (New Jersey)	Mike Bamber (So. California)
Atts Ono (So.California)	Carl Hegge (Virginia)
Roy Farley (Oklahoma)	Hanson-Dalsey (Washington)
Rogers-Rogers (No.California)	Bob Williamson (Canada)
Harry Hall (Pennsylvania)	Selkirk-Bork (Illinois)
Don Eisner (So.California)	Carter-McGavock (Kentucky)
Roger Garten (So.California)	Busse-Fout (Illinois)
Hrudka Bros. (Ohio)	Dale Kersh (So.California)
Bob Panella (No.California)	Meredith-Newton (So.California)
Dan Hix (Kansas)	John McDougall (Canada)
Wiesner-Owens (Colorado)	Don Montgomery (So.California)

The "Dark Horse" was a '33 Willys built by Chuck Finders (So. Calif.) in late 1963. It debuted in December in Stone-Woods-Cook blue and with Tim Woods' 400" Olds engine. The car was apparently the one that Eddie Thompson and Chuck Finders had campaigned successfully in the unblown A/G class earlier in 1963. After a test in B/GS the car moved up to A/GS and soon cranked out a best of 144.69 mph and a very good 9.88 sec. At precisely the same time that Chuck was testing the '33 Willys, Big John Mazmanian and "Bones" Balogh were demonstrating what Chrysler power could do. The result was that Tim Woods and Doug Cook were busy converting to Chrysler power and the "Dark Horse" project died. Chuck ran it until April and then it came out in May as the 389" Chevy powered, Altizer-Finders-Kibler A/GS Willys. (Photo courtesy of Charles Strutt)

65

The "new" 1964 Stone-Woods-Cook Willys was painted black and it had a new engine. The team skipped the Bakersfield meet and then in April the rumored Chrysler powered Swindler A appeared. Within five weeks the Willys had recorded times of 145.18 mph and 9.80 sec. In August they went East for about three months. Match races were run with George Montgomery, Eddie Sanzo and other cars, including dragsters. At U. S. 30 "Swindler A" made a 150.00 mph pass through the lights (8-18-64). The 440" Chrysler continued to push the 2740 lb. Willys to speeds over 145 mph and E.T.'s in the 9.80 to 9.90 sec. area after returning to Southern California. Doug Cook recalls that the magazine people told him that they should not have painted it black because magazines feature bright (red, yellow, etc.) cars. But even if Big John's red car did get lots of publicity the Stone-Woods-Cook car did too, because they earned it. (Photos courtesy of Don Prieto, Ray Tognarelli and Junior Thompson - Front view by Charles Strutt)

..AN OFF THE "CUFF" DRAG RACING INTERVIEW..

... Between FRED STONE of S-W-C Cars and Mr. Bull-Cam Grinder, spokesman for Big June and Little June and their Chrysler power A-Gasser....

... FRED STONE to Mr. Bull (Question): Are you the guy that spread the big lies and propoganda from Coast to Coast for a certain Cam Company on the West Coast, better known for its unreliable performances?....

Mr. Bull (answer): Well, man seeing how this is just between you and I, and not for publication,...yes, you might say that's my job...spreading their marlarkey in the DRAG NEWS and any other drag paper that will print it... You know man, if you tell a big enough lie... somebody will believe it... STONE to Mr. Bull:... Now that you and I understand your position...you don't mind answering a few questions on how you help Big June and Little June deceive the Public with propoganda and plain lies about the STONE WOODS COOK car in the past four issues of Drag News....

Mr. Bull... No sir— fire away, if you were not so honest, you might pick up a point or two from my boss, Big June?

QUESTION: Isn't it a fact, Mr. Bull that at Long Beach, California on February 2, in the first race we beat Big June and completely eliminated his car?

ANSWER: Yea, that's true.

QUESTION: And Mr. Bull, will you admit that the second race was a 'kick' race?.... And we still beat your E.T. in that race almost fifteen hundreds of a second...

ANSWER: True.., True...

STRAIGHT FROM THE BULLS MOUTH - - -

QUESTION: Is it not true that Big June is an officer in UDRA with Authority to appoint his choice of starters?
ANSWER: Right, that's Big June alright..man he is a gasser...
QUESTION: Well, then did he change starters in that race in order to get the jump on Doug Cook at the starting line?
ANSWER: Yea, man, you sure can call it correct....
QUESTION: Then Mr. Bull how do you explain our car turning better E.T. at every track, yet you claim superiority in A-Gas Super Charge?
ANSWER: By spreading more bull.....
QUESTION: How do you explain 825 Horse Power being defeated and outclassed by approximately 650 H.P.?
ANSWER: Big June will fix that with his a pointed starters..If you can't beat them, trick them.....
STONE to Mr. Bull: Over 9,000 fans saw our car pull ahead by two lengths off the line in the first race eliminating you completely...
Comment by Mr. Bull: I was amazed...
QUESTION: Isn't it a fact that Big June refused to race the dark horse on Saturday night after being slapped twice on the back by Chuck Finders' Driver...
ANSWER: Yes, that's right...
QUESTION: Why didn't he race?
ANSWER:. We didn't want any part of that so called dark horse, even with our choice of starter, we couldn't win anyway.. Lies are just not big enough to make such a claim...
STONE:... Lets review a few facts now; The dark horse, a new car.. 1st day out..POMONA.. 9.88 - 144.79...
Long Beach 1st day out 9.89 - 143.08 with 400 cu. inch we claim only 600 h.p. however, we realize that we have the Engle Cam which accounts for the difference. Big June was a big mouth in the Pits, making false claims, like a 150 miles per hour, and that we are afraid to race him and etc., etc., etc... Isn't it a fact Mr. Bull that we raced Big June in A-Gas Super Charge six times and defeated him five times out of the six; twice in Detroit, twice in Pomona and once in Long Beach? .. In a so called B-Gas Chevy powered with the weight pulled, he was in A-Gas Super Charge.
BULL: Yes, so what?
STONE: Well, beating Big June is nothing to brag about because we feel that he is still in the minor leagues... BESIDES having a car in competition, no sportsmanship..making phony claims about what he is going to do in order to sell equipment, for a certain Cam-Grinder.
BULL: We got away with it for ten years.
STONE: We made him buy that Chrysler, he couldn't win with a Chevy. That Chrysler hasn't shown us anything as yet.
BULL: Have to admit, it is a disappointment, even to my Boss.....
STONE: Now, Mr. Bull we will take the Ex-Champ, George Montgomery. There is real sportsmanship to be respected, no propoganding, lie spreading bull... In fact, he denied Cam-Grinder's accusations about S-W-C and called him a 'liar' in Drag News...
BULL: Yes, you see he is driving Stock Cars now..Man he's fired..
STONE: Big June's time at Long Beach was not 9.97, top time was not 144.95.
ANSWER: Big June exaggerated both E.T. and time.... That's us...
QUESTION: At Inyokern on January 26th, Big June was blown off by a Small Chevy Dragster, his best time... 10.64.
ANSWER: You could have beat him with your B-Gas Car..How naive can you be? Haven't you learned yet, that honesty just doesn't pay...
STONE: We think it does. We rely on a good competitive car, an expert driver, a reliable Engle Cam, a B & M Hydro Stick, sportsmanship and an honest race...
We'll see you after the 'Nationals'.... Mr. Bull...

FRED STONE

One of the best remembered of the A/GS Willys was the steel '33 coupe built by K. S. Pittman in 1964. It was quickly built, much of it in B&M's shop, to replace Pittman's '41 coupe. Competition had heated up considerable with Big John's move into A/GS and Tim Woods subsequent switch to Chrysler power. Dave Zeuschel assembled a 420" Chrysler for the coupe. The engine used was the 354" Chrysler rather than the larger 392" Chrysler. The 354" was popular because it was approximately 50 lbs. lighter than the 392" Chrysler engine. The life-span of the Pittman Willys lasted only one year. After the car was destroyed at a Texas strip (after clocking 149.67 mph), K. S. quickly built a '41 Willys to fill his match race bookings. (Photo courtesy of George Montgomery - Photo by Don Brown)

68

While Big John and Doug Cook were battling it out in early 1964, K. S. Pittman was home working on his new A/GS race car. In May he reappeared in this distinctive '33 Willys. It was red, had a Dave Zeuschel built 420" Chrysler engine and had his sponsors logo (S & S Racing Team) on the doors. A coil rear spring setup was used. The front axle was done by Don Long. After a few checkout runs K. S. and the new, tall Willys went on tour. The Willys hit speeds up to 148.76 mph and E.T.'s as low as 9.70 sec. in match races with the Mallicoat twins, Mazmanian's Willys (driven by Hugh Tucker now) and others. The highlight of the 1964 season for K. S. had to be his participation in the Dragfest tour in England. Prior to being rebuilt to Pittman's specifications, the car had been a A/GS racer (Page 42). Pittman's sponsor, Chuck Stolze (S & S Auto Parts) had purchased it from Jim Clinton. The Willys set both ends of the NHRA records (146.10 mph, 9.99 sec.) at the Nationals. Unfortunately the Willys was destroyed at a strip near his home town in Texas (5-2-65). (Photo courtesy of Ray Tognarelli)

Bob and Harry Sheffler (Penn.) competed in the B/GS class. In spite of the use of a fiberglass hood and fenders the car retained the 1940 Willys look. This was accomplished by retaining the steel front panel and grills and putting all the trim pieces on the fiberglass hood. Like most of the Willys the hood was not hinged like the stock one was, it was held by wingnuts and hood latches ('32 Ford style). Access to the engine was accomplished by merely lifting off the lightweight hood. In the 1980's the Sheffler Bros. started building complete fiberglass Willys bodies. (Photo courtesy of John Hellmuth)

After leaving John Mazmanian's team in the summer (1964) Bob Balogh teamed with Gary Dubach to run Gary's '33 Willys coupe. A 364" Chevy pushed the A/GS Willys to 142.18 mph on the initial outing, (12-13-64). After a few months of racing with Chevy power (143 mph) Joe Pisano joined the team with a 454" Chrysler engine. The team of Bones-Dubach-Pisano (shown in the warm-up photo - Bones in car, Dubach beside engine and Pisano in front) quickly hit 150 mph. After only a few runs a broken axle resulted in a totaled Willys. The team spent the next six months building a new car (shown in primer with the original door lettering still showing). The Willys recorded best times of 155 mph and 9.38 sec. before Joe Pisano moved on to Fuel Altered and Funny Car racing in late 1966. The 2780 lb. maroon Willys was one of the nicest looking Willys on the drag strips. Bones has been a Venolia (Joe Pisano's company) employee since the Bones-Dubach-Pisano A/GS days. (Photo courtesy of Bob Balogh)

Jack Coonrod and Wayne Harry (Oregon) teamed to run this Chrysler powered '33 Willys pickup prior to their "Kamakazi Koup" (Page 60). The pickup raced the black Stone-Woods-Cook Chrysler powered Willys at the Woodburn (Oregon) strip as shown in this 1964 photo. Tim Woods was able to get many more bookings this year than the previous year. The Willys traveled to Northern California, the Northwest, Midwest, East and the Southwest before returning to Southern California. Often a local A/GS competitor like the Coonrod-Harry Willys or even a Dragster, was match raced. The match races helped many of the supercharged gassers with promotional publicity. (Photo courtesy of Jack Coonrod)

Gene Ciambella of C&O Hydro (So. Calif.) jumped into the A/GS wars with a '40 Willys pickup. After running in B/GS (1964) with Chevy and Chrysler engines, Gene moved up into A/GS with a 420" Chrysler. The MGM team was Gene Modlin, Gene Ciambella and Steve Montrelli. After the switch to A/GS in June, 1965 the team worked the times up from 143 mph to 151.51 mph by the end of the year. The Willys had a one-piece fiberglass, lift-off, front end. The color was candy red. The transmission was a Hydro by C&O (naturally). The 2550 lb. pickup dropped down to a good 9.85 sec. E.T. before the end of 1965. Almost immediately after this Gene and the MGM team put the Willys aside and built a little Austin pickup. (Photo courtesy of Vern Hicks - Photo by Gary Traviss)

It was almost standard procedure to update a 1937 to 1940 Willys to look like a 1941 model. But the change was not done just because the racers wanted a newer car. The new look was done with the switch to a light weight fiberglass front end which was most readily available in the '41 Willys style. This '39 Willys (Page 48) was the Wayne Arteaga-John Hellmuth (Missouri) B/GS car after being upgraded to a '41 model. Wayne is on the right and John, left, in the photo congratulating each other after their first run over 130 mph at Union Grove, Wisc. The race photo recorded the start of a B/GS race between the Arteaga-Hellmuth Willys and the Paul Radici-Pat Curran '55 Chevy at Wentzville, Missouri. Incidently the '41 look was not the only change the Arteaga-Hellmuth had made, the powerplant now was by Chrysler instead of Olds. (Photos courtesy of Wayne Arteaga, Tom Horace and Bob Rothenberg)

New York was a "hot bed" of blown gasser activity and Eddie Sanzo was one of the top A/GS racers. This '40 Willys pickup was built in 1964 by the team of Eddie Sanzo, Vinnie Pellicane and Bob Siediecki. It was built with fiberglass hood, fenders and doors and an aluminum bed to compete in the top class, A/GS. The engine was a 375" small block Chevy. The pickup hit speeds up to 143 mph in 1964. Although the speed was not up to the fastest Chrysler powered A/GS cars (150 mph) Eddie's 9.99 sec. E.T. made him very competitive with the top A/GS cars. Match races were run with K. S. Pittman and Stone-Woods-Cook (in photo). Eddie, who worked for Jack Merkel (see on doors), continued to race in 1965 until July when a wheel-stand cracked the frame and damaged the body. One year later Eddie's rebuilt pickup flipped in New York while experimenting with low tire pressures. (Photos courtesy of John Hellmuth and Doug Cook)

John Mazmanian Ad
DRAG NEWS — 2-29-64

The Speed Engineering '40 Willys pickup was a BMG (AHRA class) blown gasser in Phoenix, Arizona. It was run by Bob Harrington who was the owner of the Speed Engineering Co. The Willys looked different than other pickups because of the low bed it had. The engine was a 352" Chevy. Later the Willys jumped into the A/GS class with the change to a '57 Chrysler engine. Bob generally raced at the Bee Line Raceway (Phoenix) and was able to get occasional match races with visiting blown gassers like Junior Thompson's. He named the Willys, the "Bush Master". (Photo courtesy of Charles Strutt)

Like many of the gasser competitors Bob Ida (New Jersey) started in BB/G class with a '55 - '57 Chevy. Bob's '56 was unique in that the engine was perhaps the only 409 Chevy engine to be competitive in the blown gas coupe classes. Bob had to make his own blower manifold since nothing was made for the 409. He was also on his own for ideas because there was no one else developing that engine, unlike the small block Chevy where hundreds of racers were continually making improvements. The photo was taken at Englishtown, N.J. (1966). (Photo courtesy of Bob Ida)

The Shaker Racing Enterprises entry in the B/GS class was this '41 Willys with 327 Chevy power. The team was the racing efforts of Rich Szabo, Tom Meuleman and Dave Bohl. Their home was South Bend, Indiana. The wheels on the Shaker were the popular American Racing wheels. (Photo courtesy of John Hellmuth)

By 1965 both K. S. Pittman and Doug Cook had become touring professionals. They left California in the spring and didn't return until November. Each scheduled as many dates as they could manage. Match races were run with A/GS cars like George Montgomery, Eddie Sanzo or Big John Mazmanian and occasionally with Funny Cars (Mr. Norm-Gary Dyer, Don Nicholson, etc.) or Dragsters. Generally the guys got $500 to $750 for a show (3 races or runs). This year was very good for Doug as he won the Nationals with a best of 152.54 mph and 9.53 sec. E.T. This match race with K. S. was three weeks later. Pittman had to work extra hard this year because his '33 Willys crashed in May. He quicky built a '41 Willys, installed his Chrysler engine, and was back filling his scheduled dates in June. The best part is that the '41 was competitive (151.65 mph, 9.76 sec.). (Photo courtesy of Doug Cook)

76

The ultra high set 1941 Willys A/GS pickup in the far lane was Mike Bamber's (So. Calif.). In 1964 the original red color had been changed to silver and Mike named the Willys "The Silver Dollar". It had a 340" Chevy engine and a B&M Hydro. The photo shows a 1964 race against the black Stone-Woods-Cook Willys at Lions (Long Beach). The front end on the Silver Dollar seemed to be the highest of all the blown gassers, at least it sure looked like it in 1964. Mike only ran this car about two years before dropping out of drag racing. He still has the car. Best speed - 139 mph. (Photo courtesy of Mike Bamber - Photo by Rod Stender)

Although it was not always done at many local strips the NHRA events required that the weight be checked. The neat yellow '41 Willys on the scales at Santa Maria, Calif. (1964) was the C/GS entry of Tommy and Jimmy Rogers (father and son) from Northern California. It had a 292" Chevy engine. The team usually raced at the nearby Fresno drag strip in DMG class (AHRA). It apparently was an all steel car (unusual). (Photo courtesy of Sherm Porter)

The only guy to have his blown gasser record erased because his performance was too good was Ron Nunes (No. Calif.). In late 1965 Ron's '41 Willys bombed the NHRA B/GS record by almost a half a second to 9.94 sec. The two racing photos show Ron's coupe racing Bob Panella's pickup and Gene Ciambella's Willys pickup (hidden behind the coupe) at Half Moon Bay on that record day (both A/GS and B/GS records broken). The record that the 327" Olds powered Willys set was a disaster for the B/GS class racers who raced in the NHRA (handicap) Eliminator brackets. Most of them could not qualify close enough to the record to make the Eliminator programs. Two years later the NHRA erased the record and set 10.44 sec. as the B/GS minimum (record). Ron continued to run Olds engines until he was almost the last top blown gasser competitor with one. He then switched to Chrysler, as shown in the spark plug changing photo. (Photos courtesy of Ron Nunes - Engine photo by Rich Welch)

Bob Panella (No. Calif.) jumped into B/GS racing by purchasing the Willys pickup previously run by Al Del Porto in the A/GS class. Bob rebuilt the car and added a 327" Chevy engine (675 hp) built by Bones Balogh in 1963. The beautiful little pickup was an excellent advertisement for the Panella Bros. successful trucking business. Bob's Willys, driven by Joe Morris, won numerous events including the Winternationals. The frontal view was taken at Bakersfield (1965) while the match race against the Airoso Bros. was at Fresno where each received $550. The pickup was sold in 1966 and Bob turned his attention to building a new B/GS Anglia. (Photos courtesy of Sherm Porter, Joe Airoso and Bob Panella)

One of the major problems for the blown gasser racers was broken axles in the early 1960's. Most of the cars were using Olds, Pontiac or Chevy truck rear ends. The stock axles were more than adequate at first, but with the continuing power increases and the improving traction from better tires the axles became over-stressed. Broken axles could be dangerous (Page 70). The '33 Willys waiting for a new axle, shown here, was the Lee Bros. (Michigan) A/GS entry. Ed and Jack Lee had one of the A/GS entries to run the late 426 Chrysler Hemi engine. Prior to running in A/GS the coupe had used a Pontiac engine to compete in the unblown A/G class. The 2600 lb. coupe was used mostly for match racing. (Photo courtesy of Kevin Perry)

The C&O Hydro Willys pickup was the C&O "Factory" car run by Gene Ciambella, an owner of C&O Automotive. (C&O stood for Ciambella and O'Brien. Pat O'Brien raced in A/GS in 1960.) The pickup raced in the B/GS class with a Chevy engine in 1964 until July when a Chrysler engine was installed. One month later a giant wheel-stand broke the front end of the car. Although Gene recorded good perform-ances up to 133 mph with the B/GS pickup better days were ahead when the pickup moved up to A/GS with a bigger 420" Chrysler engine. The photo was at the 1964 Nationals. (Photos courtesy of John Hellmuth & Charles Strutt)

The 1965 season started well for K. S. Pittman and his tall steel '33 Willys coupe. He won the Winternationals (145.86 mph, 9.87 sec.) beating Stone-Woods-Cook and Altizer-Finders-Kibler (in photo). The single run at Lions was at a Supercharged Gas Coupe meet where K.S. won over Bones-Dubach and Big John Mazmanian (Dick Harryman driving) and then lost to Doug Cook. The Willys was destroyed at Mineral Wells, Texas on May 16, 1965. Stone-Woods-Cook and K. S. were to have a match race there. Apparently K. S. ran out of shut-off area after an almost 150 mph run. Note that the roll bar kept the top up allowing K. S. to get out with minor injuries. He immediately hurried to his Eastern base (Falls Church, Va.) and built a new '41 Willys. (Photos courtesy of the author, Jack Coonrod and K. S. Pittman)

There probably were not too many 1933 Willys panel delivery trucks made (2100 lbs. and sold for $445 new) and only a few of them made it to the drag strips. This very nice red one was the CC/G entry of Joe and Tom Hrudka (Ohio) in 1966. It was powered by a destroked Chevy (233") engine driving through a Borg-Warner four-speed manual transmission. The original Willys suspension was retained with strong spring anti-windup (traction) bars added. The small engine allowed a 4-71 blower to be used. At 2800 lbs. the Willys was one of the lightest CC/G cars running. The panel was put up for sale in 1967 and the Hrudka's moved into AA/G with the former Lee Bros. Willys (Page 80). Today the Hrudka's company, Mr. Gasket, is one of the major high performance equipment manufacturing firms in the business. (Photos courtesy of Dean Court and Barbara Hamilton Advey)

Jeg Coughlin's (Ohio) company was in the high performance business and he was a blown gas class racer in 1966. Jeg campaigned this Austin in the AA/G class with best times in the 151.20 mph and 9.38 sec. area. Jeg Coughlin became the second AA/G class car to move up into the BB/Altered class to set an NHRA record (9.46 sec.) after Jack Merkel had done it three months earlier. The Cragar wheeled Austin was raced by an O-Hemi-An, (a Hemi from Ohio?). Coughlin later switched to a Chrysler powered Camaro for his AA/GS racing. Today Jeg's High Performance is one of the largest mail order firms. (Photo courtesy of Jeg Coughlin)

One of the problems when you are touring from strip to strip, racing every date you can, is finding a place to work on the race car. In addition to regular maintenance often repairs were required. Pros like Doug Cook and K. S. Pittman were quickly able to make many friends and find places to work on their cars. In St. Louis, Missouri they were the guests of Wayne Arteaga. The guys leaning on the S-W-C trailer were (from left) K. S. Pittman, Wayne Arteaga, Doug Cook and Tiny Roberts. In the garage was K. S. Pittman's '41 with Wayne Arteaga and K. S. (on right). Doug Cook was having some milk in the background. This visit to St. Louis was in 1966. (Photo courtesy of Wayne Arteaga and K. S. Pittman)

Doug Cook's turn in Wayne Arteaga's garage in St. Louis (1966) looked like this. Doug (on right) and John Hellmuth seem to be trying to decide what to do next. The best part about fiberglass front fenders and hoods, or one-piece front ends, was how easy it was to work on the engine after removing them. That is why the one-piece front end that was hinged to open or merely lift off was so popular.(Photo courtesy of Kevin Perry - Photo by Wayne Arteaga)

In 1966 Southern California racers Doug Cook and John Mazmanian filled their schedules with match races. This photo was at the New York National Raceway. Previously Dick Harryman had been building the engines and driving for Big John but in early 1966 John switched to Dave Zeuschel built engines and hired Dick Bourgeois to do the driving. (Photo courtesy of Bob Ida)

After winning the unblown B/G coupe class at the 1965 Nationals, Jim Oddy (New York) decided to move up to the blown AA/G class. He built a nice Austin with a 398" Chrysler engine, a Torque-flite transmission and an A-1 (Anderson) fiberglass one-piece hood and fenders assembly. The weight of 2420 lbs. put the Austin into the AA/G class. It was quickly competitive blasting a 9.43 sec. E.T. plus setting the NASCAR record for A/GS at 145.16 mph. Jim ran the Austin through 1968 in the AA/GS class although it often ran in the BB/A class at NHRA meets. In 1969 Jim moved into the BB/GS and in 1973 his Opel GT set the NHRA BB/GS speed record (158.17 mph). Jim's engines were built at Gor-Den Automotive where Jim was the shop manager. By 1968 the AA/GS Austin had hit 162.74 mph and 8.82 sec. (Photos courtesy of Dean Court and Mike Hanlon)

Early in 1965 it was apparently obvious to George Montgomery that the little foreign cars (Anglias, etc.) were coming into the blown classes. It could also be that George felt that his Willys-Chevy combination had reached about the end of its potential while his competitors with the larger Chrysler powered cars still had more room to improve. So he built a "compact" A/GS race car. His choice was a Prefect (four-door Anglia) which had an A/GS legal 94" wheelbase. Just prior to the 1965 Nationals the Prefect proved that it was competitive with 141 mph and 10.07 sec. times. Although the Prefect was built with George's usual care, the NHRA tech officials ruled that the floor-boards were not acceptable. So the "Gasser Passer", as he called it, missed the Nationals. Although George continued to race the Prefect until June of 1966 (both AA/GS and BB/A classes), with a best of 152 mph and 9.60 sec., his major efforts by then were on his SOHC Ford powered Willys. (Photos courtesy of Junior Thompson)

George Montgomery (Ohio) divided his time between two cars during the 1964 season, his Chevy powered '33 Willys and a Comet A/FX (Factory Experimental) stocker. But it didn't seem to hurt his A/GS performances. George won the Nationals again with a win in the much anticipated race against Doug Cook. He also made the trip to England for the Dragfest in September. His best time in 1964 was 145.1 mph (8-18-64). It is interesting to note that even as late as 1964 George did not have any lettering on the car, except the class number. But he was already earning money with match races and certainly that car was well known. This photo, at the 1964 Nationals, shows an early round race between Ohio George and Ed Sanzo and his very quick Chevy powered Willys pickup.   (Photo courtesy of George Montgomery)

Competing against big Chrysler powered A/GS cars with a small block Chevy had made George Montgomery the "under-dog" in the eyes of many racing enthusiasts. But that all stopped in 1966. After losing at the 1965 Nationals George decided to make an engine change to a 427" Ford SOHC engine. The early Ford rear end was replaced by a Pontiac rear axle modified to retain the torque tube drive. The '33 Willys weighed about 2400 lbs. Only one month after the initial runs Ohio George's Willys tied the NHRA E.T. record at 9.71 sec. The Willys immediately started a full schedule of match races (S-W-C, K. S. Pittman, Jeg Coughlin, Jack Merkel, Lee Bros., Kohler Bros., etc.). When the 1966 season was completed George had captured the NHRA records for the AA/G class at 155.97 mph and 9.34 sec. His best time was 158.7 mph that year. (Photos courtesy of K. S. Pittman and George Montgomery.)

In the late 1950's one of the lightweight cars that was popular in the gas classes was the 1951 to 1954 Henry J's. Their original weight was 2300 lbs. However their short lived popularity faded quickly. One reason can be seen in the photo where the engine and the driver share the same space. Very few Henry J's were still competing in the blown classes when Grant Merideth and Gary Newton (So. Calif.) brought this one out in 1965. Being one of the last Henry J's in A/GS, it was perhaps the most hi-tech with fiberglass hood, fenders, doors and deck lid plus a nicely finished aluminum interior. The engine was a big 478" Ford. The team raced "Snoopy II" for a year to a best of 141.52 mph and 9.96 sec. before being selected (drafted) to serve in the Army. (Photo courtesy of Gary Newton)

After winning the B/GS class at the Nationals twice with his '39 Willys (Page 44), Jack Merkel built this '33 Willys for a shot at the A/GS class. It was very light, 2184 lbs., and was powered by a 364" Chevy. The little yellow coupe ran in the 144 mph and 9.80 sec. area. A win over George Montgomery's Chevy powered Willys at the Nationals earned him much more publicity than his B/GS car had received. That publicity was more than welcome to help Jack with his speed shop business. After racing this engine setup for a while Jack made the switch to a big block Chevy (1966). When Jack Merkel and George Montgomery retired their small block Chevy engines in 1966 that was really the end of the "mouse motor" in the AA/GS class. (Photo courtesy of Junior Thompson)

Much of the credit, or blame, for the Anglias crashing into the Southern California A/GS picture is due Jim Shores and Skip Hess. They built this very beautiful 384" Chevy powered Anglia to compete in the unblown A/G class. The metallic red "Critter" was one of the top A/G cars along with their local competitors, the Kohler Bros. In November of 1965 the Shores and Hess Anglia appeared as a blown gasser. Although the NHRA did not allow blown Anglias in the A/GS class, the local AHRA strips did - Lions, Irwindale. Within a few months the Anglia was in the 149 mph and 9.50 sec. area. The team progressed from a four-speed manual transmission, to a B&M Hydro and finally an Art Carr Torqueflite. After the Kohler Bros. had moved into A/GS with a big block Chevy powered Anglia it was only logical that the Shores-Hess Anglia would also be upgraded to a "Rat motor". (Photos courtesy of Junior Thompson and Skip Hess - Front view photo by Dan Bott)

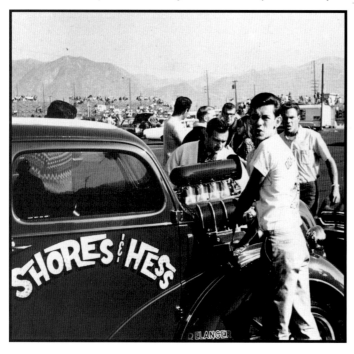

The drag racing fans at Martin, Michigan had a chance to see the popular Stone-Woods-Cook Willys match race against a local A/GS racer. The '33 Willys in the near lane was owned by Tom Prock from Detroit, Michigan. Tom's Willys had the stock bodied look popularized by George Montgomery, K. S. Pittman and Gordon Selkirk. Note that the injectors were the forward facing throttle type, commonly known as "bug catchers". Tom's times for this race were 150 mph and 9.34 sec., obtained with big block Chevy power. (Photo courtesy of Tom Prock)

After moving his A/GS Willys pickup (Page 80), with Chrysler power, to a 151.26 mph speed, Gene Ciambella decided to make a change. In three weeks Gene, with the help of Ted Brown (Fletcher & Brown), built the first Chrysler powered Austin pickup for the A/GS class. The big 467" Chrysler helped Gene win both the 1966 AHRA and NHRA Winternationals in the Austin's initial meets. Unlike most of the A/GS race cars this one did not have fiberglass components; it was all steel. It was also ran at record times including a 9.04 sec. E.T. In June (1966) after five months of competition, Gene put the Austin up for sale, $6500 in turn-key condition. But he still continued to run the Austin with success that resulted in a Drag Racing Magazine rating of No. 1 in the country. (Photo courtesy of Don Prieto - Photo by Chester Kirk)

Chuck Finders' '33 Willys (So. Calif.), ran with the Stone-Woods-Cook colors (and Olds engine) for only five months in 1964 (Page 65). After separating from Tim Woods' team, Chuck joined with Bill Altizer and Neal Kibler to campaign the car. A big small block Chevy engine (389") was installed in the newly painted red Willys coupe. Only one month after leaving Tim Woods' team the coupe was back on the drag strips (5-10-64) hitting an excellent 143.86 mph and 9.95 sec. clocking. In August a Howard cam ad called the Altizer-Finders-Kibler the "Worlds fastest, quickest Chevy A/GS" and was looking for competition (using a Howard cam). In November the Willys (called the "Traveler") hit excellent 146.57 mph and 9.76 sec. times. Now Chet Herbert cams said the Herbert cammed "Traveler" offered a challenge to all the A/GS competitors. After Chuck Finders moved on, the Altizer-Kibler team continued to run the coupe which was later campaigned by Roger Garten. (Photo courtesy of Charles Strutt)

It would be natural to assume that Pat Dakin (Ohio) would put his blown Chevy engine in a '55 Chevy or a Willys to run in the CC/G class. But Pat's very nice blue race car was a 1947 Ford. The engine had a displacement of 292". By 1968 the Ford coupe had turned times of 134.35 mph and 10.94 sec. Pat Dakin then moved up to faster cars. (Photo courtesy of Barbara Hamilton Advey)

In 1965 Junior Thompson decided the little Anglias running in the A/GS were writing the epitaph for the larger Willys, like his (Page 49). So he put the Willys up for sale in May of 1965 and started to build a 1950 Austin. Chuck Finders did the chassis work while Junior built a 341" Chevy. The Austin appeared at Lions in October. In early 1966 the Austin set the AHRA record down to 9.52 sec. The influx of big block Chevy and Chrysler engines in Anglias and Austins encouraged Junior to install a Chrysler. Jim and Don Cassedy provided a 392" Chrysler. The 2400 lb., burgundy colored Austin, in July 1966, recorded 155.85 mph and 9.17 sec. at Fremont, California. This car was Junior's entry into work as a full time, professional racer. (Photos courtesy of Harry Hall and Don Prieto - Still photo by Chester Kirk)

STONE-WOODS-COOK TO MEET GEORGE MONTGOMERY Conditions And Times Set Up By Eskimo Cam Grinder

At last on August 16, 1964, you have finally given your permission to your boy George Montgomery to race the Stone-Woods-Cook A/GS coupe at Dragway 30 near Gary, Indiana. It is my understanding that you have set up certain unsportsman-like rules to be enforced as a condition for this race. Although my partner Tim Woods signed the contract without my consent, I want the public to know that you have refused to let George Montgomery race us unless we agree to race without any warmup runs prior to the race. We have never demanded or even requested that a competitor come directly off the trailer and run against us, especially when they are over 2,000 miles away from their home strip.

We have a few questions:

1. Is it not true that Montgomery lives near this particular strip and will have an advantage in being tuned for that climate?

2. Is it true that you refused to let Montgomery race us unless we agreed to race without tuneup prior to race time?

3. If there are not your requests and demands, will you see that our friend George or yourself make arrangements with Dragway 30 manager to set up clocks 2 days before the race for trial runs and extend both cars an invitation to come? Each cars time and E.T. should be withheld from the other in order to subdue the possibility of either car disappearing. If there are any terms with which you are unhappy, we will be most happy to discuss them with you.

Mr. Cam Grinder:

Also we would like to extend our congratulations to Bones Balogh for his fine sportsmanship and ability to tolerate Big June's torments. Example of Big June's torments:

1. Bones blamed for June's defeat at the 1964 Winter-nationals by Stone-Woods-Cook.

2. Bones blamed for June's defeat at Long Beach on the best 2 out of 3 match race with Stone-Woods-Cook.

3. Bones blamed for the inability of the big June's candy coupe not being able to duplicate the 150.25 turned by Stone-Woods-Cook on the same clocks at the same strip, although June's rapid Willys was able to come within 3 mph and 1/4 second of E.T. of Stone-Woods-Cook's times.

Big June on the Run

Big June disappointed over 6,000 spectators at Half Moon Bay when he failed to appear after having agreed to race Stone-Woods-Cook 2 out of 3. He blamed this on an engine failure, however, we know he has 3 or 4 extras.

Big June disappeared at San Diego one day before race date...we were there. As a climax, Big June told all UDRA members, who incidentally are his friends, to go jump in the lake.

Signed
Fred Stone

P.S. Is this not playboy June's way of saying to Stone-Woods-Cook: 'Boys, I have had it!'

Fred Stone (Stone-Woods-Cook) Ad
DRAG NEWS — 7-18-64

HYDRO-MOTIVE: DO YOU HAVE TO TELL LIES TO SELL A PRODUCT?

In the Sept. 26 issue of Drag News, in your ad you stated that "...his (George Montgomery's) Hydro-Motive equipped A/GS coupe was the fastest gasser in the world. The fact is that of the 4 well known A/GS cars at the Nationals, George Montgomery had the slowest...running as much as 6 mph slower on his BEST run. K.S. Pitman turned 146.10 mph; Stone-Woods-Cook 145.86; John Mazmanian 143 (with an ailing engine); George Montgomery only 140 mph.

You also state "Incidentally none of his (George's) competitors could get below 10.30." Fact: K.S. turned 10.05, 10.03, 10.00 and 9.99. Stone-Woods-Cook turned 10.11, 9.96, 10.05, 10.04, 10.04, and 10.00. George turned 10.41, 9.96, 10.03, 10.13, 10.20 and 10.31. As our cars made more runs, our times got consistently better due to the dependability of our equipment. George's runs got progressively worse...resulting finally in his retiring the car after the first round of Street Eliminator DUE TO EQUIPMENT FAILURE (was it the same product that failed at Gary, Ind.?).

It' widely known in drag racing circles that the underdog has the advantage in close competition under the Christmas tree light starting system. The slower car has everything to gain and nothing to lose by jumping the lights. George took a chance and lucked out winning with a 5 mph slower time and .09 worse e.t.

Proof that you can't always luck out is evident by the three out of five match race held three weeks before the Nationals at Gary, Indiana. With the conventional starting system, Stone-Woods-Cook beat George 2 straight and George couldn't even make round 3 due to a MECHANICAL FAILURE.

We, the undersigned, race as a hobby. We have an untold amount of time and money invested in our cars and cannot sit dily by while a business belittles our efforts with lies. Many of our sponsors advertise our performance and the products we run. Our sponsors are proud to advertise our cars because we run all year around proving the performance and durability of their products. How can you establish performance and dependability when your most advertised car runs so seldom even during the Eastern drag racing season? We take out cars back to the East Coast and to the Nationals year after year. Why is it your cars never show up on the West Coast even after being offered money to come?

Sincerely,
Stone-Woods-Cook
K.S. Pitman
John Mazmanian

Stone-Woods-Cook, K.S. Pittman and John Mazmanian (B&M) Ad
DRAG NEWS — 10-3-64

A SIMPLE TOSS OF THE COIN

Have you ever noticed that some people are always cheerful when they are winning, yet the smile fades when they lose? This adage holds especially true for Pebble, Pulp and Chef, since we have beaten them for the past three weeks straight. Unfortunately they cannot take a loss without losing all perspective of self-control. This weekend before we raced them in the final round of the Fontana A/GS Championships, we approached Tim Pulp and asked him if he would like to flip a coin for lane choice. He wouldn't. We then approached Dough Chef and asked him, and he wouldn't. Finally we tossed the coin with one of their crew members, who appeared hot at us for winning the first three rounds. It is unfortunate that some racing teams cannot maintain good sportsmanship when they are on a losing streak.

FLASH:

MGM C & O Hydro takes top over a fifteen car gas super-charged field at Fontana. MGM beats Pebble-Pulp & Chef again, this time in the final round. Once you break the ice, it's not hard at all to beat P-P & C. Is it time for Dough Chef to step down from the throne?

We would like to express our appreciation to the fine manufacturers whose products enable us to compete.

- Mickey Thompson Equipt. Co.
- Schnieder Racing Cams
- Henry's Machine Shop
- Syverson's Porting Service
- Roto-Faze Ignitions

Special thanks to Fletcher & Brown of Bellflower for the excellent job they did in setting up the running gear and chassis. Also to C & O Hydros for their reliable product.

STRIP MANAGERS ATTENTION:

If you are interested in obtaining the MGM-C & O Hydro A/GS Chrysler/Austin for an appearance at your strip, call Gene Ciambella at (213)-678-3997. This is the team which won the NHRA Winternationals, the AHRA Winter Nationals, the AHRA Nationals, and the Fontana A/GS Championships.

Signed, MGM

LEGAL (le'gal) adj. In Accordance With The Rules or Laws

Junior Thompson's A/GS car is in accordance with the rules. It is a legal A/GS machine. This may not surprise you, but you may be surprised to know that certain so-called A/GS cars were classified as AA/Altereds at the Hot Rod Magazine Championship meet this weekend. Junior's wasn't one of them ... his car won A/GS class at the HRM Meet, just as it did at the Bakersfield Championships. Junior's car is LEGAL, and passes NHRA inspection.

THE BURGUNDY BANDIT — Junior Thompson's beautiful Chrysler A/GS Austin nabbed top honors in A/GS class at the tough Hot Rod Magazine Meet this weekend. It has run a best of 9.49–154.87. Quite creditable, since it is a legal A/GS car which does not violate the "sacred" tradition of the gas coupe class rules.

Junior is tired of racing against AA/Altereds, and wants to race against legal A/GS cars, in the manner that the class was established and meant to be. If you would like to have Junior Thompson race at your track against any legal A/GS car, just call:

JUNIOR THOMPSON
(213) UN 8-2761
(For best results, call about 6:00 p.m.)

Why a legal A/GS car? Why do you have rules? Junior Thompson doesn't present a hassle, an argument, or a sit-down strike. All he wants to do is race against cars in A/GS class, and he is willing to travel to do it. Why not give him a try? When is the last time you had some drag racing at your track?

AN OPEN LETTER TO DRAG RACE FANS EVERYWHERE

We feel that now the time has come for us to bare some unpleasant facts to the drag race public. Until now we have stood passively by and watched the traditional give-and-take between others participating in A/GS. Now the challenge has been passed and we stand ready for all comers. It is no secret that our infamous "RAT MOTOR" has revolutionized A/GS racing. Since the "RAT MOTOR" has been running, California has seen a mass exodus of A/GS cars. In the light of recent events we feel a responsibility to ask these pertinent questions for you, our loyal friends and fans. Please consider these questions and try to supply honest answers. We feel that you will arrive at the same conclusions we did.

1. Is it true that a well-known Chrysler-Austin owner has refused to race against the Chevy-Anglia on the grounds that its short wheelbase exhibits unsafe handling characteristics. If we may be so bold as to ask, Mr. Austin owner when did you last make three consecutive, full power runs in competition that could be labeled "safe"?

2. Is it true that a Chrysler-Austin owner recently said that the Anglia was unfair when equipped with a 454" Chevy, while his own car was powered by a 460" Hemi?

3. Why does the Burgundy Bandit moan and groan about our 92" wheelbase? Could the reason be that we spotted him 1/2 pound per cubic inch at Riverside by running AA/A? Unfortunately the Bandit's 92" wheelbase didn't handle well enough to survive the first round. Maybe its just as well, we ran quicker anyway.

4. Which of the three dominant combinations in A/GS (Chrysler-Austin, Chrysler-Willys, Chev.-Anglia) is responsible for A/GS being known as "SQUIRRELY CARS"?

5. Is it true that the day of the "WHALE-BLOCK" Hemi is nearing an end and that the only motor to run in A/GS is the Super "RAT MOTOR"?

6. Is it true that the entire issue could be resolved in one weekend?

The answers to the preceding questions are extremely enlightening in view of charges leveled in a recent drag racing weekly. If we receive no response to this letter it will be evident that someone didn't come to race.

SIGNED: SHORES & HESS

Time to race! John Mazmanian's Willys is shown during the starting procedure. Rich Siroonian has the oil squirt can, filled with gas, and is feeding gas into the injector scoop. Because the injector fuel lines drain down while the car is sitting, the initial feed will include spurts of air. The engine could start and then starve for gas. The result would usually be a backfire through the blower which could damage it. So the squirt can adds fuel until the engine is fully running. (Photo courtesy of Bob Balogh)

Here are two photos of Big John Mazmanian's Willys at the NHRA Nationals. The 1963 photo shows three guys in front of the B/GS Willys. Two of them, John Mazmanian and Rich Siroonian, are wearing B&M T-shirts. The guy without the B&M T-shirt is Bob Spar (owner of B&M). The group gathered next to the Willys in the other photo includes Bob Spar, Rich Siroonian, Don Nicholson and Dave Zeuschel. (Photos courtesy of Junior Thompson and John Hellmuth)

This 1964 outdoor hot rod show in Hollywood featured Big John Mazmanian's Willys along with other rods and even custom show cars. Dick Harryman's name was listed on the door as the driver. Several drivers handled John's Willys including Bob "Bones" Balogh, Dick Harryman, Hugh Tucker and Dick Bourgeois. (Photo courtesy of Leo Duchaine)

Don Long, the talented chassis builder, and Big John Mazmanian (on right), posed for the record, shaking on a deal to build John's new '35 Willys A/GS race car. Unfortunately just before Don could tear into the project the Willys was stolen. John then passed on a Willys project and moved on to build a controversial A/GS Austin. (Photo courtesy of Don Long)

Included in the fastest and best known Southern California AA/G competitors were Ron Bizio and the Kohler Bros. Bizio's blue '33 Willys pickup, originally built by Chuck Finders, was powered by a Chrysler while the Kohler Bros. red Anglia had a big block Chevy engine. Note the front wheels on the Anglia turned when the weight was transferred to the rear (wheelstand). (Photo courtesy of Tom Willford)

PROGRESS AND CHANGES

- 1 9 6 7 -

The outlook for the blown gassers starting the 1967 season was very good. The previous year had been probably the most exciting and competitive in the short history of the A/GS coupes. Racing continued hot and heavy throughout the winter of 1967 in California with four or eight-car A/GS shows almost every week at Irwindale, Long Beach and the brand new Orange County dragstrips. The payout for the four-car shows was $100 - $50 - $25 (total purse $200) or $150 - $75 - $25. Eight-car shows normally paid $200 - $150 - $100 - $50 (total purse $750). The March Bakersfield Fuel and Gas Championships scaled up to $400 for the winner of the A/GS class. The future looked so good that a loosely knit A/GAS Super Association was formed. They were able to coordinate with the strips to insure that enough A/GS cars would be available and also organize scheduling.

In spite of the fact that 1967 was a very good year for the A/GS cars, there were some things happening that would influence the future success of the blown gas coupes. One of these things was the runaway success of the Funny Cars which was taking much of the drag racing publicity and also the money. But still the A/GS cars were doing pretty well.

A little noticed item in the NHRA's National Dragster commented that "hot car" entries (defined as everything except stock or modified stock cars) were declining even while the total entries at NHRA strips were increasing. The figures the NHRA gave were that "hot car" entries had dropped from 25.7% of the total entries to 13.7% from 1964 to 1966. One reason was the availability of all the new factory built "hot rods" and high performance stock cars. This resulted in a reduction of interest for the Roadsters and other "hot car" classes. But probably the real reason was that the costs for a competitive "hot car" entry were escalating faster than anyone would have predicted. The reason that the costs were going up so fast was that drag racing was leaving the hobby phase behind and starting to be a professional activity. When money was awarded to the winners then the competition got very serious. Serious competition forced the purchase of new components, testing new ideas or even building new cars. All it took was more money. It was obvious from NHRA's data that a smaller number of competitors would stay in the game as the costs increased. And indeed the numbers of Supercharged Gas Coupes were not increasing except where A/GS shows or match races offering cash awards were being run.

It was to be expected that the 1967 NHRA rules would be influenced by the Special 1966 Division 7 AA/G rules, and they were. The weight breaks for all three blown coupe classes were moved down. The new numbers were AA/G: 5.00 - 7.99 lbs./cu.in. (was 6.00 - 8.99); BB/G: 8.00 - 10.99 lbs./cu. in. (was 9.00 - 11.99); CC/GS: 11.00 lbs./cu. in. or more (was 12.00 lbs./cu. in. or more). Now all the AA/G cars could run legally at NHRA meets at 5.0 lbs./cu. in., as they had been running at AHRA strips. In addition, the blown cars could now use fiberglass bodies although they still had to use a frame made by an auto manufacturer and the door had to open (no flip-top Funny Car styles). The most interesting items in the new rules were the elimination of the requirement that Anglias had to run small block engines and the continued ban of Anglias in the Supercharged classes. So although Anglias were racing in A/GS events and match races around the country, the NHRA put them into Altered Class (usually BB/A) at NHRA events.

The big changes in 1966, especially (1) many new Anglias and Austins and (2) big leaps in performance, made most of the major blown gas coupe competitors take another look at their 1967 programs. The result was major changes in most of them. John Mazmanian sold his famous '41 Willys and had a "trick" Austin built. K. S. Pittman again parked his '41 Willys and built a beautiful chopped, all fiberglass '33 Willys. George Montgomery continued to race his Willys until mid-year when he debuted a sleek new Mustang, powered by his strong SOHC Ford engine. Stone-Woods-Cook continued to race their faithful old '41 Willys, "Swindler A" but their major effort was with the new Mustang Funny Car that Doug Cook took on tour this year. The Lee Bros. replaced their Willys with an Anglia and Jeg Coughlin jumped into AA/G with an Austin. Then Big John's old '41 Willys rejoined the AA/G competition with new owners, the Hill Bros. Gene Ciambella, formerly with the MGM team, moved up into Funny Cars using the name Gene Conway.

The first meet of the year (1-6-67) at Orange County set the pace for the year with terrifically quick times that most of the cars would not see again for some time. Big John's new Austin (which the NHRA said was not a legal AA/G Class car) hit 8.68 sec. and 161.87 mph. The Korney-Montrelli Anglia recorded an 8.84 sec. time (with its new, stronger chassis) and Jim Shore's Anglia with John Herrera's big "rat motor" blasted through at 8.72 sec. and 158.50 mph. Ray Cook drove the big Stone-Woods-Cook Willys to a quick 9.06 sec. time. In the subsequent meets most of the top cars recorded E.T.'s in the 9.20 to 9.50 sec. area.

The Winternationals proved to everyone how much the cars had improved. The NHRA AA/G winner was George Montgomery with best times of 9.01 sec. and 155.70 mph while the Kohler Bros. won the AHRA A/GS class with 9.23 sec. and 152.28 mph clockings.

The NHRA BB/G class winner was the Marrs Bros., moving up from CC/G, with a 10.32 sec., 136 mph time; while CC/G was again won by Charles James' Ardun powered Willys.

Two weeks later at Bakersfield the Kohler Bros. hit a 9.12 sec. clocking on the way to the A/GS victory. The Airoso Bros. Willys nailed the B/GS trophy with excellent 10.08 sec. and 139.10 mph times. Ray Cook showed everyone that they shouldn't overlook the Stone-Woods-Cook Willys when he blasted through for 9.07 sec. and 155.97 mph times.

Match racing got off to an early start for the A/GS cars when George Montgomery and Stone-Woods-Cook were booked at Long Beach for a January 28th race. Stone-Woods-Cook won when George was unable to get the traction he needed. His victory at the Winternationals a week later shows that he was quickly able to solve his traction problems. Match racing started in the East (weather permitting) in April. Naturally the "Big Four" - Stone-Woods-Cook, George Montgomery, K. S. Pittman and John Mazmanian were there. One interesting item was that the car that had "Big John Mazmanian" on the door was actually Junior Thompson's Austin. Junior had an agreement with John to fill in for Big John's contract dates while John's Austin stayed home. Many successful match races were run, sometimes two and three a week. Eastern cars like the Lee Bros. Anglia, Paul Frost's Willys, Jeg Coughlin's Austin, Jack Merkel's Willys and the Hill Bros.' Willys got into the action. Oregon's Jack Coonrod ('33 Willys) also joined the touring professionals, Chuck Finders went back to drive the Stone-Woods-Cook's Willys and then in June Jim Shores took his Anglia on tour.

What was the effect of the A/GS touring? Most of the guys worked hard, had a lot of fun and came home with money in the bank. The touring A/GS cars became well known among drag racing enthusiasts and were probably the most important factor in the growing popularity of the Supercharged Gas Coupes. So the touring not only benefitted the racers, it helped all the blown gas coupes with gobs of publicity.

Back in California the stay-at-home A/GS cars were also busy. A few of the top competitors were Herrera and Sons, the Kohler Bros., Bones-Dubach, Jim Kirby, Altizer-Kibler, Steve Korney and John Lombardo. New entries included Ernie Nicholson, the Zeller Bros. and Ron Bizio. Perhaps taking the suggestion from the Funny Cars, many A/GS cars were being given names (Fuel Altereds were also adding car names at this time). The ads for A/GS shows would often list pre-entries including the Agitator, Goldfinger, Traveler, Challenger and the Super Stude.

The publicity ad war continued in full swing. This year most of the ads were placed by the competitors instead of the manufacturers. The challenges and counter charges made the ads one of the top topics of discussion among drag racers. An example of the ads was K. S. Pittman's ad charging that Big John's (Jr. Thompson's) Austin actually had an Engle cam in it. Isky's ad the following week said that the Pittman ad was obviously ghost written, but did not actually say that Engle Cams had written the ad. Once again most Drag News and Drag World readers looked forward to the weekly A/GS competitor "bashing" ads.

The NHRA National winners were George Montgomery for AA/G, the Airoso Bros. in BB/G and Bill Lindner, Jr. in CC/G. The interesting item is that the AA/G winner was not a Willys, Austin or Anglia, it was a Mustang. This AA/G car did not look like a 20 to 30 year old style gasser Willys, Austin, etc. It looked like a new 1967 Mustang. In fact the typical spectator might have had trouble distinguishing it from a Funny Car. A columnist in a Drag News column commented on George Montgomery's Mustang by writing "Don't jam all these new "Super Cars" down everyone's throat - it is still a Funny Car". A petition was even circulated asking for a ban on late model cars in the Supercharged Gas Classes. The 1967 Mustang was typical of George Montgomery's excellent workmanship and proved to be exceedingly fast. But by being on the leading edge of progress, perhaps George Montgomery was the first to blur the distinction between the Supercharged Gas Coupes and the Funny Cars. It was not long before other new style AA/G cars would appear. It is impossible to be certain what effect the new style cars had on the blown gassers but it seems that some of the crowd appeal faded away. And even today when drag racing enthusiasts talk about the old Supercharged Gassers they will usually talk about the Willys and Anglias and rarely about the newer model cars that competed in the late 1960's and early 1970's.

As the 1967 season wound down, the West Coast continued to offer eight-car shows for the local cars and the returning touring A/GS cars. The Hill Bros. even made a winter tour to the West Coast. Big John's Austin was hitting record times (8.65 sec., 162.87 mph). Other cars recording excellent times included K. S. Pittman (8.66 sec.), the Hill Bros. (8.69 sec.), Shores-Herrera (8.95 sec.), Steve Korney (8.92 sec.) and Jr. Thompson (8.99 sec.). The typical field trying to qualify for the 8-car A/GS shows was about 12 to 14 cars. It was not uncommon for a B/GS car to qualify into the A/GS show because the stress and strains of qualifying often put out a few cars.

It must be noted that the strong cars "back East" were also going fast and quick. George Montgomery with his new 12.00-16 M & H tires recorded a sensational 8.50 sec., 166 mph run. Jack Merkel was also keeping pace with an 8.81 sec. time. His '33 Willys was now propelled by a big block Chevy engine.

Somewhat lost in the limelight were the BB/G and CC/G cars. Basically the A/GS match races and eight-car shows were the main activities for the Supercharged

Gassers. About the only racing for the BB/G and CC/G competitors was to run Super or Competition Eliminator (handicap) brackets. This generally meant that they had to run the bigger NHRA events since most smaller strips did not have enough cars to run a Super Eliminator bracket. Naturally they could and did run at local strips, usually running in a handicap bracket, and rarely meeting another BB/G or CC/G car. The blown cars were at a disadvantage racing many of the more E.T. consistent unblown gassers or dragsters.

In spite of the lack of publicity, there were some strong BB/G and CC/G cars running. Although the big '41 Willys' were almost obsolete in AA/G, most of the fastest BB/G and CC/G competitors were using them. Billy Holt, the Marrs Bros., Bill Lindner Jr. and the Airoso Bros. were at the top of the list. Paul Pittman un-retired the old K. S. Pittman '41 Willys with BB/G times of 9.92 sec., 147.78 mph while Don Toia, Barb Hamilton and Bob Lombardi were all pushing their '40 to '41 Willys' to excellent performances.

The NHRA records were rewritten in the names of AA/G - George Montgomery (8.93 sec., 162.16 mph); BB/G - Marrs Bros. (10.43 sec.) and Pittman-Edwards (139.96 mph); and CC/G - the Marrs Bros. (10.75 sec., 130.43 mph). The improvements were obvious in all places except in the BB/G E.T. record column. The 1965 record that Ron Nunes had established had so handicapped the BB/G class competitors that the NHRA erased it before the end of the year.

Once again the AA/G competitors had completed a successful year. Change was again in the wind as evidenced by George Montgomery's new Mustang. The modernized '33 Willys like the Hill Bros. and K. S. Pittman had proved competitive but the old big '41 Willys was now demoted to the BB/G and CC/G classes. In addition the "touring pros" were making some money and local cars, especially in California, were also winning some cash. As for the BB/G and CC/G cars the only place to really race them was in the handicap eliminator brackets and the NHRA National events. Interest in the BB/G and CC/G classes was indeed waning.

- 1 9 6 8 -

Drag racing was going through major changes in 1968. The professional aspect touched and would soon affect every segment of the drags. Naturally the Supercharged Gassers were also involved.

The push into professionalism was not just about racers getting paid, it was really about the drag racing promoters learning that better racing programs drew larger crowds and more money. The successes of the program scheduling over the past few years were used to plan for even more successes. Each individual strip promoter had to work out a schedule balancing costs and projected income, as in any business. Most strips could not afford an expensive program every week because major sized crowds would not come every week. So most promoters scheduled one to two expensive shows or match races in a monthly schedule. Then less expensive programs were scheduled in between the major shows.

In 1968 the most expensive shows or match races were the Funny Car or Dragster programs. Depending on the drag strip location and potential crowd, a Funny Car match race could cost around $3000 while an eight to sixteen-car show could cost $4000 to $8000. Interestingly the former "King" of the dragstrips, the Top Fuel Dragsters, no longer commanded top money. In fact, with the exception of the top competitors like Don Garlits, most Fuel Dragsters could get only 50 % to 75 % as much as the Funny Cars. The reason was that the crowds just didn't come out for the Dragsters. Some people attributed this to the advances in tire and clutch technology which had virtually eliminated the dragster's exciting tire smoking and often "squirrely" blasts down the strip. In addition, the Funny Cars had introduced a complete presentation of burnouts and backing up that kept them "on stage" two to three times longer than the Dragsters.

The strip managers did a lot of experimenting with their "off" weeks. It was important to offer some kind of a show or only the racers would be there and that would be disaster to the profit. Less expensive programs using slower class cars were tried. The most successful lower cost programs were those with Top Gas Dragsters, Junior Fuel Dragsters, AA/Fuel Altereds, AA/GS Supercharged Coupes or the Super Stocks. So, typical limited cost programs would have one, two or three of the mentioned groups in four, eight or sixteen-car shows or match races. It was great for these competitors as it gave them a chance to earn some money and publicity. Naturally most AA/GS racers were anxious to participate.

The growing professionalism convinced many of the racers that they should get together to help schedule races, promote their particular group of cars and, most importantly for many of them, have a say on the cash arrangements. In Southern California the Professional Dragster Assn. (PDA) was promoting high payouts for Dragsters while the Midwest United Drag Racing Assn. (UDRA) was actively scheduling a series of races for Dragsters, Funny Cars and Gassers. Texas had a Pro Fuel circuit and Northern Californians formed a circuit, Northern California Drag Racing Assn. (NCDRA), that included Gas Coupes. The Southern California AA/GS racers had the loosely organized group they had formed in 1967. The group called itself the A/Gas Supercharged Organization with Steve Korney as the President.

The 1968 NHRA rules had a number of changes that seemed to indicate that no clear agreement of what a Supercharged Gasser should be was found. Some items were relaxed while others were retained. Instead of solving problems the rules helped add to the confusion.

The first change for 1968 was the class designation initials. The new initials were AA/GS, BB/GS and CC/GS. It will be remembered that in 1966 and 1967 the initials were AA/G, BB/G and CC/G. And back in 1965, and earlier, the initials were A/GS, B/GS and C/GS. Now that the initials were clarified, the confusion was gone - wrong! Most AHRA strips were still calling them A/GS, etc., and when most strips advertized the Supercharged Gasser programs they called them A/G Supercharged. This was true for both NHRA and AHRA dragstrips and for most drag racing enthusiasts. A/GS was still the most popular name. But it didn't really matter because they all meant the same cars.

The new rules replaced the requirement for an original automobile frame and deleted the word "American" from the auto body maker paragraph. The rules now allowed 2" x 3", .120" wall, tubing to be used to fabricate a custom frame. The wheelbase limit was reduced to 90" minimum. Thus the Anglias were now legal in the Supercharged classes. Also the driver's seat could be repositioned 10" back compared to 4" by the previous rules.

Perhaps the most important new rule was the relocation of the Supercharged Street Roadsters (AA/SR) into the Coupe classes (AA/GS). In 1958 the NHRA had tried to combine the Roadster and Coupe classes and now finally in 1968 they partially accomplished it;

partially because it did not combine unblown street roadsters and coupes. Although this was a major rule change there were only a few supercharged street roadsters running then so time would tell what the impact of this rule change would be.

The new rules did solve some of the old problems including recognizing that Anglias were running at A/GS meets. The rules also allowed new, stronger and safer frames to be built to replace the lightweight, fifteen to thirty year old Willys and Anglia frames or be built into late model unit body cars.

Unfortunately the rules were having difficulty keeping up with the cars. Not only would 1968 see some all-fiberglass cars with race car interiors (not street interiors) but even AA/GS versions of the Funny Cars - flip-top bodies and all. The Southern California AA/GS circuit had several very nicely done flip-top cars including the Zeller Bros.' Willys and John Herrera's Austin. Indeed when some of the A/GS circuit cars ran in NHRA Championship events most of them were put in the BB/Altered class.

"Some say the AA/G Supercharged class is dead and others say it is only the beginning". This statement, printed in a 1968 Drag News issue referred to the changes being brought by the new model AA/GS cars hitting the strips. Steve Korney, President of the A/GS Organization and owner of an "old style" Anglia, commented that the "class should be restricted to old reliables because the spectators can't really tell the

Big John Mazmanian's Willys raced in the A/GS class from 1964 to 1967. In 1967 it was replaced by John's new Austin. In spite of only competing less than three years, it is one of the best remembered blown gassers. By June of 1967 the Willys was back on the Eastern match race circuit. After extensive modifications the much lighter Willys, with a late Dodge 426 type Hemi engine, was campaigned by Bill and Pete Hill (Ohio) as the "Red Baron". But about six months later they replaced it with a new '33 Willys. (Photo courtesy of Erik Chaputa)

new Mustang AA/G gassers from the Funny Cars". Certainly George Montgomery's excellent performances in late 1967 had caused a lot of thinking to be done. Perhaps the racers saw that most of the old cars were still using traditional upgraded street type chassis' while the new cars had essentially Funny Car chassis. So the AA/GS ranks started filling up with new style cars. Skip Hess built a beautiful Mustang as did Stone-Woods-Cook. Ohio suddenly had two new AA/GS Camaros built by Jeg Coughlin and Joe Hrudka. Ernie Nicholson replaced his '41 Studebaker with a new Barracuda. But not everyone used an American body. Norm Paddack was one of the first to use a German Opel in the AA/GS class.

Progress was now introducing the late model cars in the Supercharged Gas Coupe classes. Although many Willys', Anglias and Austins continued to run in the Supercharged Coupe classes, the new cars soon became dominant. Perhaps 1968 was the beginning of the end of the popularity of the Supercharged Gassers as the racers moved on to newer and better cars. It could be that the fans of the old Stone-Woods-Cook Willys, George Montgomery Willys, K. S. Pittman Willys, Steve Korney Anglia, Shores-Hess Anglia and Junior Thompson Austin found it difficult to transfer their allegiance to the new cars. It is not possible to say that is exactly what happened, but when fans reminisce about the A/GS cars they usually talk about the Willys, Anglias and Austins.

With drag racing's new professional direction publicity became extremely important for every competitor. Unfortunately for the AA/GS racers most of the publicity was going to the Funny Cars. The drag racing papers and magazines concentrated on the Funny Cars and a few of the Top Fuel Dragsters. The cam and transmission manufacturers' ads that used to mention the AA/GS cars often now only occasionally commented on the Supercharged Gassers. And the race results for weekly races became narratives about the feature program or match race - Funny Car, Dragster, etc. - and rarely mentioned the other class racers such as the Supercharged Gassers. Most results in Drag News and National Dragster no longer listed all the trophy winners. This meant that unless a Supercharged Gasser won a Super or Competition Eliminator or ran a feature AA/GS or BB/GS show his name usually did not appear in the drag newspaper or magazine. This general lack of publicity was especially felt in the BB/GS and CC/GS classes.

It is important to realize that the Supercharged Gassers were not the only cars affected by this problem. The drag racing leaders knew that the successful professional growth of drag racing required lots of spectators. And spectators wanted fast, competitive and exciting racing. This could be provided by the Funny Cars (AA/FC) and Fuel Dragsters (AA/FD). Both the AA/FC and AA/FD classes offered the fastest

performances and most importantly they did not run the handicap starting procedure that the majority of spectators did not like. Thus professional success was tied to "professionalizing" the Funny Cars and Dragsters while allowing the remainder of the classes to become "sportsmen". Naturally publicity, money and sponsorships were guided into the professional area. So not only the Supercharged Gassers suffered from a lack of publicity so did almost everyone else except the Funny Cars and Dragsters.

The exception to the lack of publicity rule was the supercharged cars that ran AA/GS shows, Super Eliminator meets or match races. Some of the drag strips advertised the pre-entries and then printed the results of the Supercharged Gasser shows which did help get many of cars known. Naturally the "big four" touring cars - George Montgomery, Stone-Woods-Cook, Junior Thompson and K. S. Pittman received good amounts of publicity. The Southern California AA/GS program publicity helped the names of Ron Bizio, Steve Korney, John Herrera and Skip Hess get to drag racing enthusiasts all over the country.

Just as drag racing was changing so the Supercharged Gasser roster was also. Both the cars and the racers were changing. It has already been mentioned that many racers had updated to newer model cars. And many of the new cars at the AA/GS meets were not legal by the NHRA rules because of major things like flip-top bodies or little things like no interior upholstery. The costs of racing a Supercharged Gasser were escalating rapidly. John Mazmanian apparently looked at the costs and return equation, sold his AA/GS Austin, and went into Funny Car racing. Tim Woods also built another Funny Car to replace the one that had crashed, but also continued to be involved in AA/GS.

Action started early in 1968 with AA/GS meets at Irwindale and Orange County (OCIR) and then the Winternationals (AHRA and NHRA). The competition was fierce with the quickest cars running in the 8.70 to 9.00 sec. area. Most of the cars were clocking between 150 and 158 mph. Both Irwindale and Lions were running about one AA/GS show every five to six weeks while OCIR (a new NHRA strip) was trying some Super Eliminator shows and an occasional AA/GS show in an effort to get a successful formula. By the middle of the year OCIR gave up on the Super Eliminator (handicap racing) shows and scheduled AA/G shows approximately every five weeks. So the local Southern California strips in 1968 approached three AA/GS shows every five weeks. The pay scale was typically $300, $200, $100, $50 for an eight car meet.

The local AA/GS competitors at these AA/GS shows included Ron Bizio, Skip Hess, Jim Kirby, John Lombardo, Steve Korney, Herrera and Sons, the Zeller Bros., Hicks-Galli and Gary Densham. K. S. Pittman and Junior Thompson ran initially but then left on their Eastern tour. Other AA/GS cars running the eight-car

AA/G shows were Ernie Nicholson, Meyer-Cluff from Phoenix, and the Northern California entries of Nunes-Murray, Del Rio-Carlson and Mike Mitchell.

Interestingly in spite of all this activity, each week saw the same basic group of cars qualifying for the show (Note that each car had to qualify into the program, they were not booked shows). Usually there was about ten to fourteen cars trying to qualify for the program. Occasionally due to broken cars or too few entries, a BB/GS car could qualify into the show. So even with good racing and some money available, the ranks of the Supercharged Gassers were not actually growing.

In the Eastern half of the country the touring "pros" were very busy. In addition to the "big four" (Montgomery, Pittman, S-W-C, Jr. Thompson) other AA/GS racers active on the road included Jack Coonrod, the Lee Bros., Prock-Howell, Jim Shores, the Hill Bros., Paul Frost and Jim Oddy. Most of the rest of the Supercharged Gassers had to compete in Super or Competition Eliminator (handicap racing) shows to get their racing.

The New Jersey area had a number of strong running BB/GS cars that often turned the Super Eliminator program into a BB/GS show. Eddie Sanzo, Bob Chipper, Bob Ida, Bob Lombardi, Harry Bickford and the Jersey Engineering car were running in the 9.90 to 10.50 sec. area with speeds of 133 to 139 mph. On August 7, 1968 the drag strip at Englishtown announced the meet had the "Finest BB/GS field every assembled" with all six of the listed Willys there.

In Southern California the only meets for the BB/GS cars, and the few CC/GS cars left, to run was the Super Eliminator events which would soon be only at NHRA Championship meets. However starting with Lions and then Orange County, Don Montgomery was able to get four car BB/GS shows scheduled. These shows were usually backup shows to a AA/Fuel Altered or AA/GS show. The BB/GS cars were running 9.90 to 10.50 sec. with speeds 130 to 142 mph. Even though there was only about one show every six weeks it was not easy to insure a full field for a four car show. At one meet an unblown A/Gasser had to fill in and often the last qualifier was not very competitive. The problem was a lack of competitive cars. The cars running the BB/GS meets included Paul Pittman, the Marrs Boys, Don Montgomery, Dave Fentress, Jack Carlson and the Airoso Bros. But the number of cars did increase so that eight-car BB/GS shows were run the next year.

The NHRA Nationals were won by George Montgomery (AA/GS), Bob Chipper (BB/GS) and Bill Lindner Jr. (CC/GS). George Montgomery owned the AA/GS records (8.72 sec. - 163.04 mph). The BB/GS records were held by Billy Holt (9.89 sec.) and the Marrs Boys (143.76 mph). Bill Lindner set the CC/GS record at 10.69 sec. while the CC/GS speed record was held by the Marrs Boys' 1967 time of 130.43 mph.

So on the surface 1968 had been a good year for the Supercharged cars. The touring AA/GS cars were earning $800 to $1600 per week while in Southern California AA/GS cars had chances to win money about every two weeks. Even the Southern California BB/GS cars were starting to get their own shows. Also some of the AA/GS and BB/GS cars were getting some paying match races.

But the overall picture shows that the AA/GS and BB/GS ranks were really not growing. Basically it was the same guys competing. Many built new cars. A little new blood came in and some moved on to other classes. Where there was strong competition and racing programs the classes remained active but elsewhere they seemed to fade away. Another thing that seemed to fade away was the interest in the CC/GS class. It cost as much money to run CC/GS as to run BB/GS or AA/GS with little opportunity to earn some money, like the AA/GS and BB/GS guys could.

- 1 9 6 9 -

The NHRA reported that 1969 was a record year. The number of spectators and contestants at the NHRA sanctioned events were said to be up 27% and 35% respectively. They also announced that 75% of the U.S. and Canadian drag strips were operating with NHRA sanctions leaving the remainder to AHRA sanctions or independent operations and insurance. The NHRA's racing schedule included four National meets (Winternationals, Springnationals, Indy Nationals and World Finals) and six regional points meets in each of the seven divisions.

Most of the racing for Supercharged Gassers at the NHRA meets was in the Super Eliminator competition. The Super Eliminator races combined twelve Fuel or Supercharged classes running time handicaps based on the class records. Super Eliminator competitors were basically the fastest group of cars that did not run heads-up (both start at the same time) races. The gassers did get the opportunity to race heads-up against similar class cars in class eliminations at the four National meets. But the time limits and lack of numerous entries in many of the classes resulted in most NHRA regional events running the Super Eliminator races without the class runoffs for the Supercharged Gassers. Unfortunately winning handicap races did not excite the spectators like the straight heads-up drag races did. So the publicity for the Super Eliminator racers was minimal, with the possible exception of George Montgomery whose many Eliminator victories resulted in lots of publicity for him. Thus the Supercharged Gasser competitors who raced the NHRA regional meets or at local NHRA drag strips had to race in a version of what is today called "bracket" racing.

The 1969 NHRA rules were basically unchanged from the previous year. The only actual rule change

Ron Nunes' (No. Calif.) '41 Willys ran in the B/GS long enough (10 months) to bomb the E.T. record in 1965 (Page 78) and then it stepped up to the AA/G class. With partner Dennis Murray, Ron replaced the Olds engine with a 430" Chrysler and reduced the weight of the Willys by 800 lbs., to about 2150 lbs. Fiberglass fenders, hood, doors and deck lid from Cal Automotive helped them get the weight down. A B&M Tork-Flite transmission was used. In 1968 the Willys stopped the clocks at 156.80 mph and 9.17 sec. It is possible that some Oldsmobile enthusiasts were happy to see the "Olds" name on the hood but the engine smoking the tires was by Chrysler.(Photo courtesy of Ron Nunes)

was to reduce the weight break for the CC/GS class from 11.0 lbs/cu.in. to 10.0 lbs/cu.in. The change was probably made to induce more entries in the CC/GS class as the interest seemed to be fading. The minimum weight breaks for AA/GS and BB/GS remained as they had been (5.0 and 8.0 lbs/cu.in.). Interestingly no effort was made to catch up with the increasing number of AA/GS cars that were "pushing" the rules. By making no effort to resolve the growing problem of illegal AA/GS cars, the NHRA apparently left the problem to resolve itself. In reality the new AA/GS cars were race cars while the rules still considered them to be "street" cars.

Once again Supercharged Gas Coupe racing in the East concentrated on match racing or Super Eliminator handicap racing. The group commonly referred to as

the "Big Four" (George Montgomery, Junior Thompson-John Mazmanian, K. S. Pittman and now Stone-Woods-Bones) returned for another successful season of match race touring, with changes in both cars and personnel. Junior Thompson's AA/GS racer this season was a new model (1969) Opel Kadett. K. S. Pittman was using the sleek Austin that he had purchased from John Mazmanian and George Montgomery brought out yet another AA/GS Mustang in mid-year. Bob "Bones" Balogh was now campaigning the Stone-Woods-Bones AA/GS Mustang. After recovering from his accident Doug Cook had joined John Mazmanian's team to work on John's Barracuda Funny Car. The "Big Four" ran probably the most successful match race program of all the so called "Sportsman" class cars; that is the non-pro classes which excludes the Top Fuel Dragsters and Funny Cars. Their races drew excellent crowds and their names are still well remembered today.

Another four car group of AA/GS racers was also touring throughout the Eastern half of the country. This group had a slightly different sales pitch. They were billed as "Nitro Gassers". They ran fuel because it helped them get more scheduled dates. The group included the Hill Bros. ('33 Willys), Chuck Finders (Anglia), Tom Prock-Jay Howell ('33 Willys) and Jim "Fireball" Shores (Anglia). All four cars had flip-top fiberglass bodies. The "Nitro Gassers" were recording E.T.'s as low as 8.16 sec. and 160 to 176 mph speeds. However the E.T. and speed performances were not improved by the fuel induced horsepower as much as might have been expected. The reason was probably that the short wheelbase AA/GS (?) cars could not "get hold of the track"; the same problem the Fuel Altereds were having. It is interesting to note that the 90" wheelbase Anglias of Finders and Shores apparently measured 98". The "Nitro Gassers" put on a fast, exciting and unpredictable show with truly early style cars. This was perhaps the last group to tour the Willys and Anglia bodied Supercharged Gassers. But, they weren't actually gassers.

Another group scheduling AA/GS meets was the Midwest UDRA Super Gasser circuit. Although not as successful as some of the other Midwest UDRA circuits (Funny Cars, Dragsters, Super Stocks), the Super Gasser circuit had some fine running cars including the Rich Ratliff-Bill Bisby Corvette and the Gordon Selkirk-Saul Bork Camaro.

The remainder of the Supercharged Gassers racing in the East was predominantly in Super Eliminator or other local Competition Eliminator programs. The most successful racers in these programs were the BB/GS racers. The New York area had strong competition with Bob Lombardi ('41 Willys), Bob Chipper ('33 Willys), Albers-Minnich (formerly Jack Merkel's '33 Willys) and Jim Oddy (Austin, formerly AA/GS). Several other areas also had strong gasser competitors like Florida's Tommy Shinholster (CC/GS), Iowa's Nelson Bros. (BB/GS) and Alabama's Billy Holt (BB/GS). In addition to the Super Eliminator racing some of the Supercharged Gassers were able to get a few match races at local area drag strips.

In Southern California things were great for the Supercharged Gassers. That is there was plenty of AA/GS and BB/GS heads-up racing with lots of confusion about what the rules were. Irwindale, Lions and Orange County drag strips were scheduling shows with two or three different classes of cars on their off-weeks between the major events of Funny Cars or Dragsters. The AA/GS Supercharged Coupes had a program at one of the three strips usually at two to three week intervals. Most of the programs were eight-car shows with typical payouts of $350 - $150 - $100 - $50. In November

Orange County even produced a sixteen-car AA/GS show. Generally the AA/GS Gassers shared the spotlight with a show of Junior Fuel Dragsters, AA/Fuel Altereds, Top Gas Dragsters or BB/GS Gassers.

The competition was strong at the AA/GS shows with most cars recording E.T.'s from 8.50 to 9.0 sec. All the qualifying cars were clocking over 150 mph with the 169 mph time by Li'l John Lombardo's topless Corvette being probably the fastest. Whereas in 1968 the AA/GS car that seemed to be a little ahead of the pack in the So. Calif. circuit was Ron Bizio's '33 Willys pickup, the 1969 Southern California season was dominated by John Lombardo's Corvette with Manuel Herrera doing the driving. John's record included a string of six victories in seven races. The regular competition included Ernie Nicholson, Ron Bizio, Steve Korney, Gary Burgin, Rogers-Johnson, Mike Mitchell, Skip Hess, Gary Densham, Doolin-Stroup, Vern Hicks, Ron Zeller, Bryan Raines and Meyer-Cluff from Phoenix. Also coming down from Northern California were the AA/GS cars of Warren Bros.-Nunes, Jim Jennings and Terry Rose. When they were home K. S. Pittman, Jr. Thompson, and Bones Balogh joined in too.

Most of the AA/GS racers tried for improved performance with a new car in 1969. Four new super small and light '27 T street roadster entries joined the circuit, run by Gary Burgin, Ron Zeller, Bryan Raines and Bilby-Densham-Plueger. Brad Anderson came out with a 160 mph big late model Dodge Dart while both John Lombardo and Mike Mitchell replaced their Willys with Corvettes, topless style. The Warren Bros.-Nunes entry was a Corvette also. There were still a few traditional style Anglias (Vern Hicks, Doolin-Stroup, Rogers-Johnson, Jim Jennings) and Willys (Garten-Braskett, Ron Bizio, Brasher-Cummings, Ron Rinauro) running in the AA/GS programs. Other new style cars included the Mustang of Skip Hess and the two Barracudas of Ernie Nicholson and the Mallicoat Bros. In addition to the cars mentioned several other entries were still working out problems in order to qualify into the shows. All of these programs were open to all AA/GS entries with the quickest eight making the show.

"What has happened to the AA/GAS Supercharged racing in Southern California? How does John Lombardo's AA/Altered run as a AA/Gasser and advertise as one when the car is so far out of class that it isn't even funny?" This question was posed by a Drag News reader from Columbus, Ohio (Nov. 1969). And indeed Drag News readers in the East had to wonder about the flip-top, topless Corvettes and the '27 T Street Roadsters running without the radiator shell, hood or front fenders that were pictured in the weekly drag newspapers at the AA/GS meets.

The letter to the editor from Ohio brought a response from John Lombardo. He said the reason his

Corvette did not run NHRA meets as an AA/GS class car was because of a few technical rules variations including Flip-Top Body, no correctly opening doors, no headlights and center steering. He further stated that "for the sake of a better show the AA/GS guys had met with the Southern California Drag Strip operators and agreed to run under their own rules". The new Southern California AA/GS circuit rules were very simple. The AA/GS circuit rules said the cars must (1) Meet the weight break (5.0 lbs/cu.in. minimum), (2) Have a stock appearing, full fendered body, (3) Run pump gas and (4) Have a 10% maximum engine set back. Incidently by the latter part of the year some of the AA/GS shows were being advertised as "Open Gas Supercharged" shows.

The Southern California AA/GS circuit presented an interesting situation to the 1969 drag racing scene. The AA/GS circuit was successfully running meets at the three major Southern California strips. They were being treated as performers, getting a good chunk of publicity and running for money. They even made their own rules. The first question for a California racer became how to build his AA/GS race car. If he built a fully legal NHRA AA/GS car, it might be difficult to be a winner in the Southern California AA/GS circuit. Or if he made a So. Calif. "legal" AA/GS car his chances in the circuit meets might be improved but the NHRA would derail him into the BB/Altered Class where publicity was nil. This decision was usually made based on what type of meets the racer preferred. Some racers were primarily interested in the NHRA National meets or points meets. Naturally their race cars were set up to be NHRA legal. Many other racers were anxious to run the AA/GS circuit meets for any number of reasons, including a chance to race more often, heads-up racing, more publicity and an opportunity to earn some money. Most AA/GS circuit cars were forced to take full advantage of the rules, or lack of them, to remain competitive thus the numbers of illegal cars, by NHRA standards, continued to grow. The only solution that seemed to be available would be to change the Supercharged Gasser rules to reflect the true race car status that had already arrived.

In spite of rules problems, the illegal AA/GS circuit was a success. The racing was good, the guys won some money, got lots of publicity from National Dragster and Drag News and were treated like professionals rather than the somewhat uninspiring treatment that the average drag racer seemed to receive most of the time.

Perhaps one measure of the success is in the numbers. The once a year NHRA Nationals had ten pre-entered AA/GS competitors drawn from all over the country in 1969. But in the Southern California area alone the AA/GS meets were recording ten to fifteen pre-entries for programs run every two to three weeks.

Instant success and long term effects are often entirely different things. In the case of the AA/GS Class the instant success stimulated interest, brought out new cars and promoted technical improvements. But what about the lasting effects? One effect of the many illegal cars was to cause racers to question the sense of racing in a class where some cars didn't follow the NHRA rules. It is also possible that the NHRA found it difficult to live with the newly successful AA/GS circuit racers who were promoting heads-up racing while the NHRA was promoting handicap racing for the "Sportsman" racers. However the most important factor to the long term prospects of the AA/GS class was the late model cars. Corvettes, Mustangs and Barracudas made great race cars and the public appreciated them in the Funny Car ranks. But when they appeared in the AA/GS ranks the public did not seem to readily accept them. Perhaps to the majority of the spectators they looked like Funny Cars, but didn't go as fast or sound as good. And some of the AA/GS cars even blurred any differential between the Funny Cars and AA/GS cars by running Funny Car meets on fuel. John Lombardo's Corvette was able to qualify into Funny Car shows with 7.80 sec. performances on fuel. So perhaps the long term effect of the new model AA/GS cars would be the most important of all the things that went on in 1969.

Perhaps the most unexpected item in the 1969 season was the success of the Southern California BB/GS circuit. A total of 18 shows were run. All were four-car programs except the California BB/GS Championship meet at Orange County which was an eight-car show. Although there was not a formal BB/GS organization, the BB/Gassers had their own points race with trophies to the top cars at the end of the season given at the 1969 BB/GS season banquet. Scheduling, publicity, promotion and trying to get the racers out was done by Don Montgomery, while Silas Pittman, K. S. and Paul's younger brother, wrote the "BB Gasser Report" column in Drag News. Articles and photos in the programs at Orange County Lions and Irwindale helped to promote the BB/GS racers. In addition both National Dragster and Drag News occasionally commented on the BB/GS Supercharged Gassers. One of the Drag News columnists wrote about the BB/GS racers (June, 1969), "These guys have spurred a lot of attention lately in what many thought was a 'dead' class".

The BB/GS shows were inexpensive programs that a strip manager could combine with another show, such as AA/GS Supercharged Gassers or AA/Fuel Altereds, to offer a full night of racing entertainment. The typical payout for a four-car BB/GS show was $100 - $70 - $35 ($240 total). The eight-car 1969 BB/GS Supercharged Championships was actually billed as a feature show running with an AA/Fuel Altered eight-car program. The eight-car show paid $175, $100, $70, $40 (total $470).

Southern California had several very strong running BB/GS cars but unfortunately not too many. For whatever of the many reasons available the class had not grown in numbers since the days around five to six years previously when the B/GS racers included Stone-Woods-Cook, K. S. Pittman, Junior Thompson, the Mallicoat Bros. and John Mazmanian. So the BB/GS programs early in the year had difficulties getting more than three to five pre-entries. But as the year progressed more competitors joined in so that the pre-entries moved up into the eight area, for the four-car shows. The Drag News report on the 1969 California BB/GS Championships said that the eight-car show had "the greatest selection of BB/Gassers ever massed". (Note: The word "selection" probably should have been "collection" and the "collection" may not have been the greatest ever massed but it was a great and successful show which led to more eight-car shows in 1970).

Sixteen cars scored points in the Southern California BB/GS circuit during the 1969 season. The top scoring cars included the Pittman Bros., Neil Stein, Marrs-Lukens, Don Montgomery, Jack Hayworth, Larry Holt (who won the Championship meet), Jon Anderson and Fentress-Jones. Some of the meets drew entries from Northern California (Bob Panella, Ed Roberts, Gary Brookshire and Steve Woods) and Don Toia came over from Arizona.

In contrast to the "happenings" in AA/GS, the BB/GS were all legal NHRA cars. They were predominately Willys and Anglias plus a few '37 Chevys, Corvettes and an Austin. Three of the BB/GS circuit cars strongly competed in the NHRA Points races (Pittman Bros., Marrs-Lukens, Bob Panella) running in the Super Eliminator competition. Very few new cars were built to run in the BB/GS ranks and perhaps the most obvious reason was why spend the money. The earnings were meager and if you have money to spend why not build an AA/GS car which could easily double the earnings (of course a little more in a Funny Car yielded much more money, which is what many of the racers did). Two noteworthy new BB/GS cars were the Pittman Bros.' Anglia (formerly Jim Shores' AA/GS car) which replaced the Willys that K. S. Pittman had campaigned in years past and Neil Stein's pro-built '56 Chevy which Neil had run in the unblown classes previously.

The BB/Gassers were recording E.T.'s generally in the 9.60 to 10.30 sec. range while the fastest cars were running in the 140 to 145 mph region. It is important to note that although the West Coast BB/GS cars were getting the publicity in the drag papers, many BB/GS competitors in other parts of the country were also recording excellent times. Both Bob Panella and Bob Chipper broke the NHRA BB/GS records during the year but the final records (9.58 sec., 146.81 mph) were owned by Holt-Suski-Fowler from Alabama.

The publicity given to the BB/Gassers in 1969

helped generate interest and races for them in 1970. Some new cars moved into the class. But actually the total number of BB/GS cars was not high and not increasing. The NHRA Nationals had seventeen pre-entries in BB/GS Class and ten of the top forty-five cars in the NHRA Super Eliminator Points standings were BB/Gassers. So even though the number of BB/Gassers was not increasing, the racing was still competitive and good.

The NHRA CC/GS records were captured by the Shinholster-Lehman team, from Florida, at 10.26 sec. and 136.15 mph. There were ten CC/GS pre-entries at the NHRA Nationals and two CC/GS teams were in the top forty-five NHRA Super Eliminator Points lists. Unfortunately the CC/GS guys got very little publicity. A few CC/GS cars moved up to BB/GS to get some action. But CC/GS was actually dying. Indeed the 1970 season would be the final season for the CC/GS Class.

The 1969 season had been an interesting and exciting season. The AA/GS cars had confused everyone including the NHRA, the spectators and the competitors. Some cars were NHRA legal and some were not. Some of them were running fuel and most of the new cars looked like Funny Cars. In the NHRA Super Eliminator Points race there were not any AA/GS cars in the top forty-five spots. After the AA/GS pre-entries to the NHRA Nationals only totaled ten, it was obvious the AA/GS cars were "doing their own thing". The BB/GS guys in Southern California were enjoying success, the BB/GS entries in the NHRA Super Eliminator races were doing well and a few BB/GS cars around the country were getting some match races. As for CC/GS, it was a well kept secret with the possible exception of Tommy Shinholster's very fast Willys. In spite of all the confusion the Supercharged Gassers had a very good year in 1969.

- 1 9 7 0 -

There were really no changes in the 1970 NHRA rules that affected the Supercharged Gassers, but important changes in drag racing were having a major impact on the blown gassers.

Drag racing was still trying to become a professional sport. Almost all major drag strips were paying for shows or match races in an effort to draw more spectator's admittance fees. Many drag racers were sharing in the payouts including those running Funny Cars, Dragsters, Fuel Altereds, Supercharged Gassers and the Super Stockers. But most of the racers were not happy. The match racers were complaining that they were running for the same money that they had earned three and four years before. Racers in most of the shows felt that the payouts should be more, especially for the non-winners. And the rest of the racers in classes where little or no cash was being paid naturally wanted a chance at the money. The racers felt that the growing spectator crowds meant that there should be more money for the racers. Basically they felt that drag racing needed to pay enough to support the racers as most professional sports do. And although a number of racers were being financially supported by their racing earnings, the majority were not. In fact there were too many racers looking for support from the drag strips income. This resulted in a spread out distribution of money and a general dissatisfaction with professional drag racing as it was in 1970.

Many different classes of cars were earning money at the drags by 1970. The top paychecks were going to the Funny Car racers. The second highest paid racers were the Fuel Dragster guys; although the interest in the Dragsters was lagging and many Dragster "heroes" were jumping into Funny Cars (including Don Pruhdomme, Connie Kalitta). Next on the money list was the match race and show programs put on with groups of Supercharged Gassers, Fuel Altereds, Injected Funny Cars, Junior Fuel Dragsters, Top Gas Dragsters or Super Stockers. Almost every area had a mini-circuit with at least one group of cars requesting a share of the money.

The major change in 1970 was a focusing of the direction into professionalism for drag racing. The NHRA pretty well laid out the ground rules with their 1970 NHRA competition rules. The new rules made a defined split between Professional racers (Group I) and Sport racers (Group II). The Professional Classes (Funny Cars, Top Fuel Dragsters, Top Gas Dragsters and the brand new Pro-Stocks) would run heads-up and would be the featured show while Sports racing would combine all other competitors in handicap brackets (4). The new rules recognized that the Funny Cars had become the dominant force in drag racing by giving them a professional status and heads-up racing. Prior to this Funny Cars had to run in the Super Eliminator handicap brackets and were conspicuous by their absence at NHRA events. In addition the new Pro-Stock Class allowed the new factory backed Stock racers to be featured in heads-up racing instead of competing in the Super Stock Eliminator (handicap) bracket. The Pro-Stock Class encouraged factory participation with greater publicity opportunities.

The establishing of the Professional group with only four classes simplified the selling of drag racing to sponsors and the media. The result was more publicity and much more money. This year the NHRA was even able to get the first live television broadcast of a drag race. The NHRA's decision to set up the Professional category in 1970 was perhaps one of the most successful actions in their history.

The new Professional category may have been good for drag racing but it did not help the Supercharged Gassers. They were classified as Sports racers running handicap races. Publicity would soon become difficult to get for the AA/GS guys because the drag racing

associations, drag strips, sponsors, manufacturers and media were focused on the Professional classes. The opportunities for the Supercharged Gassers to share in the increasing dollars in drag racing were greatly diminished. But although the AA/GS, BB/GS and CC/GS classes were actually dying, most of the competitors didn't realize it.

In the East the most successful AA/GS guys were once again the "Big Four" (George Montgomery, Jr. Thompson, K. S. Pittman, Stone-Woods-Cook). They were able to secure dates almost every week for two- or four-car shows or individual appearances. On occasion one of them would get a match race with another of the Eastern Supercharged Gassers. But this year it required traveling longer distances to fill the calendar and in spite of the continuing increases in costs to compete the pay-offs were no greater than those of five years before. The other AA/GS cars in the East, including Dave Mason, Ellison-McGarvey, Sachs-Milanese and Norm Paddack, had to run Competition Eliminator events and an occasional match race.

The West Coast AA/GS cars continued to run their Open Gas Supercharged shows. The first eight-car show at Orange County Raceway in January drew twenty-three entries to qualify. The AA/GS guys were averaging a meet every three to four weeks. The competitors were running roadsters (Gary Burgin, Ron Zeller, Densham-Bilby-Plueger, Brian Raines), Corvettes (Warren Bros.-Nunes, John Lombardo, Terry Rose, Mike Mitchell), Mustangs (Skip Hess, Vern Hicks) Barracudas (Mallicoat Bros., Ernie Nicholson) and other interesting models ('37 Chevy - Sherman Gunn, '69 Dodge - Keith Bush, Anglia - Steve Korney and Willys - Ron Bizio). The AA/GS cars were hitting E.T.'s in the 8.50 sec. to 8.90 sec. area and speeds from 155 to over 160 mph. Competition remained stiff throughout the year with as many as twenty-two entries signing in for a sixteen-car program in September. Very few of the West Coast AA/GS cars ran the NHRA meets. The cash awards remained the same as in 1969. In addition to the Southern California shows the Northern California AA/GS cars had shows and some match races in their area.

Once again the East had a strong contingent of BB/GS racers. The majority of the racing for BB/GS cars was in Competition Eliminator bracket (handicap) racing. Competitors like Jim Oddy, Bob Lombardi, Joe Amato, Bob Chipper and Paul Day were running at record pace. In fact there was apparently more BB/GS activity than AA/GS action in the East, not counting the "Big Four" touring AA/GS guys.

The West Coast BB/GS group had a great season in 1970. A total of twenty-four meets were raced. Both four and eight-car shows were run with the payoff for the eight-car show equal to $175, $100, $70, $45 ($595 total purse). The Southern California BB/GS Points race had sixteen cars scoring points this season. The

In 1966 Billy Holt (Alabama) won the NHRA Nationals BB/G title with final times of 132.36 mph and 10.78 sec. Three months earlier Holt's Willys had recorded a 138.51 mph run. It was a repeat of Holt's 1965 victory. He returned in 1967 and was the runner-up in the BB/G class. The '41 Willys was propelled by a 327" Chevy engine and driven by Gary Fowler. The team set BB/GS records in 1968 and again in 1969. They also replaced the '41 Willys with a '33 Willys. Billy Holt's Willys were certainly among the best blown gassers to come out of the South. In 1967 Billy had to build a new, but identical car, when his Willys was totaled in a crash. It had hit E.T.'s as low as 9.77 sec. before this. (Photos courtesy of Bob Balogh and Mike Hanlon)

BB/GS competitors included Marrs-Lukens, Steve Woods, Paul Pittman, Jon Anderson, Don Toia, Bob Panella, Larry Holt, Neil Stein, Fentress-Jones, Ed Roberts, Don Vance, Don Montgomery, Charlie Saucedo and Stewart-Cook.

The BB/GS cars were recording times in the 9.40 sec. to 9.90 sec. range with speeds of 140 to 146 mph. The NHRA records for 1970 were set by the California BB/GS cars of Marrs-Lukens (9.39 sec.) and Steve Woods (151.00 mph) and the best E.T. at a Southern California BB/GS meet was a 9.27 sec. time by Steve Woods.

There were not many CC/GS competitors running in 1970. Eddie Flora, Shinholster-Lehman, Bill Lindner, Claudie Meador and Tom Hrudka were among the strongest of the CC/GS racers. The NHRA records were the property of Eddie Flora (10.00 sec.) and Shinholster-Lehman (136.15 mph, set in 1969). The owners of cars in this class usually found most of their racing in Competition Eliminator bracket (handicap) events.

The trend to newer model cars continued this year. Most of the AA/GS competitors were now running Corvettes, Opels, Mustangs or Barracudas. The BB/GS and CC/GS racers were still predominantly racing their early model Willys, Anglias and Austins. But even in the BB/GS class some late model cars were starting to compete including Bob Lombardi's Opel GT, Paul Pittman's Gremlin and Bob Chipper's Barracuda. Since most of the new cars utilized new chassis designs their performances generally left the older cars with a distinct E.T. disadvantage. Naturally this meant that the general opinion was that a new car was needed to remain competitive in the AA/GS and BB/GS classes.

It is interesting to note that the 1968 rule change that had allowed roadsters to run in the Supercharged Gas Coupe classes had not resulted in a flood of roadsters competing. In fact it appears that only several roadsters ran in the Southern California Open Gas Supercharged (AA/GS) meets and that was it. And the roadsters that did run the Open meets often neglected to run with grills, hoods or fenders. The Southern California BB/GS Circuit ruled against roadsters at their meets. It wasn't a problem anyway because none of them showed up to run in the heavier weight break class.

The 1970 season had been a good one in the minds of most of the competitors. But things are not always as they seem. In fact some disturbing things were happening. After continuing gains in the number of contestants each year the 1970 figures showed a decline. The number of drag racing events and total spectator count was still slightly increasing although the NHRA's figures actually showed a reduction in the average spectator count per event (Incidently the average spectator count was approximately 1700 per drag race event). The result of this apparent end to continual growth in drag racing was cutbacks in the drag racing programs. The most notable changes were the experiments by many managers to replace shows of Supercharged Coupes, Fuel Altereds, Gas Dragsters or Injected Funny Cars with inexpensive bracket racing programs. Basically the idea was to forget about offering a show every week and switch to a big Funny Car or similar program about every three or four weeks. This trend appeared to begin late in the year so did not greatly affect most of the racers. But the handwriting was actually on the wall for all to see.

The Supercharged Gassers did get some publicity during 1970, but it was only a fraction of the kind of publicity they had received five years earlier. The magazines did do some articles on individual Supercharged cars (Spiegel Bros. Bob Lombardi, Nunez-Dillon and others) and the drag papers wrote up the stories on the AA/GS and BB/GS meets. Other than that most race results only seemed to mention a Supercharged Gasser when it raced a Competition Eliminator final race. Although around the country Supercharged Gassers were running at various events rarely did their names get in print. The manufacturer's ads that used to highlight many of the Supercharged Gassers now almost never mentioned them. Unfortunately when the Supercharged Gassers were mentioned in the magazines comments like "vanishing AA/GS breed" seemed to be the prevailing thinking.

When the AHRA reporter wrote that 1970 was "the first true Professional racing season yet seen for drag racing", he was probably correct. Elevating the Funny Cars to heads-up racing brought them back to NHRA events and the new Pro-Stock class was an instant success with a welcome influx of factory money. Unfortunately for the Sports Racing (Group II) guys all this success, and money, was for the Professional (Group I) racers. So by the end of the season many Sports racers were unhappy with the money situation. So while one columnist in Drag News was writing that it's "time the actors' stopped paying to put on the show" and "there are a lot of unhappy racers" another magazine writer was predicting more money for the Professional racers.

The 1970 season had been a good one for the AA/GS and BB/GS racers, especially where match races or shows were being raced. But the total entries at the National events were dropping and the number of Supercharged Gassers in the NHRA Points lists were also declining. So it now appears that the Supercharged Gas Coupe classes were "over the hill" by the end of the 1970 season.

Some of the other Supercharged Gas Coupe competitors in the 1967 to 1970 period were:

Smith-Goldenstein (Minnesota)
Jim Buckwheat (Michigan)
Nail-Holzman (Kansas)
Jim Mack (Ohio)
Gene Schwartz (Ohio)
Coy Martin (No.California)
Gary Morgan (Alabama)
"Big" Wilson (Ohio)
Bob Ida (New Jersey)
Ratliff-Bisby (Illinois)
Stoltz-Velasquez (Indiana)
George Gray (Canada)
Johnson-Nobuyai (So.Calif.)
Mike Steinberg (No.Calif.)
Wilko Bros. (New York)
Sammy Loria (Texas)
Hank Greenleaf (Kansas)
Glenn Lazzar (New York)
Jack Halsey (No.California)
Harry Bickford (New Jersey)
Charles Farley (Oklahoma)
Jeff Larkin (Minnesota)
Joe Pirrone (Maryland)
Mel McGinnis (Pennsylvania)
Busse-Fout (Illinois)

J. B. Graziano (Illinois)
Jim Stohr (Minnesota)
Paul Paolozzi (So.California)
Kohler-Vassar (So.California)
Vinnie Crawford (New York)
Jack Williams (Canada)
Chuck Poole (No.California)
Larson Bros. (So. California)
Royal Langford (Ohio)
Eddy Bryck (Canada)
Pete Gretz (Indiana)
Bob Riffle (Ohio)
Carl Hegge (Virginia)
Pat Dakin (Ohio)
Cameron Cogsdill (Michigan)
Kroona-Deeb-Sandberg (Minn.)
Paul Van Woensel (Colorado)
Mickey Hart (Ohio)
Henry Lawson (Illinois)
Jim Rhea (Maryland)
Leone-Fruge (Louisiana)
Burgess-Steed (Massachusetts)
Ken Silvestri (No.California)
Hutchinson-Hope (So.Calif.)
Cottrell-Reichard (Maryland)

Ed and Ray Kohler (So. Calif.) had one of California's fastest unblown Anglias in 1965. Then they followed Skip Hess and Steve Korney into the A/GS class. But they did it a little differently when they installed a big 454" Chevy engine. The Anglia had almost immediate success recording E.T.'s as low as 9.23 sec. It only took a few months before other Anglias and Austins were re-engined to Chryslers or big block Chevys. Perhaps the Kohler's biggest contribution to the blown gas class was in helping to popularize the Torqueflite transmission. The Anglia's excellent performances with the Torqueflite transmission built by Art Carr, who even drove the Anglia on occasion, resulted in a stampede to install Torqueflites in other A/GS cars. In early 1966 the Anglia won the Eliminator bracket at the AHRA and NHRA Winternationals and Bakersfield (9.12 sec.). (Photo courtesy of Don Toia)

111

Perhaps the neatest appearing A/GS Austin pickup was this blue one from Phoenix, Arizona. Larry Meyer and Ed Cluff raced it in 1968 at the local AHRA events and at many Southern California A/GS programs. The 1950 lb. pickup had fiberglass doors and a one piece front end by Dave Anderson (A-1 Fiberglass). The blown Chrysler engine pushed the Austin to 162 mph and 8.90 sec. times. In 1969 the car, ready to run, was offered for sale at $4000. (Photo courtesy of Don Toia)

By the time of the 1967 Nationals Jack Merkel's '33 Willys looked very different than it had before (Page 87). The previously tall Willys was now low and a big "rat motor" had replaced the "mouse motor". The steel Willys body was gone and a neat fiberglass body was on the chassis. The front wheels were the weight reducing Halibrand spindle mount (no hubs) model. Later (1969) the Willys was campaigned in the BB/GS class by Albers-Minnich (New Jersey) with a Chrysler engine. And the name on the front was "Glass Ruler". Before he sold it Jack was recording 156 mph and 8.80 sec. times. (Photo courtesy of Dean Court)

Here is the Bob Balogh-Gary Dubach Willys (1967) after Joe Pisano had moved on to other projects (Page 70). The Willys was still red, beautiful and 470" Chrysler powered. Although the lettering said "B&M Hydro", Bones had installed a Torqueflite (Aug. 1966). Note the 8" wide Cragar rear wheels. The narrow wheels and wide slicks were the wrinkle-wall, low pressure concept tried in the 1966 period. This car competed in the Southern California A/GS programs. The running weight of 2560 lbs. was actually a little heavier than most of their A/GS opponents. (Photo courtesy of Junior Thompson)

One of the top A/GS racers in the Southern California area was the "Goldfinger" Anglia. It was originally built by Steve Korney with an unblown Chevy to compete in the A/G class. In late 1966 Steve Montrelli's blown Chrysler and a B&M Tork-Flite were added. After rebuilding the frame (it wouldn't handle the Chrysler power) the 153 mph performance had convinced Steve that he should build a Chrysler engine. He did and the "Goldfinger" Anglia became one of the top A/GS cars in Southern California going below 9 sec. early in 1967. Steve added an interesting gimmick to the Anglia with a multiple colored light bar connected to a loud sound system. The flashing lights showed nicely at the many night programs the Southern California A/GS racers had. (Photos courtesy of Steve Korney)

Bob Ida (New Jersey) parked his '56 Chevy (Page 75) and switched to a Willys in 1967. The '40 Willys was a four-door sedan. The sedans were seldom used because they were considered to be much heavier and not as nice looking (actually the sedans were 75 lbs. heavier than coupes). Bob put his 409 Chevy engine in the Willys with his own reworked Hydro-stick transmission. The 3300 lb. sedan recorded a best of 135.73 mph and 10.24 sec. Bob often ran the Super Eliminator (IHRA and NHRA) events in the New Jersey area against many of the New York area blown gassers. In 1969 Bob changed again, to an Austin-Healy with a Chrysler Hemi engine (BB/GS). (Photos courtesy of Bob Ida)

One of Indiana's entries at the 1967 NHRA Nationals was the candy red '40 Willys run by Nelson Stoltz and Raymond Velasquez. The AA/G coupe had a Hemi Dodge under the hood. They ran in 1966 and 1967 recording 145.39 mph and 9.84 sec. In 1968 the team announced that they were moving to the Super Stock class with a Hemi-Barracuda. (Photo courtesy of Mike Hanlon)

There were many car club entries at the drags in the 1950's. But as drag racing became more competitive and expensive, club entries faded away. The Stags Car Club (Ogden, Utah) starting racing this '40 Ford coupe in 1960. By the late 1960's the club had moved up to the BB/GS class. The power came from a blown 392" Chrysler engine driving through a Clutch-flite transmission. The Ford's best times were 134.47 mph and 10.12 sec. in 1970. These were good times for the high altitude (4600') Bonneville drag strip. The race photo shows the Stags Car Club Ford lined up with Paul Pittman in the Pittman Bros. Willys at a 1968 NHRA points meet. (Photos courtesy of Don Palfreyman of the Stags Car Club)

John Herrera (So. Calif.) campaigned one of the best running unblown B/G Anglias in Southern California before jumping into the Supercharged Gas Coupe classes. After seeing the "fun" that the Anglias of local area racers (Kohler Bros. and Shores-Hess) were having in the A/GS class, John had to join up. He built an Austin (steel body) with a 427" Chevy engine built by Jack Bayer. It started running the Southern California A/GS shows in late 1966. By the end of the year the Austin had recorded times of 156.52 mph and 9.15 sec. The photo was taken at the 1967 AHRA Winternationals (Phoenix-January) where 155.70 mph was recorded by John Herrera and Son's (Manuel, Richard & Phillip) burgundy colored Austin. Three months later the Austin dropped below 9.0 sec. (8.95 sec.). (Photo courtesy of Don Toia)

After a winning season in Stock class with his factory fuel injected '57 Chevy, Claudie Meador (Texas) decided he wanted to go faster. So the Chevy hard-top got a 4-71 blown 310" engine and competed in the C/GS class in 1968. Note that AHRA was still using C/GS instead of CC/GS (NHRA). Claudie competed in the AHRA divisional points series, winning it that year. In 1969 the Chevy was retired and replaced by an Austin. The C/GS Chevy ran in the low 12 sec. area with speeds up around 120 mph. The race photo was taken at an independent central Texas track - Temple Academy. (Photos courtesy of Claudie Meador)

The "Agitator" was the '40 Willys pickup owned by Vern Hicks and Lou Galli. It had been raced very successfully before under the name "MGM" by Gene Ciambella of C&O Hydro. Initially renamed "HGM" for Hicks, Galli and Modlin, the name was changed to "Agitator". Early in 1967 the car was reworked, including a chopped top, by Chuck Finders. Gary Densham, Gene Modlin and Chuck Finders all drove the "Agitator". The Vern Hicks built Chrysler engine was a 392 increased to 467". On 10-8-66 the truck recorded a 9.65 sec. E.T. By the end of the year (1967) times of 152.02 mph and 9.27 sec. had been recorded running the Southern California A/GS programs. The Willys was sold and later reappeared racing in Ohio with new owner Paul Day (April 1968). (Photos courtesy of Junior Thompson and Vern Hicks)

After finishing the 1966 season with the '41 Willys, K. S. Pittman came home and built a new '33 Willys for the next season. This one used a Cal Automotive fiberglass body. The chassis was built by Chuck Finders and the engine was a Dave Zeuschel product (420" Chrysler). The transmission was a Tork-Flite by B&M. In the first few weeks K. S. hit 158.90 mph and 8.95 sec. Once again K. S. Pittman spent most of the year successfully earning his living on the Eastern tour. Late in the year, before returning home the Willys recorded times of 163.70 mph and 8.55 sec. After John Mazmanian moved to Funny Car competition K. S. Pittman and Jim Foster purchased John's Austin. Both cars campaigned running match races under the Pittman name. Harry Hall (Penn.) purchased the Willys in 1968 and ran it until the summer of 1972 when it crashed at Englishtown, N. J. (Photo courtesy of Harry Hall)

The Stone-Woods-Cook "Swindler A" continued to tour in 1967 but Tim Woods and Doug Cook were already building a Funny Car. The new "Dark Horse 2" Funny Car was a Mustang. Doug Cook raced the Mustang early in 1967 while his brother Ray drove the AA/GS Willys. By March both the Funny Car (Doug) and the AA/GS Willys (Ray) had left on tour. The next month found Chuck Finders behind the wheel of the Willys. Ray and Chuck completed the 1967 tour while Doug concentrated on the Funny Car. In September the Funny Car crashed at 180 mph putting Doug in the hospital and finishing his driving career. In January 1968 the Willys hit 158 mph in 8.90 sec. and Tim Woods stated that he was building a new Mustang AA/GS car and the Willys was to be retired. (Photo courtesy of K. S. Pittman)

Steve Woods (No. Calif.) had been racing a Gas class Prefect until he moved up to the Supercharged ranks. This '41 Willys was Steve's BB/GS entry. The "Bad Habit" had a 331" Chrysler engine (and a loose rear fender). Steve traveled to two of the Southern California BB/GS meets in 1969 with the Willys. In 1970 he put the Chrysler engine in the Prefect and that combination won many races and records. (Photo courtesy of Phil Quinto)

Barbara Hamilton and Nancy Leonello (Ohio) were the first women to race in the Supercharged Gas Coupe classes. It was very difficult for Barbara to even get an NHRA drivers license. Finally in 1964 she got an NHRA license, but in 1967 they revoked the licenses of all five licensed women drivers. The NHRA was concerned about the effect of an accident with a woman at the wheel (Shirley Muldowney was applying for a Dragster license at the time). The Hamilton-Leonello CC/G Willys was brought to California in August of 1967 to try and convince the NHRA to reinstate the license. The photo shows the car running at Lions. The license was reinstated in 1968 and they raced the car until 1972, first in CC/GS and then in BB/GS, when Barbara felt the car was no longer competitive. The Willys used Chevy engines (265" and 294") and a B&M Clutch-flite (1968 on). In 1968 Chapman Automotive rebuilt the suspension to clear up handling problems. (Photos courtesy of Barbara Hamilton Advey and Bob Balogh)

This chopped top '41 Willys was called the "Challenger". It was owned by Harry Bickford (New Jersey). It had a 420" Chrysler to race in the AA/GS class. It had a Tork-flite transmission and a nice firemist aqua blue paint job. The gold leaf lettering came later. Southern California fans remembered the "Challenger" when it ran the Southern California A/GS meets. It was raced by it's builder Jim Kirby who had put it up for sale in late 1968 for $1500 (less engine and trans). (Photo courtesy of Harry Hall)

Here is another '55 Chevy in the C/GS class. This blue hard-top belonged to Ron Rinauro (No. Calif.). It is pictured at Fremont where it stopped the clocks at 124.30 mph and 11.13 sec. (Dec. 1965). The engine was a 292" Chevy. The name was "Blown Hell" (perhaps the Chevy was a distant relative to "Pure Hell", the famous Northern California Fuel Altered). The engine was built by "Terrible" Ted Gotelli. (Photo courtesy of John Chambliss)

Lil' John Lombardo (So. Calif.) - we already had a Big John - ran this Chrysler powered '41 Willys pickup. John ran it in the 1967 and 1968 Southern California A/GS meets. The engine was a 392 type Chrysler and the transmission was an Art Carr Torqueflite. In January 1968 the Willys qualified into an A/GS show with an excellent 9.70 sec. E.T. (149.56 mph). But the Willys was soon replaced by a new Corvette. This photo was taken at Art Carr's Arcadia transmission shop. (Photo courtesy of Art Carr)

History repeated itself when Vern Hicks and Lou Galli bought Gene Ciambella's second pickup after buying the first one (Page 117). The Austin pickup inherited the "Agitator" name in place of the "MGM - C&O" name previously painted on the doors. A Vern Hicks built 467" Chrysler fit right in because Ciambella had also been running a Chrysler. Interestingly the new owner of the Hicks-Galli '40 Willys pickup retained the name "Agitator" on the truck and used it on his next car also. Gary Southern drove the Austin pickup to 151.59 mph and 9.16 sec. in 1968. (Photos courtesy of Tom Chambliss and Vern Hicks)

The BB/G entry of Cameron Cogsdill (Michigan) was a '33 Willys with a 331" Chrysler engine. It is shown here at the 1967 NHRA Nationals and previously when it was bronze in color. The Willys had Halibrand "Mag" wheels (spindle mount fronts) and a Logghe coil-over front suspension system. (Photos courtesy of Barbara Hamilton Advey and Mike Hanlon)

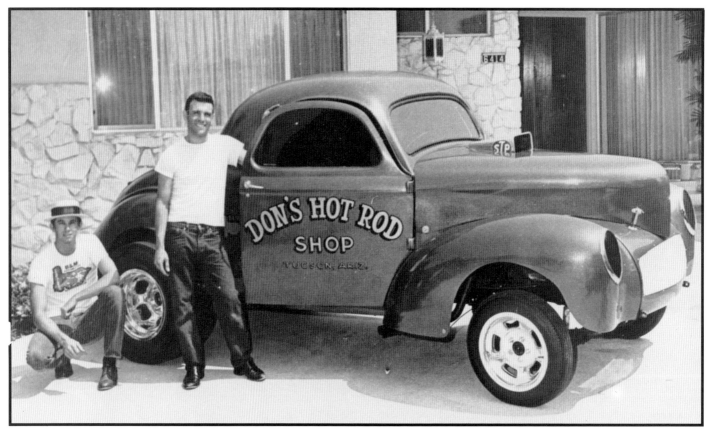

Don Toia (Arizona) bought a "dead" '39 Willys in 1966. After much work the completed B/GS Willys looked nice painted metallic maroon. He first ran a Chevy engine (1968) but then changed to a 354" Chrysler (1969). Since Arizona was "AHRA country" Don had to get an NHRA license to run the Southern California BB/GS shows. He did this in Oct. 1969 and recorded 141.50 mph and 10.04 sec. at the BB/GS Championship meet in November. After winning Competition Elimator at the 1970 AHRA Nationals Don built a Maverick for BB/GS competition. He kept the Willys. Don is the President of Don's Hot Rod Shop in Tucson, Arizona. (Photos courtesy of Don Toia)

Jack Coonrod (Oregon) took the "Kamakazi Koup" (Page 60), after Wayne Harry cut back on his racing, and continued to race it in the A/GS. Jack had Chuck Finders rework the car. After his 152 mph Willys had a good year in 1966 Jack decided to get serious about racing. He spent the 1967 and 1968 seasons as a "touring pro". Jack "The Bear" Coonrod scheduled races with most of the other touring AA/GS cars including the Hill Bros., Jim Shores, Paul Frost, Stone-Woods-Cook, K. S. Pittman, the Kohler Bros., Junior Thompson, Jim Oddy and so on. The yellow '33 Willys used a 430" Chrysler and a Tork-flite transmission to hit 165.13 mph in mid-1967. Jack returned to the tour in 1969 but everything was changing. Some of the AA/GS "pros" had changed to nitromethane (Hill Bros., Jim Shores, etc.) and touring was becoming less profitable for the AA/GS competitors. So Jack dropped out at the end of his 1969 season. Jack is shown on the left (with the plug wrench) with Ray Cook. (Photos courtesy of Jack Coonrod - Speed Center display photo by Carlson Drag Photos)

Often the touring AA/GS competitors had to help with publicity for their match races or shows. This was usually done by displaying the cars before the races, sometimes with local radio interviews. This photo shows four of the successful AA/GS "pros", from left - Junior Thompson (So. Calif.), Jim Shores (So. Calif.), Paul Frost (Ohio) and Jack Coonrod (Oregon) in Oct. 1968. (Photo courtesy of Jack Coonrod)

John Mazmanian had started the 1967 season with a new car (Austin) and a full tour racing schedule. But then John and Junior Thompson made a deal to have Junior fill in to race with K. S. Pittman, Stone-Woods-Cook and George Montgomery on the Eastern tour. Thus the Austin that ran with Big John painted on the door was actually owned, tuned and driven by Junior Thompson. The Austin ran in the 8.99 sec. to 9.20 sec. with speeds in the 155 mph area in 1967. (Photos courtesy of K. S. Pittman and Junior Thompson)

In July of 1968 Ed and Jack Lee came out with a new AA/GS car to replace their Willys (Page 80). The photo was taken at Tri-City Dragway, Saginaw, Mich. (8-25-68). The Anglia and the Prock-Howell Willys are shown in the process of "staging". The way most drivers tried to stage or set the car in the light beams was to just barely roll into the beam and hold it there. This meant the car could move a short distance forward before causing a red light or foul start. Thus the driver could go a split second earlier without fouling. (Photo courtesy of Tom Prock - Photo by Dale E. Smith)

Tom Prock and Jay Howell (Michigan) built the "F Troop" Willys at the Logghe Stamping in 1967, where Jay Howell was shop foreman. The AA/GS '33 model was built similar to a Funny Car with a tilt-up fiberglass body. It was built for match racing and was not NHRA legal. A 482" Chevy engine, connected to a Torqueflite, powered the coupe to 158 mph speeds. In 1969 Tom and Jay took part in the Hill Bros. promotions of "Nitro Gassers". These were AA/GS cars running fuel to offer faster races. A 480" late Hemi Chrysler engine was installed to run Nitro. The "F Troop" Willys recorded 186 mph and 8.03 sec. on about 70% Nitro but found it difficult to get traction. With AA/GS bookings getting more difficult to get the team sold the Willys and moved on to Funny Car races. (Photos courtesy of Tom Prock - Photos by Eric Brooks)

The standard drag racing supercharged early Willys looked like this in 1970. This steel bodied (most of the ones being built were fiberglass by 1970) '33 Willys was raced by Tony Del Rio and Elwin Carlson (No. Calif.). The photo was taken at an AA/GS meet at Fremont in 1970. On a warm day it could be very uncomfortable to sit in a closed car with a firesuit on and safety belts buckled. This driver was one of the few fortunate enough to get air conditioning via a stock push open windshield. Naturally he closed it when he made his "pass" down the drag strip. (Photo courtesy of John Chambliss)

"Nice Vice" was the very nice appearing '41 Willys raced by Jim Stohr (Minn.). It was Chevy powered. It is interesting to note how few signs or decals were on Jim's coupe. By the 1970's many of the cars were starting to become traveling signboards. Although Jim had a one piece fiberglass fender and hood assembly he had retained the stock grill and headlight rims (1941/2 models). After virtually disappearing from the AA/GS ranks, BB/GS was the supercharged class where most of the late style (1937-42) Willys could be found. This photo was taken at the NHRA Nationals. (Photo courtesy of Mike Hanlon)

In the mid 1960's the AA/GS class races could almost have been called the Willys races. This race was at an AA/G eight-car show at Fremont, Calif. in July of 1967. Both cars had been recently finished. The '33 Willys in the near lane was owned by Bill Brasher and Cotton Cummings (No. Calif.) while the one in the far lane was Ron Rinauro's (No. Calif.). Both had big block Chevy power and both had steel bodies with Cal Automotive fiberglass everything else. Rinauro's Willys held on to the lead to win this race.
(Photo courtesy of Tom Chambliss - Photo by Rich Welch)

The Bill Brasher-Cotton Cumming's Willys chassis was rebuilt for AA/GS racing by Tom Chambliss in 1967. The previous owner had run in A/G with a Chevy engine. Tom narrowed the frame in the rear to allow the wide tires to pull in under the fenders, built a roll cage and motor plate and set up the front end using parallel quarter elliptic springs. A 462" Chevy engine and Torqueflite transmission provided the propulsion. The chopped top and light pearl purple paint job was done by Tony Del Rio (Page 126). After a year Terry Rose joined the team and a 462" Chrysler engine replaced the Chevy. The NHRA legal AA/GS weighed 2320 lbs. with about 250 lbs. of ballast, including batteries. The team raced the Willys until 1970 when it was sold. They ran numerous AA/GS shows in Northern and Southern California, plus match races. Their best times were 162.31 mph and 8.59 sec. (Photo courtesy of Terry Rose)

After experiencing the "joys" of C/GS class racing (Page 120) Ron Rinauro (No. Calif.) moved up to AA/G class racing. He purchased a '33 Willys that had been running an unblown Chevy in the B/G class. Tom Chambliss updated the chassis for a Ted Gotelli built 427 Chevy engine. Interestingly Tom Chambliss rebuilt this car at the same time that he did the Brasher-Cummings Willys. Both cars were set up similarly with coil springs and Watts linkages in the rear. However Rinauro's coupe retained the semi-elliptic front suspension while the Brasher-Cummings car changed to quarter-elliptic springs and then coil springs. Ron's Willys was Chevy powered for less than a year. Then a 462" Chrysler was installed. The car weighed about 2200 lbs. and was NHRA legal. The little red coupe recorded 161.30 mph and 8.79 sec. prior to being sold in 1969. Ron named this car the "Super Fox".
(Photo courtesy of Tom Chambliss - Photo by Rich Welch)

One of the best known Willys in the Southern California AA/GS circuit was the '36 pickup owned by Ron Bizio. It was originally built by Chuck Finders. The "Tall Texan" was initially Chevy powered (and rumored to be illegally too light in weight) and then Dave Braskett's Chrysler was installed in the Cal Automotive sponsored truck (1965). Eventually after some problems between Chuck and his sponsor the truck was rebuilt and Ron Bizio became the owner. In early 1966 Ron and Chuck already had the truck up to 155 mph. In 1967 the car was rebuilt by Steve Plueger of S and R Race Cars, the firm that took over the chassis business when Chuck Finders went East. The beautifully finished blue pickup with a 448" Chrysler, and an aluminum bed, became a favorite to win on the Southern California AA/GS circuit with a string of victories in late 1968. After recording a best of 166.35 mph and 8.43 sec., Ron advertised the "Beaver Shot" for sale (6-69). (Photos courtesy of Tom Willford and Bob Balogh. Bizio racing (OCIR) photo by Jere Alhadeff. Bakersfield photo by Bob McClurg)

The gold colored Willys raced by Bob Lombardi (New York) was one of the top BB/G cars in the East. The 1939 coupe had a 327" Chevy engine and Vitar Clutch-Flite transmission. The fenders, hood, doors and deck were fiberglass components from Anderson Industries. The Willys set an NHRA record in 1968 at 10.25 sec. (1968). The suspension was the original Willys quarter elliptic setup. Bob raced often at Englishtown, N. J. where most of the top Eastern BB/G racers came to compete in the Super Eliminator bracket. In addition the Eastern Automotive (Bob's business) Willys ran the NHRA meets and some match races. In 1970 Bob changed to an Opel GT but not before the Willys had recorded 138.67 mph and 9.86 sec. times. (Photo courtesy of Mike Hanlon)

"Mac's Taxi" was the Prefect owned by Jim Mack (Ohio). Jim built (1968) it with Chevy (288") power to race in the BB/G class. The B&M Clutch-Flite was operated by a Chrysler push button board. Although the Prefect weighed about 2400 lbs., almost 700 lbs. was ballast so the car was very light (about 1700 lbs.). After getting the sedan up to 144.00 mph Jim decided to move up to the AA/GS class. So from 1970 to 1972 the "Mac's Taxi" car was racing in the AA/GS class with a 432" late Hemi Dodge and a Torqueflite transmission. His best times were in the high 150's mph and close to 9.0 sec. E.T.'s. Jim moved out of the AA/GS competition in 1972. Note that all the Prefects (four-door Anglias) had fiberglass Anglia front ends. The two main reasons the fiberglass companies saw no reason to make Prefect fronts were (1) no demand, and (2) they were ugly. When Jim bought the car his first quarter mile was across a muddy field being towed by one of the farmer's cows. The car show photo was of the Dodge powered AA/GS blue and white Prefect. (Photos courtesy of Jim Mack)

By 1970 the AA/GS meets were full of Corvettes, Mustangs, roadsters and other new style blown cars. So when Ken Silvestri (No. Calif.) brought out his '37 Chevy for AA/GS competition the crowds may have believed that time moved back about 10 years. Ken named it the "Old Master" (Chevy models in 1937 were "Master" and "Master Deluxe"). Ken's blue coupe was appreciated by the fans at both the drag strip and car show. Ken retired the "Old Master" and built a Corvette for the AA/GS meets. The photo was at Fremont. (Photo courtesy of Ron Arcangeli)

The NHRA rule book was not needed to build a car to race the Southern California AA/GS circuit. Ron and Ray Zellar jumped into the AA/GS meets in 1967 with this beautiful flip-top Willys. Steve Plueger (S & R Race Cars) built the chassis. The late Hemi engine of 430" drove through a B&M Tork-Flite. The "Ambition" coupe raced the Southern California AA/GS circuit hitting speeds up to 159.57 mph and E.T.'s down to 8.93 sec. It was one of the nicest early Willys among the Southern California blown gassers. The next Zeller project was a AA/GS roadster. (Photo courtesy of Kevin Perry)

After a year of C/GS competition with his '57 Chevy, Claudie Meador (Texas) decided to move up into the B/GS class. He purchased an Austin from a wrecking yard and built this blue colored race car. Using his 310" Chevy engine he competed in both C/GS and B/GS at AHRA strips and BB/A at NHRA strips. When CC/GS was eliminated (1971) Claudie parked the Austin (he still has it) and joined the Funny Car competition. (Photo courtesy of Claudie Meador)

The "Royal Kahuna" was the BB/G class Anglia run by Royal Langford (Ohio). It had a Hemi Chrysler for power. This photo was taken at the 1969 NHRA Nationals. Note how the rear end and frame have been narrowed to keep the wide tires inside the fenders. (Photo courtesy of Barbara Hamilton Advey)

Len Cottrell and Kenny Reichard (Maryland) ran this Austin from 1967 to 1970. It had an all fiberglass body by Contemporary Fiberglass with a top chopped by Chuck Finders, who then had moved to Ohio. The front end and doors were also fiberglass, supplied by Anderson Industries. The 467" Chevy was connected to a B&M Tork-Flite. Len Cottrell built the chassis. The Austin was raced mostly at local area strips. (Photo courtesy of Joe Andulics - Photo by R. F. Bissell)

Ohio's Paul Frost jumped from the unblown B/G class to AA/G in 1966. He built this Chrysler powered, purple colored '41 Willys. He ran some NHRA meets and then mostly match races, including those scheduled by the Hill Bros. About the same time the Hill Bros. changed to a '33 so did Paul Frost (April 1968). After 1969 Paul enlisted in the Pro Stock ranks, where the money was. During his AA/GS match racing days Paul scheduled up to 50 to 60 match races in a season and recalls that he made money. The photos were taken at the 1967 Nationals. (Photos courtesy of Mike Hanlon)

Jim Jennings and Dennis Miller (No. Calif.) raced this Anglia in the AA/GS class in 1969 and 1970. The blue Anglia raced mostly in Northern California and occasionally in the Southern California AA/GS meets (also called "Open Gas Supercharged" by then). The photo was at Fremont (Aug. 1970). Ron Nunes is standing behind the Anglia while Dennis Miller is shown on the far side (striped shirt). (Photo courtesy of Ron Arcangeli)

Skip Hess (So. Calif.) after helping to crash the Anglias into the A/GS class (Shores-Hess, Page 88), built his own new car for the 1968 season. It was a 1968 Mustang powered by a SOHC Ford. The chassis was built by Jim Kirby and the C-6 transmission was an Art Carr product. The Mustang (fiberglass by Cal Automotive) debuted in February, one month before the Stone-Woods-Cook AA/GS Mustang. By the end of 1968 Skip had recorded times of 162 mph and 8.80 sec. The Mustang continued to run the Southern California AA/GS meets until they died (1972). A 8.53 sec. E.T. was recorded. Skip also entered a couple of Funny Car meets as did several other late model AA/GS competitors. Skip Hess' business ability enabled him to get two solid sponsorships - Revell and Meguiar. Skip's major sponsor, Revell, was strongly involved in the plastic model car kit business, thus the name "Revell Kit". (Photos courtesy of Skip Hess - Wheelstand promotion photo by Roger Marshutz)

After the second "Agitator" pickup (Pages 117 and 121) was sold to Paul Paolozzi, Vern Hicks (So. Calif.) put his 467" Chrysler engine into an Anglia. The "Hicks and Son" (for Vern and Randy Hicks) was usually driven by Gene Modlin or Jim Adolph, and raced the Southern California AA/GS races in 1969 and 1970. Lots of horsepower and better tires were making the short wheelbase Anglias with "beefed" stock frames difficult to handle. In fact the larger Mustang and Camaro AA/GS cars were now competitive with the little Austins and Anglias because they were more easily able to control their horsepower. The photo was taken at Irwindale (4-25-70). (Photo courtesy of Vern Hicks - Photo by Harvey Miller)

Although Terry Rose (No. Calif.) was involved with the engine in the Brasher, Cummings and Rose Willys (Page 127), he also had his own AA/GS car. The "Dawg Trainer" was Terry's 1968 Camaro. It was powered by a 427" Chevy engine and raced at the Northern California AA/GS meets at strips like Fremont, Vacaville and Half Moon Bay. Terry's Camaro raced from 1968 to 1971. The 1968 season was the real beginning of the Funny Car style, late model AA/GS cars. (Photo courtesy of Terry Rose -Photo by Steve Reyes)

One of the fan's favorite BB/G cars was Bob Panella's (No. Calif.) Anglia. It was the only successful BB/GS car still using a manual transmission then. The steel Anglia, with Fiberglass Trend's doors and front end had a chassis built by Exhibition Engineering (Ron Scrima). The 301" Chevy was put together by Fred Miner. The 2400 lb. Anglia, driven by Ken Dondero, set NHRA BB/GS E.T. records (9.79 and then 9.74 sec.) in 1969 and raced it until 1970. It was replaced by a new Opel GT in 1972. Named "Il Padrone" (The Boss) the car raced NHRA events, Northern California gasser races and Southern California BB/GS circuit shows. Although best noted for the quick E.T.'s the Panella Trucking Anglia did record speeds up to 149 mph. The photo shows Bob (right) showing the car to Union Oil Co. representatives in 1969. (Photo courtesy of Bob Panella)

Bill and Pete Hill (Ohio) got their "feet wet" in A/GS racing after buying John Mazmanian's '41 Willys in 1967. They liked it enough to have Chuck Finders rebuild a '33 Willys they bought from Tom Hrudka. So after running the '41 Willys only about six months, the new "Red Baron" was racing. The team visited Southern California (Nov.-Dec. 1967) when this photo was taken. The steel bodied Willys (said to weigh 2150 lbs.) had a 489" late Chrysler Hemi engine. The Hill Bros. became successful match racers. They raced against most of the touring AA/GS racers and soon they were booking shows for themselves and others including Coonrod, Shores, Frost, Merkel, Kohler Bros., etc. In 1969 they put together "Nitro Gasser" programs with their new flip-top Willys, Prock-Howell, Jim Shores and Chuck Finders. The steel car was sold in 1968 (to Fred Gartner) after hitting 163.63 mph and 8.69 sec. times. (Photo courtesy of Dan Lau - Photo by Jere Alhadeff)

Oregon's Jack Coonrod (Pages 60 and 71) was back out in AA/G in late 1966. After "dialing" the Willys into good performances and some chassis work by Chuck Finders and Woody Gilmore, Jack loaded up and became a professional racer on the Eastern tour (June 1967). Jack (Chuck Finders also drove) raced most of the other professional AA/G racers (Pittman, Stone-Woods-Cook, Hill Bros., etc.). In 1968 the Willys was completely rebuilt and the "Bear" was one of the "toughest" AA/GS cars on the tour. Speeds over 160 mph and E.T.'s in the high 8 sec. area yielded Jack a full season of bookings at $375 to $500 per date. Jack raced through the 1969 season and then sold the car. The photos were taken in 1968 in New England. (Photos courtesy of Jack Coonrod - Photos by Paul Wasilewski and R. F. Bissell)

With two successful seasons (1967, 1968) of making his living as a professional AA/GS racer, Junior Thompson decided a new car was required to keep up, or ahead of, the competition. Once again Chuck Finders helped with chassis. The new Thompson AA/GS car was one of the first Opel Kadetts to run in the blown gasser classes. The engine was a 448" Chrysler with a C&O Torqueflite bolted to it. Junior started his Eastern tour only a few weeks after finishing the car. Once again the car doors said Junior Thompson and John Mazmanian (Page 124) and it ran the "Big Four" races (Stone-Woods-Cook, George Montgomery and K. S. Pittman) plus numerous other dates. Within a few months the nice little Opel Kadett had recorded 165 to 167 mph speeds and 8.35 to 8.57 sec. E.T.'s. The Opel proved to be quicker and faster than the Austin had been. The display photo was for pre-race publicity with the Stone-Woods-Bones "Swindler A". The Kadett was run by Norm Day (Ohio) in 1972. (Photos courtesy of Junior Thompson)

The real Big John Mazmanian Austin (see Page 124) was this one. The chassis was done by Ron Scrima (Exhibition Engineering). It had a uniquely chopped steel body with Anderson Ind. fiberglass front end, doors and deck lid. The 427" Chrysler was put together by Dave Zeuschel and connected to a B&M Tork-Flite. The Austin had such a distinctive look that the NHRA said it could not and would not be an AA/GS car. At the first AA/G meet at OCIR in 1967 the car recorded great 161.87 mph and 8.68 sec. times. It raced locally with first Dick Bourgeois at the wheel, and then Rich Siroonian. It won many match races and AA/GS programs running in the California area. Then in 1968 John started to build a Funny Car and the Austin was put up for sale. The car, which had been nicknamed the "Football", quickly passed from one AA/GS racer (Big John) to another (K. S. Pittman). (Photo courtesy of Tom Willford)

In mid-1968 John Herrera replaced the steel Austin with a fiberglass bodied Austin (body and chassis by Contemporary Fiberglass). This AA/GS car had a flip-top body. A Jack Bayer built 480" Chevy engine did the work through an Art Carr Clutch-Flite. The Herrera and Sons (Manuel, Richard and Phillip) Austin recorded times of 157.89 mph and 8.79 sec. by the end of 1968. The Austin raced in most of the Southern California AA/GS meets in late 1968 and early 1969. Both Manuel and Richard drove the car. The flip-top Austin shown here was unusual in that it had an opening door. (Photo courtesy of Tom Willford)

The "Agitator" '33 Willys was Paul Day's (Ohio) BB/GS racer in 1970. Prior to that Paul had campaigned a 1941 Chevy coupe in CC/G and a '41 Willys pickup in BB/GS. The Willys was the old C&O and Vern Hicks "Agitator" (Page 117). In 1968 the team of Paul Day-Jerry Baird set BB/GS records (142.85 and 143.31 mph). Unfortunately the pickup crashed, so Paul switched to this '33 Willys (ex-Bob Chipper) in 1970 still using a 327" Chevy engine. In 1972 Paul moved on to a BB/FC Vega. (Photo courtesy of Ross Martin)

The "Aggrivator" was formerly Paul Day's CC/G race car. It had a 30l" Chevy in it. Paul put it up for sale in 1969 ($3500). The new owner was Bob Easterbrook (Ontario, Canada). This photo was taken in 1969. Bob raced it in CC/GS and then put it up for sale in 1972. (Photo courtesy of Ross Martin)

The United States had an "Ohio George" and Canada had an "Ontario George". George Gray built his '33 Willys to run the AA/GS class. The 427" rat motor drove through a Turbo Hydro (by Hydro Motive). The Willys hit times up to 155 mph. George raced mostly with the UDRA AA/G circuit. This photo was probably in 1969. (Photo courtesy of Ross Martin)

One of the most unusual AA/G cars was the Graziano-Cundiff and Yungerman coupe. It was a much modified '32 Ford five-window coupe. It was candy red and powered by a Chrysler Hemi engine. This car was a regular on the UDRA AA/GS circuit. (Photo courtesy of Ross Martin)

After competing in the 1968-1969 seasons with a Willys (Page 119), Steve Woods (No. Calif.) returned to his Prefect. Steve's 335" Chrysler quickly made the Prefect one of the top BB/GS cars in the West. Steve ran the NHRA meets and the Southern California BB/GS circuit meets. In 1970 he set a NHRA - BB/GS speed record (151.00 mph) that lasted until 1972. The Prefect set low E.T. and won many of the BB/GS circuit meets. It was cleaned up and painted after a fiberglass Anglia front end replaced the Prefect sheet metal. The car was named "Hypocrite II". Steve had good success in the 1972 and 1973 seasons winning events and setting records in AHRA, IHRA and NHRA events. After that the car was retired and Steve built a Plymouth Cricket. (Photo courtesy of Steve Woods and the Author)

Paul Frost (Ohio) put his '41 Willys (Page 131) aside and switched to a new light and low AA/GS '33 Willys for the 1968 season. The engine was a 450" Chrysler. The fiberglass body was made by B & N Fiberglass. The purple and silver Willys raced on the match race circuit about 50 to 60 times that season. Paul also ran some NHRA meets. The Willys was often included in the Hill Bros. scheduled match races with Coonrod, Shores and the Hill Bros. Then in 1970 Paul switched to the Pro Stock class. (Photo courtesy of Jack Coonrod - Photo by R. T. Manning)

The 1967 Opel Kadett raced by Dave Mason (Indiana) had a Chrysler Hemi engine. It had a steel body and fiberglass doors and front end. The weight was 2290 lbs. This car had been built and raced by Norm Paddack (Indiana). Norm started work on his Opel GT in late 1968 and sold the Kadett. Dave Mason campaigned the AA/GS Opel at NHRA meets as this photo at the 1970 NHRA Nationals shows. Dave was the 1970 UDRA Supercharged Gas Coupe season points winner. (Photo courtesy of Barbara Hamilton Advey)

"Big" Wilson (Ohio) ran this '48 Austin in the AA/GS class (1971). The name "Hart and Soul" referred to Wilson's association with Mickey Hart. The brown and green Austin was used mainly for match races. (Photo courtesy of Barbara Hamilton Advey)

The team of Bob Silva (Austin) and Ron Nunes (engine) joined together to race some A/GS events in Northern California. Here the Chrysler powered, 2285 lb. Austin is shown racing Mike Mitchell's Willys. (Photo courtesy of Ron Nunes - Photo by Rich Welch)

The Boyd Bros. campaigned this '33 in 1970. It had a 426" Hemi Chrysler engine and ran in the AA/GS class. It had previously been raced in the AA/GS class by Joe Pirrone. Later Joe bought the car back. "Pure Acid" hit speeds in the 150 mph area. (Photo courtesy of Harry Hall)

The bright red '40 Willys run by Rich Ratliff and Al Carothers (Illinois) was powered by a 470" Chrysler engine. It had Cal Automotive fiberglass body parts. Note that the fenders were trimmed up to the body line as Stone-Woods-Cook had done on the "Swindler A". A Don Long front axle was used. In 1967 the car ran 9.50 sec. times at 146 mph as the Ratliff-Bisby entry. Then in 1969 the Willys was replaced by a Corvette which was raced in the UDRA A/GS events. (Photo courtesy of Mike Hanlon)

Carl Hegge (Virginia) was the owner of this nice '42 Willys pickup which was Chevy powered. Note that the engine was mounted lower than most of the cars so tubes were added to the injectors to raise the scoop up through the hood. Like many of the Willys pickups the stock bed had been replaced with a fabricated bed. Carl's sponsor, Big Ed's Speed Shop, immortalized the pickup by putting it on the cover of their mail order catalog. (Photo courtesy of Mike Hanlon)

Bill Lindner Jr. (New York) built this '37 Willys coupe to race in the CC/G class (1967). The 288" Chevy engine was bolted to a four-speed manual transmission. The gold colored Willys, named "C C Rider", raced NHRA events with much success. Included in Bill's list of victories was the 1968 Nationals (CC/G at 126.93 mph and 11.15 sec.). He also set an NHRA record (10.69 sec.) in 1968. The Willys was one of the top CC/GS cars in the 1967 to 1969 period. (Photo courtesy of Dean Court)

"Rampage" was a 1959 Corvette BB/GS class racer run by Bud Fentress and Dale Jones (So. Calif.). A Clutch-Flite transmission was used to transmit the power from the 327" Chevy engine. The team competed in the Southern California BB/GS circuit, finishing 7th in the 1969 BB/GS points. In 1970 the Corvette was replaced by an Anglia. (Photo courtesy of the author)

Perhaps the biggest blown gasser that raced in the Southern California BB/GS circuit was a '52 Chevy sedan delivery "Blue Power". The pretty silver and blue Chevy was raced initially by Jack Carlson (1968) and then by Milt Stewart and Bill Cook (1970). The power came from a 327" Chevy engine driving through a C&O Torqueflite transmission. Unfortunately the small Anglias and Prefects had a major advantage over the big Chevy delivery. (Photo courtesy of the Author - Photo by John Ewald)

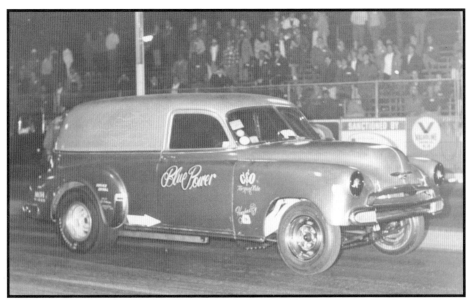

The Airoso Bros. (Page 59) continued to race their '40 Willys into the 1969 season. After running smaller De Soto and Chrysler engines Joe and Lee moved up to a 392" Chrysler in 1967. A Don Long front axle and a B&M Tork-Flite transmission were also added. The team raced mostly in Central and Northern California and raced a few of the Southern California BB/GS circuit races. In addition they won several NHRA or AHRA events including the BB/G class at the 1967 NHRA Nationals. The top times for the Willys were 144.90 mph and 9.77 sec. The car was sold to Gary Brookshire who also raced at BB/GS circuit meets in late 1969. (Photo courtesy of the Author)

Larry Holt's (So. Calif.) Anglia was one of the top cars in the Southern California BB/GS circuit. The red Anglia (formerly an unblown B/G car) joined the BB/GS circuit in late 1969. In 1970 Larry won the Southern California BB/GS Points Championship. The 289" Chevy engine and B&M Clutch-Turbo combination pulled the steel Anglia to times of 144 mph and 9.50 sec. It was one of the most consistently quick BB/GS cars in Southern California. Larry's sponsor was Speed Specialties (where he is still the owner). (Photo courtesy of the Author - Photo by John Ewald)

One of the Southern California BB/GS circuits most popular cars was the '56 Chevy owned by Neil Stein. After running in C/G class Neil had the chassis reworked by Don Long and by Steve Plueger. An Ed Pink built 350" Chevy was installed along with a B&M Clutch-Flite. The result was a beautiful BB/GS racer. The 2800 lbs. Chevy two-door raced the Southern California BB/GS circuit from 1969 to 1971 finishing second in the 1969 points race. The photo was taken at OCIR/ (Photo courtesy of the Author)

This was a Southern California BB/GS circuit event at OCIR. The race pitted the Marrs-Lukens Corvette against the Pittman Bros. Willys. (Photo courtesy of the Author - Photo by Jim Kelly)

After good success with a CC/G Willys Mel Marrs (So. Calif.) switched to a '63 Corvette. Phil Lukens did the driving. The engine was a 396 Chevy and the transmission was a B&M Clutch-Flite. The Corvette usually ran in the BB/GS class at NHRA meets and the Southern California BB/GS meets. In 1968 the Marrs-Lukens team set NHRA records in BB/GS at 9.96 sec. and 143.76 mph. It also ran an NHRA points meet in CC/GS (Paul Pittman's 335" Chrysler). Mel and Phil switched to a 354" Chrysler and then in 1970 sold the car after getting it down into the 9.40 sec. E.T. area. (Photo courtesy of the Author)

This familiar looking Willys was the 1968 BB/GS racer campaigned by Paul and Silas Pittman (So. Calif.). The Willys was the older brother K. S. Pittman's AA/G machine (Page 76). The Pittman Bros. ran the car in 1967 and 1968 at NHRA events, local Super Eliminator programs and Southern California BB/GS shows. The Willys hit times of 141.28 mph and 9.96 sec. and then was retired (again) when Paul picked up a Jim Shores Anglia. The engine and transmission were 354" Chrysler and B&M Tork-Flite. The car won the 1968 NHRA Division 7 Super Eliminator points competition. (Photo courtesy of the Author)

The Pittman Bros. (Paul and Silas) new car for 1969 was this Anglia that Jim Shores had been using. They built a 335" Chrysler to put the 2700 lbs. Anglia into the BB/GS class. The Anglia raced the Western NHRA events and the Southern California BB/GS circuit. Paul and Silas won the 1969 Southern California BB/GS Points Championship. In early 1970 the Anglia (it was considered to require careful driving) was destroyed at the NHRA Winternationals. Paul almost immediately started to build his (future) record setting Gremlin (American Motors) which he debuted six months later (8-70). (Photo courtesy of the Author)

Mel Marrs and Phil Lukens purchased a new nearly completed Anglia in late 1970. Jim Kirby had built the chassis and Contemporary Fiberglass had built the body. The car had been built to race in Open Gas Supercharged events and the frame did not meet the NHRA rules. Since Mel and Phil planned to run the NHRA events they had to correct the frame. This was done by carefully splitting and welding a new 2" x 3" frame over the existing frame. A 300" Chrysler (destroked 354") was built and installed with a B&M Clutch-Turbo transmission. The team raced the NHRA events and the Southern California BB/GS circuit. They set an NHRA record (BB/GS) in 1970 at 9.39 sec. E.T. and hit speeds in the 145 mph area. After Mel moved Phil continued to campaign the "Blair's Speed Shop" car to the end of the Supercharged Gas Coupe classes (1975) and beyond (CC/A). Phil Lukens is now the owner of Blair's Speed Shop. (Photo courtesy of the Author)

Another one of the fast New York based blown gassers was this '33 Willys owned by Bob Chipper. He raced local meets, match races and NHRA events with the Chevy, later Chrysler, powered Willys. In 1969 Bob set NHRA records (144.92 mph and 9.76 sec.) in the BB/GS class. He also won the class at the NHRA Nationals. In 1970 he switched to a BB/GS Barracuda and the Willys was sold to Paul Day. (Photo courtesy of Mike Hanlon)

After building and campaigning his AA/GS Opel Kadett (Page 150) for only a short time, Norm Paddack (Indiana) built what was apparently the first Opel GT gasser. He obtained a body from Germany in 1968. The new "Mini-Brute" had a 480" late Hemi Chrysler engine for AA/GS competition and weighed 2350 lbs. It quickly became one of the top AA/GS cars with times like 163.33 mph and 8.67 sec. (1970). In addition to performing well the two Opels (Kadett and GT) that Norm built showed other racers what Norm's building talents were. As a result Norm Paddack, with the help of his wife Vicki, went into the business. Paddack Racing Enterprises built both gassers and Funny Cars. The photo shows Norm's brother Dwight ready to "light the fire" with his gas squirt gun. Norm continued to race NHRA and UDRA events and match races before going to alcohol Funny Car class with a Vega. (Photo courtesy of Vicki Paddack)

Carl Hegge (Maryland) joined the early Willys owners when he replaced his '42 pickup truck (Page 141) with this '33 model. It had a Chevy engine and a Vitar built transmission. Carl's Willys was unique in still retaining a steel grill instead of an all fiberglass front end. The photo was taken at the 1969 NHRA Nationals. Paul Day's "Agitator" (ex-MGM) was pitted beside Carl's Willys. (Photo courtesy of Mike Hanlon)

The switch to late model cars in the Supercharged Gas Coupe classes had already started when the NHRA finally allowed custom frames and fiberglass bodies. The Larry and Gary Warren Corvette (No. Calif.) was constructed in late 1967. The chassis was built by Tom Chambliss. The fiberglass body was made by Fiberglass Trends. Before the car was finished Ron Nunes joined the team with his 433" Chrysler engine. The red and orange "Vette" had best times of 167.34 mph and 8.53 sec. The 2000 lbs. AA/GS race car was raced from 1968 to late 1969 and then sold to Fred Schimer, who also raced it in the AA/GS class. (Photos courtesy of Tom Chambliss - Photo by Mike Bognod)

Rod Barker's (No. Calif.) topless Corvette was an example of what was happening in California's Open Gas Supercharged class. The Corvette (1940 lbs. + 370 lbs. of ballast) was built by Tom Chambliss in 1969. Ron Rinauro installed his 462" Chrysler and the team went AA/GS racing. It was one of the top AA/GS cars in Northern California and part of the controversy about Funny AA/GS cars. Rod even dropped back to the B/Altered class with an unblown Chevy to get away from the arguments. Then Bill Brasher put his 462" Chrysler in the Corvette, running the 1971 season. The best performances were 167.20 mph and 8.54 sec. Only a few topless Corvettes competed in the AA/GS meets. They were not NHRA legal and probably caused many drag racing fans to question where the AA/GS class had gone. (Photo courtesy of Tom Chambliss - Photo by Rich Welch)

All doubt that the Willys were dying disappeared when major Willys competitors like George Montgomery and Stone-Woods-Cook switched to late model cars. George Montgomery's "Malco Gasser" appeared in June, 1967 and the Willys was retired. The Stone-Woods-Cook Mustang was built for the 1967 match race season. The driver was Doug Cook's brother Ray. (Doug Cook went touring with the Mustang Funny Car). This photo was taken at an AHRA sanctioned strip (Thompson Drag Raceway - Ohio) in May of 1968 where George recorded 161.3 mph and 8.74 sec. (Photo courtesy of George Montgomery - Photo by Steve Suhajcik)

This was an AA/GS show at Thompson Drag Raceway (Ohio) in August of 1968. The performers were George Montgomery and the Hill Bros. (shown here) and Jim Shores and Paul Frost. The summer months were the peak match racing period. In addition to the regular touring AA/GS cars, a few other cars joined in by extending their trip to the Nationals (Sept.). George Montgomery, for example, had nine bookings in August of 1968 prior to the Nationals at the end of the month, where he won the AA/GS class. (Photo courtesy of George Montgomery - Photo by Steve Suhajcik)

For the 1969 season Tim Woods made a deal with "Bones" Balogh to have "Bones" run the ex-Stone-Woods-Cook AA/GS Mustang. The Mustang toured that year as the Stone-Woods and Bones "Swindler A". Bones represented Tim Woods in the "Big Four's" match races (George Montgomery, Junior Thompson, and K. S. Pittman). In 1970 Tim made a deal with Steve Korney to run the Mustang for the AA/GS tour. (Photos courtesy of Bob Balogh - Photo by Chance Brockway)

In June of 1967 George Montgomery replaced his '33 Willys with a new 1967 Mustang. It was obvious to him that his sponsors at Ford would be much happier to see him racing a Ford product than the Willys. Because the NHRA rules in 1967 still required an automotive frame George had to add a frame (he used a Willys frame) to the unit body constructed Mustang. The "Malco Gasser" had his SOHC Ford engine. It was perhaps the first NHRA legal AA/GS late model car. The Mustang raced the match race circuit and the major NHRA events. The "Malco Gasser" was George's only racer until 1971 when he added the "Mr. Gasket Gasser" to his competition stable. The Mustang owned the NHRA - AA/GS records from 1967 to mid-1970 and also held BB/A records in 1968 and 1969. By 1970 Ohio George's car had recorded times as high as 169 mph and 8.46 sec. (Photos courtesy of Len Cottrell and Mike Hanlon - Photo of George (beside car) by R. F. Bissell)

Tom Shinholster (Florida) retired his record setting CC/GS Willys and replaced it with an Opel Kadett. It had a chassis by Norm Paddack. The Shinholster-Lehman Willys was the final CC/GS speed record holder when the class was discontinued. Tom moved up to the BB/GS class with his new Opel Kadett. This photo was taken in early 1972. (Photo courtesy of Norm Paddack)

Norm Paddack (Indiana) debuted this 1967 Opel Kadett for AA/GS competition in 1968. The car was purchased from a local Buick dealer (Buick sold the Opels). Norm built the car with a 440" Chrysler late Hemi engine. It weighed 2290 lbs. and Norm called it the "Mini-Brute". It was the car that launched Norm into the chassis business. The Opel hit times of 166 mph and 8.86 sec. Then Norm was off on his Opel GT project (Page 146) and the Kadett was sold to Dave Mason (Page 140). (Photo courtesy of Norm Paddack)

Mike Mitchell (No. Calif.) competed in AA/GS racing with '33 Willys from 1964 to 1970. Then Mike, who was called the "Worlds Fastest Hippie" built this 1970 topless Corvette. The chassis was built by Ron Scrima (Exhibition Engineering). A 450" Chrysler engine propelled the Corvette to 160 mph and 8.50 sec. times. It was one of the few topless Corvettes running in the California AA/GS meets and naturally helped create the controversy about the AA/GS rules. It had a flip-top body and Mike was leaning over the engine with a spark plug wrench in the photo. (Photos courtesy of Ron Arcangeli)

Don Toia (Arizona) kept up with the improving technology by building a Maverick to replace his Willys (Page 122) in 1970. Don and partner Lee Behner used a 354 Chrysler engine hooked to a B&M Tork-Flite. The "Incognito" Maverick raced at the Arizona AHRA drag strips in the B/GS class plus some of the Southern California BB/GS circuit meets. Although Don quit driving in 1973, the team continued to race the car into the 1975 season. The problem of building a unit body chassis was solved by putting the Maverick body on a '39 Willys frame. Don is the owner of Don's Hot Rod Shop. (Photo courtesy of Don Toia)

After a short stint with an Anglia (Page 133), Vern Hicks and his son Randy built a Mustang for AA/GS racing. It was called the "West Coast Gambler" and it was a Southern California Open Gas Supercharged style car with a flip-top body. Vern bought the car unfinished. He finished the car and added his 467" Chrysler and a C&O Torqueflite transmission. Built in 1970 the car raced in the Southern California AA/GS (Open Gas Supercharged) meets and even some Funny Car shows. The continual changes in the AA/GS races (topless Corvettes, Roadsters and Gas Funny Cars) made Vern decide that his Mustang was too heavy, so he built a new Barracuda. (Photo courtesy of Vern Hicks - Photo by John Ewald)

It was a little unusual to see new big cars enter into AA/GS competition in 1969. At the same time that little roadsters, Opels and Willys were dominating the class, Brad Anderson (Colorado) came out with a full sized 1969 Dodge Dart. It had a 426 Hemi Chrysler engine and quickly hit 160 mph, 8.77 sec. times. Brad only ran it for a short time and then it was sold. The new owner Keith Bush (No. Calif.) campaigned it at the California AA/GS meets for a year and then put it up for sale. Keith called it the "Bushwacker" and was shown at OCIR in 1969. Keith recorded times of 162.16 mph and 8.65 sec. (Photo courtesy of John Chambliss)

In 1968 K. S. "Tiger" Pittman bought the "Football"; formerly John Mazmanian's Austin (Page 137). Although not a legal NHRA AA/GS car, it was fine for the match racing that K. S. was doing. However Pittman's Austin did run the NHRA Nationals in 1968, winning the BB/A class with a 9.26 sec. time. K. S. ran full match race schedules in 1968 and 1969 with the Austin, racing with the more than two dozen match racing AA/GS cars running in the East. Shown standing with K. S. (right) is Ira Lichey. Ira was the booking agent at the Gold Agency (Evanston, Ill.) who handed the majority of the scheduling and contracts for the touring AA/GS competitors. He arranged dates for George Montgomery, K. S. Pittman, Stone-Woods-Cook, Junior Thompson, John Mazmanian, Paul Frost, Jack Coonrod, the Lee Bros., Jim Shores and on and on . . . . The Gold Agency charged 10% for their services and played a major part in helping many AA/GS racers earn a living in drag racing. (Photos courtesy of Tom Willford and Harry Hall - Lichey photo by Peter Pearson)

Blown Street Roadsters were added to the Supercharged Gas Coupe classes in 1968. This seemingly major change to the classes actually ended up having very little effect. Only a few "Street" Roadsters raced the AA/GS class and most (or all) ran in the California AA/GS (Open Gas Supercharged) races where there were few rules. All had fiberglass '27 T Roadster bodies and often ran without the front fenders, grills or hoods. Since the 5.0 lbs./cu. in. requirement limited the minimum weight to around 2000 to 2400 lbs. there was no particular advantage for the roadsters. So although they could run in the high 8 sec. area with speeds up to 160 mph, they never became the crowd's favorites. AA/GS class roadsters were run in Southern California by Ron Zeller ("Ambition"), Bilby-Densham-Plueger, Gary Burgin, Bryan Raines, Doug Finley and Dan Sosebee. Roadsters were not accepted in the Southern California BB/GS circuit and most (or all) were not NHRA - AA/GS legal. (Photos courtesy of John Chambliss and Ron Arcangeli)

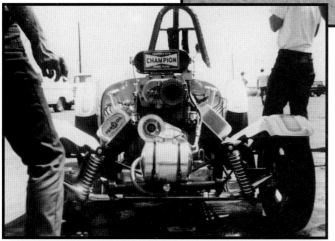

The final NHRA record holder in the AA/GS class was the Bob Panella-Fred Miner (No. Calif.) Opel GT. The final records (163.33 mph and 8.44 sec.) were set in 1975 at Fremont, California. The Opel GT was started by Exhibition Engineering and then completed by Tom Chambliss in 1972. The 301" destroked Chrysler (built by Fred Miner) initially ran with Turbochargers (1973) and then was changed to a 6-71 supercharger for the 1974 season. The initial setup used a B&M Clutch-Flite with a Crower-Glide clutch. In 1974 the Clutch-Flite was replaced by a Lenco 3-speed transmission. The body was a Fiberglass Trends product. Phil Featherston did the driving. The Opel GT was built for the BB/GS class to replace Bob's Anglia (Page 134). In 1973 the BB/GS class became the AA/GS class. (Photo courtesy of Tom Chambliss)

- THE LAST YEARS - 1 9 7 1 TO 1 9 7 5 -

Late in September of 1970, Bernie Partridge, the NHRA Division Seven Director, notified the Southern California BB/GS Circuit that the new NHRA 1971 Drag Rules eliminated the Supercharged Gasser classes - AA/GS, BB/GS and CC/GS. The thinking was that most of the AA/GS cars were illegal anyway so let them run in the AA/A and BB/Altered classes.

Since the move into the Altered classes would effectively obsolete their cars, the BB/GS racers were upset. There was only one thing to do, try to get the Supercharged Gas classes reinstated. The plan developed was to get most of the NHRA major sponsors and manufacturers to appeal to the NHRA to reinstate the blown gas classes. Excellent support was obtained from the sponsors and manufacturers, many of whom were friends or sponsors of individual blown gasser owners. In mid-October Bernie called to tell me that the Supercharged Gas Coupe classes were back. The only change was that CC/GS had been dropped for lack of participation.

The October 30, 1970 issue of National Dragster covered the reinstatement in Bernie Partridges's column:

"Don't mess with Mister-In-Between is an old saying that has new meaning where the BB/GS crowd is concerned.

This strong group of dedicated racers were quick to protest (loud and strong) the proposed NHRA move to liberalize the rules governing the blown gassers.

The rules maker's position was that most AA/GS cars were so illegal that they ran BB/A for the most part, and CC/GS had little to offer in participation. — Hence the proposal to move the whole class into the Altered bracket, where rules such as upholstery, frames, fenders, door latches, etc. are little problem.

But somebody discovered that legal BB/GS have been multiplying like rabbits and putting on inexpensive, competitive shows wherever they appeared. Consequently, NHRA received many letters and phone calls from racers, sponsors, track managers and even spectators.

For 1971 the BB/GS class will be retained; and so will AA/GS."

The Supercharged Gas Coupe classes, with the exception of the CC/GS Class, were back and would compete using the same basic rules through the 1973 season. Then in 1974 the AA/GS Class was dropped and the BB/GS Class, now renamed AA/GS, was the sole remaining Supercharged Gas Coupe Class. This new AA/GS Class competed at 8.00 lbs./cu.in. in 1974 and then at 7.00 lbs./cu.in. in 1975. This last Supercharged Gas Coupe Class was eliminated in 1976.

The Supercharged Gassers continued into the 1971 season doing the same things they had done in the successful 1970 season. Match races and AA/GS or

BB/GS shows were run as often as the guys could schedule them. In the East the "Big Four" (Montgomery, Thompson, Pittman, S.W.C.) were touring again. Other blown gassers racing in match races included Harry Hall (formerly K.S. Pittman's '33 Willys), Harry Bickford (formerly Jim Kirby's '41 Willys), Bob Lombardi, The Boyd Bros., Mickey Hart, "Big" Wilson, and Ken Mott. The BB/GS competitors included Bob Chipper, Jim Oddy, Glenn Lazzar, Paul Day, Al Page, Cam Cogsdill and Shinholster-Lehmann. Many of the guys also ran the NHRA National meets. The situation in AA/GS was confusion, as usual. The West Coast guys were running Open Gas Supercharged shows while the races in the East were said to be the Blown Gas Funny Cars. In fact, UDRA reincarnated their old AA/GS circuit as a Gas Funny Car circuit. And soon the West Coast strips also started running Blown Gas Funny Car programs instead of AA/GS shows. It didn't make much difference as the same cars ran both shows.

The AA/GS competitors in the West included most of the guys from the previous year, although a few like Gary Burgin were stepping up to the Funny Car Class. New cars included Brad Anderson's Opel GT, Meredith-Newton's Mustang, John Herrera's Opel GT and Ken Silvestri's Corvette. The AA/GS cars were tripping the clocks in the 155 to 167 mph range with E.T.'s around 8.35 to 9.00 sec.

The rules for the West Coast Blown Gas Funny Cars (sometimes called AA/GS) were (1) Gas and (2) 1900 lbs. minimum. Junior Thompson's Opel GT showed his fans what a Blown Gas Funny Car can do with a 8.11 sec., 173.07 mph performance at Lions. Most of the confusion about the Blown Gas Funny Cars was eliminated in 1972 when the NHRA set up a Blown Gas Funny Car Class, BB/FC. The basic rules were (1) Gas and (2) 1800 lbs. minimum. So now most of the illegal AA/GS cars had their own class.

The Southern California BB/GS circuit continued to run eight-car shows at the local strips plus an eight-car match race at Sacramento and at Las Vegas. Most of the regular BB/GS competitors from 1970 were back. New additions to BB/GS racing were Chris Wheeler (Anglia), Kazanian-Lemon (T-Bird), Jeff Storck (Opel GT) and Buddy Cornelius ('55 Chevy).

When the 1971 season ended the NHRA AA/GS records of 1970 had not been broken. K.S. Pittman's 8.54 sec. time had withstood a year of racing. The speed records for both AA/GS (165.44 mph by George Montgomery) and BB/GS (151.00 mph by Steve Woods) also remained at the 1970 level. Al Page set the only 1971 Supercharged Gasser record when he eased by the BB/GS E.T. record of 9.39 sec. with a 9.38 sec. clocking.

Although the 1971 season had been a good one for most of the Supercharged Gas Coupe competitors, it was obvious that the situation was not healthy.

The most important fact was that for the first time drag racing's attendance declined. Both the numbers of spectators and contestants were off by as much as 15% to 20%. That meant less income to the drag strips. The main reason for the decline was that the nation's economy was slowing down; the official name is recession. As a result of the drop in income, the drag strips started to pull back on their expenses. This was evident late in 1971 when strips started actively promoting inexpensive programs of Bracket racing, Bug-Ins, High School Nites or Antique drags. These inexpensive shows filled in between the major Funny Car shows that actually brought most of the drag strip's income. As a result, the sluggy economy was a major reason for the big drop in 1972 of shows with AA/GS or BB/GS Supercharged Gassers, Injected Funny Cars, Fuel Altereds, Junior Fuel Dragsters or Top Gas Dragsters.

But the economy was not the only reason the AA/GS and BB/GS shows were getting fewer. In the case of the AA/GS Class cars, most of them were running the Blown Gas Funny Car meets (BB/FC) and new cars were being built without the AA/GS restrictions on engine location, opening doors, upholstery, lights, etc. Most spectators could no longer see a difference between a AA/GS car and the Blown Gas Funny Car (BB/FC). Also although they looked just like the Fuel Funny Cars, they didn't go as fast and make as much noise. As a result the BB/FC shows just did not draw large crowds of spectators during the poor economy times.

The BB/GS Class was really a racer's class like most of classes in drag racing. That is, BB/GS shows would never draw big numbers of spectators. The BB/GS shows were presented as an inexpensive add-on to help fill the time of the main show, such as Fuel Altereds. So when the economy turned sour, it became more difficult to get a strip to schedule BB/GS shows.

Racing choices for the Supercharged Gassers came down to running in Blown Gas Funny Car (BB/FC) programs, running the NHRA Competition Eliminator events, bracket racing at the local drag strips or moving to another class. Indeed a look at the Funny Car lists soon showed the names of former Supercharged Gasser racers like the Hill Bros., Prock-Howell, Billy Holt,

Gary Burgin and Ray Zeller. The list of blown gasser competitors who jumped into BB/FC Class in the 1972 to 1974 period is filled with guys like Glenn Lazzar, George Montgomery, Junior Thompson, Jeg Coughlin, Joe Amato, Kazanian-Lemon, Norm Day, Bob Chipper, K. S. Pittman, Paul Day, Ellison-McGarvey, Lou Gasparelli and many others who often ran more than one of the AA/GS, BB/GS, BB/FC or BB/A classes.

Although competition continued in the original AA/GS Class, at 5.00 lbs./cu.in., through the 1973 season, the competition was very thin. The NHRA records were broken only once in 1972 when Brad Anderson dropped the E.T. record to 8.46 sec. and George Montgomery added a little to his 1970 record with a 166.97 mph speed. A little later the NHRA redesignated George's record to the separated AA/GS(T) Class; "T" for Turbocharged. This meant that no one ended up with the AA/GS record until the class died and the BB/GS Class inherited the AA/GS initials in 1974.

Action in the BB/GS Class resulted in several competitors putting their names in the record books. The speed record was raised to 154.10 mph (Shinholster-Lehmann-Holt) in 1972 and then to 158.45 mph (Paul Pittman) a few months later. But using a turbocharger resulted in Paul's record being placed on a new BB/GS(T) Class and the BB/GS speed record going back to Tom Shinholster. In 1973 Jim Oddy moved it up to 158.17 mph. The only non-turbocharged cars to set a BB/GS E.T. record in 1972 or 1973 were the Storck Bros., at 9.27 sec. and then Tom Shinholster at 9.26 sec. The Turbocharged Class E.T. record was initially set by Paul Pittman at 9.02 sec., then dropped to 8.98 sec. by Panella-Miner.

After 1973 the BB/GS cars became AA/GS racers and the old BB/GS records became the new AA/GS records. Competition in the 1974 and 1975 seasons resulted in two cars trading off the records. Panella-Miner dropped the E.T. record twice in 1974 to a final 8.88 sec. Then fellow Northern California racer Steve Woods reset the records in two steps to 8.58 sec. and 160.42 mph in 1975. The final records were back in Panella-Miner's pocket at 8.44 sec. and 163.33 mph.

At the end on the 1975 season the old Supercharged Gas Coupe Classes were gone. And they were actually gone because almost no one was left in the final surviving AA/GS Class.

Some of the other Supercharged Gas Coupe competitors in the 1971 to 1975 period were:

Hikida-McHardy (Canada)
Tom Pittman (So.California)
Steve McGee (Oregon)
Kroona-Skarda-Sandberg (Minn.)
Jerry Strickland (Texas)
Dennis Piranio (Texas)
Doug Finley (So.California)
Ron Haskins (So.California)
Ed Roberts (No.California)
Herget-Corn-Jerger (Ohio)

Mike Steinberg (No.California)
Henry Wilko (New York)
Mallicoat Bros. (No.California)
Pacini Bros. (So.California)
Fred Schimer (No.California)
Cook-Stewart (So.California)
Sherman Gunn (So.California)
Willie Johnson (Ohio)
Randy Troxell (So.California)
Sonny McMahan (Tennessee)

The last E.T. record holder in the CC/GS class was Eddie Flora (Ohio). Eddie's car, named "Locomotion", was a Prefect. The fiberglass front end was Anglia style. A 287" Chevy engine and B&M Clutch-Turbo transmission provided the energy to hit 10.00 sec. E.T.'s. In addition to racing the NHRA events (he won the CC/GS class at the NHRA Nationals in 1970) Eddie had match races with Eastern BB/GS cars like Paul Day, Bob Chipper and Jim Oddy. (Photo courtesy of Eddie Flora)

Although Mike Steinberg (No.Calif.) built this Austin in 1968 for AA/GS competition, it did not run until 1974. The chassis was built by Tom Chambliss and the body was made by Contemporary Fiberglass. Note the "legal" passenger door is actually a Dutch (half) door. It weighed 1950 lbs. with a 426" Chrysler late Hemi engine. The yellow Austin hit 164.36 mph and 8.72 sec. But by 1975 the old AA/GS class (5.0 lbs./cu.in.) no longer existed so the Austin ran in the BB/A class. (Photo courtesy of Tom Chambliss - Photo by Ron Burch)

- POST-MORTEM -

Almost everyone involved with the Supercharged Gas Coupes of the 1960's has opinions on the reasons that the classes died out. Some say the introduction of the late model cars killed them. Another reason given was the switch to the small foreign Anglias and Austins which no longer were representative of the cars the spectators drove. The rules and the illegal cars were certainly confusing to everyone and a good reason to lose interest in the Supercharged Gassers. Some of the racers back in the late 1960's said that putting the Street Roadsters into the class was the beginning of the end. Then naturally the changes to fiberglass bodies and custom frames could be blamed for allowing the cars to become too much like Funny Cars.

Although all the reasons have valid arguments, perhaps none of them are the real reason for the demise of the blown gassers. Consider, for example, what if the late model cars had not come into the AA/GS and BB/GS classes; no George Montgomery or Skip Hess built Mustangs, no Opel GTs from Norm Paddack, John Herrera and Junior Thompson or Barracudas like the Mallicoat Bros. Would that have saved the classes? Or what if in the mid-1960's the guys had stayed with their Willys and said no to the Anglias and Austins. Would that have saved the classes? Would banning the fiberglass bodies and custom frames keep the classes? The answer is probably no to all of these questions.

The demise of the Supercharged Gas Coupe Class was really due to the evolutionary changes in drag racing. The blown gas coupe classes were formed merely to remove some cars running superchargers out of the Street Gas Coupe classes. And the new Supercharged Gas Coupe classes were actually the bottom classes in the "hot car" or competition category. When the classes were first set up the "hot car" classes were 39% of the total number of classes. In the final year of AA/GS competition (1975) the Competition (hot car) bracket classes had dropped to 10% of the total classes. And the number of competitors in the blown gas classes had been declining for years, as it had been in most of the other hot car classes. The result of this decline of competition was the elimination of classes. Classes for Competition Coupes, Modified Roadsters and "Hot" Roadsters all disappeared in the 1960's. So it was probably just a matter of time before the blown gassers would be merged with other cars to reduce the number of classes. Basically survival of any class was tied to the number of competitors in the class. The classes with only a small number of competitors were the classes that were eliminated.

There never were large numbers of competitors in the Supercharged Gas Coupe classes. At first there were only a few blown gassers when the classes were formed in 1960. The numbers increased in the 1961 through 1964 years as many unblown gas competitors tried superchargers. But starting about 1965 the continuing technical improvements, (smaller cars, modern chassis designs, new transmissions) began to drive the costs escalating upward. As a result the blown gasser ranks began to decline in numbers. By the late 1960's the majority of the Supercharged Gasser activity was in Southern and Northern California, Ohio and New York. There were cars in other parts of the country but there was very little Supercharged Gas Coupe racing there.

In the early 1970's the focus of drag racing concentrated on the Professional classes and most of the activity in the blown gasser ranks faded away. A few dedicated racers like George Montgomery, Jim Oddy, Tom Shinholster, Panella-Miner and Steve Woods continued to run, with excellent performances, in the final years. But the blown gassers had just become a class in the Competition Eliminator programs, that were often dominated by things like econo-rail dragsters, by then.

The Supercharged Gassers had a great "life". The guys and the cars became much more popular than would be expected for the lowest class on the competition category list. The blown gassers were just the fastest street coupes in the beginning. Many other classes had faster cars, in fact almost all the competition, or "hot car" classes, were faster. But an interesting blend of good racing, showmanship, individuals, and publicity created a special "place in the sun" for the blown gassers.

The mention of the blown gassers to drag racing enthusiasts today will immediately bring up names like George Montgomery, Junior Thompson, Tim Woods, Doug Cook, John Mazmanian, Chuck Finders, Jim Shores, Skip Hess, Gene Ciambella, K. S. Pittman, Paul Pittman, Mel Marrs, Phil Lukens, Jim Oddy, Tom Shinholster, Larry Holt, Bob Lombardi, Bob Balogh, Jack Merkel, Bob Panella, Bob Chipper, Billy Holt, Paul Day, Mike Marinoff, Ron Nunes, Dale Moody, Sam Jones, John Lombardo, Ron Bizio, Gary and Jerry Mallicoat, Gary Burgin, Gary Densham and so many others. And many guys remember the Willys' of K. S. Pittman, George Montgomery, Stone-Woods-Cook, Jack Merkel, Big John Mazmanian and so on......

So today the Supercharged Gas Coupe Classes have been gone for over 17 years but there are many fond memories among both racers and spectators of the A/GS, B/GS and C/GS racers of the 1960's.

John Lombardo (So.Calif.) replaced his Willys (Page 120) with a new Corvette for California AA/GS racing. It was a topless, flip-top car with a Jim Kirby chassis. It also helped generate lots of controversy about where the AA/GS class was going. The 420" Chrysler engine drove John's Corvette to 169 mph and 8.50 sec. times and many AA/GS meet victories in 1969 and 1970. John, pictured in front of the car, also ran in some Funny Car shows with it. Manuel Herrera drove it in 1969. (Photo courtesy of John Chambliss)

Brad Anderson, who had competed in the AA/GS with a Prefect and a Dodge Dart (Page 151), returned to the class in 1971 with an Opel GT. It was a legal NHRA AA/GS car with no flip-top body and doors that opened. The beautiful red Opel had a body by Contemporary Fiberglass and a 414" engine (by Chrysler). Brad received the best appearing car award at the 1972 Winternationals and set the final E.T. record (8.46 sec.) for the "real" AA/GS class (5.0 lbs./cu.in.) in 1972. He ran the NHRA meets and some blown gas Funny Car (formerly AA/GS) meets. Then he moved on to the BB/FC class where many of the former AA/GS and BB/GS racers could be found. Brad Anderson Enterprises is still involved in racing. (Photo courtesy of Brad Anderson)

Probably the only 1956 Thunderbird to race in the blown gas coupe classes in the 1970's was run by Art Kazanjian-Tom and Gary Lemon (So. Calif.). It had a 427" Chevy engine. The team moved up from the unblown B/G class in 1971. Tom and Gary Lemon quickly recorded good performances of 147 mph and 9.57 sec. The photo was at an 8-car Southern California BB/GS show in 1972. (Photo courtesy of the Author)

Ron Rinauro (No.Calif.) also updated from his Willys (Page 127) to a late model car. This 1970 Dodge Challenger was built and prepared by Tom Chambliss in late 1970. It had a Fiberglass Trends body and Ron's Chrysler engine that had previously run in his Willys. It ran BB/A at NHRA events (no opening doors). The 2070 lbs. car raced mostly in Northern California in 1971 and recorded best times of 163.37 mph and 8.68 sec. Ron retired from racing in 1972 and sold the Dodge. (Photo courtesy of Tom Chambliss)

161

Junior Thompson changed cars again in 1971. He replaced his Opel Kadett (Page 136) with a new, sleek Opel GT. His 450" Chrysler engine was installed in the Jim Kirby built car. The Opel GT was Junior's race car for the match race seasons through 1973. The Opel GT raced with George Montgomery, Stone-Woods-Cook, K. S. Pittman and others in AA/GS match races. By 1973 some of the races were called "Super Gas Funny Cars" and some were called BB/Funny Cars. Junior also was active in the UDRA circuit. Match racing was Junior's job from 1967 to 1973. He toured the East from March to October each year. Originally he ran as John Mazmanian's fill-in but soon he could get the bookings under his own name. The Opel GT hit 173.07 mph and 7.92 sec. times running in blown gas Funny Car competition. (Photo courtesy of Junior Thompson - Photo by Warren and Wright)

Jeff and Larry Storck (So.Calif.) built this very nice BB/GS class Opel GT. It was a flip-top Opel GT with a body by Fiberglass Trends. The team built the 305" Chevy engine. The beautiful red with red-orange flames colored Opel GT raced the major NHRA events from 1972 to 1974. They set an NHRA record (9.27 sec.) in 1973. The 2440 lbs. car (600 lbs. was added weight) hit best times of 159 mph and 8.96 sec. Like most of the blower gassers in the mid-1970's the transmission used was a custom built racing transmission (Lenco 4-speed). (Photo courtesy of Jeff Storck)

Although this great looking '33, all fiberglass Willys, said K. S. Pittman on the doors it had been owned by Harry Hall (Penn.) since 1968. Both Pittman's Austin and Harry's Willys were used on the match race circuit. The Willys recorded times of 165 mph and 8.47 sec., with Chrysler horsepower. The photo was taken at the start of the car's final run at the 1972 Summernationals. The car was destroyed when a front wheel came off at high speed. (Photo courtesy of Harry Hall)

Here was the Panella-Miner (No.Calif.) Opel GT (Page 154) as it was built with turbochargers. The 301" Chrysler engine had Rajay turbos and a Hilborn turbo injection system. The car ran from March to October of 1973 with this setup. They set a BB/GST record (8.98 sec.) with it. The turbo setup helped them record times of 159.26 mph and 8.64 sec. The team returned to the regular 6-71 supercharger setup for the 1974 season. (Photo courtesy of Bob Panella - Photo by Barry Wiggins)

After touring the Stone-Woods-Cook Mustang for the 1970 season, Steve Korney (So.Calif.) made the decision that he needed a new car. So he built a Corvette. It actually wasn't all new because Steve basically rebuilt and re-bodied his old "Goldfinger" Anglia (Page 113). The 1969 style body was made by Fiberglass Trends. The Chrysler engine was a 1/2" stroker (450"). Steve toured in 1971 with the Corvette, recording speeds in the 168 mph area. Note that the Cook in Stone-Woods-Cooke was spelled with an E added. (Doug was no longer involved with Tim Woods). Steve owned and raced the Corvette, paying Tim Woods a percentage of the earnings to run the S-W-C bookings. Unfortunately bookings were getting more difficult to get. So 1971 was Steve's last year on the tour. (Photo courtesy of Steve Korney - Photo by Warren and Wright)

John Lo Bianco (New York) was still racing his AA/GS '33 Willys in 1973. Unfortunately the AA/GS class had actually become the BB/GS (8.0 lbs./cu.in.) so John's 392 Chrysler powered Willys was racing cars like the BB/FC Vega with K. S. Pittman's name on it. Early Willys like this were disappearing as the AA/GS class, where most of them were still running, faded away. (Photo courtesy of Harry Hall)

The Opel GT began to appear to be the "correct" car for the blown gas coupe class, just like the Willys had been in the early 1960's. This BB/GS Opel GT was Bob Lombardi's (New York) replacement for his record setting Willys (Page 129). It had a Contemporary Fiberglass body. Bob's 327" Chevy was connected to a Vitar Clutch-Turbo Hydro. The car hit speeds in the 153 mph range. Eastern Automotive was painted on the doors - it was Bob Lombardi's speed shop. (Photo courtesy of Ken Menz)

Al Page (New York) had worked for Bob Lombardi's Eastern Automotive when Bob built his Opel GT. In 1971 Al built his own Opel GT for the BB/GS competition. The car was very similar to Lombardi's (327" Chevy, Vitar Clutch-Turbo). Al set an NHRA E.T. record in 1971 (9.38 sec.) and went over 152 mph with it that year. He then decided to move on to the BB/FC class. (Photo courtesy of Ken Menz)

After their successful turbocharging efforts with their Willys in 1965, Gary and Jerry Mallicoat moved to Northern California to go to college. In 1968 they built a new Barracuda AA/GS car with a 6-71 blown 420" Chrysler. The car ran 162 mph in 8.70 sec., but they wanted more. They returned to turbocharging, working with Hilborn where Gene Adams was experimenting with injection for the turbocharging setup. With 1130 HP the rebuilt, now flip-top, Barracuda with a B&M Clutch-Flite and a Crower-Glide clutch quickly went 174 mph in 8.18 sec. The car ran BB/A at NHRA meets, setting the NHRA speed record in BB/AT (172.08 mph). The photos show the 1969 version (with 6-71 blower) and the 1971 revised Barracuda with the turbochargers on its final run in 1973. Shown receiving the best Engineering Award at the Northern California Nationals from strip manager Steve Evans (right) was Tom Chambliss (driver, on left) and Gary Mallicoat (center). (Photos courtesy of Gary Mallicoat - 1972 photo by Barry Wiggins, 1969 photo by Jerry Mallicoat)

This Northern California AA/GS meet race pitted Mike Mitchell's topless Corvette against the Mallicoat twins' Barracuda (Aug.1970). The Barracuda was the initial version with the 6-71 supercharged engine. This was its last race before being rebuilt (flip-top body and turbocharged engine). Note that the whole fiberglass front end was off of the Barracuda. It had blown off on a previous run.
(Photo courtesy of John Chambliss)

In 1972 Mas Hikida and Terry Mc Hardy (Vancouver, B.C., Canada) purchased this '33 Willys from Steve Mc Gee (Oregon). The Canadian team ran in a Northwest A/GS circuit with Jim Rockstad (Anglia), Chuck Byrd ('33 Willys), Roger Orr (Anglia), Jeff Wright (Austin) and Doug Shambarger ('67 Chevelle) in 1973 and 1974. With fewer A/GS shows being run the Hikida-Mc Hardy Willys also ran NHRA events in the BB/A class. A 426" late Hemi Chrysler engine and Torque-flite transmission drove the car down to E.T.'s in the 8.80 sec. area.
(Photo courtesy of Terry Mc Hardy - Photo by Rich Carlson)

Ernie Nicholson (So.Calif.) replaced his older AA/GS (Super Stude) with a new Barracuda in 1968. A Fiberglass Trends body was mounted on a chassis by Jim Kirby. The 452" late Chrysler Hemi engine was built by Tony Nancy and the Torqueflite by Art Carr. The Barracuda recorded times of 163.00 mph and 8.49 sec. in 1968. "Flower Power", as it was named, ran to 1971. The photo shows it at a Northern California AA/GS show (Vacaville) in late 1970. (Photo courtesy of John Chambliss)

John Herrera (So.Calif.) retired from racing when he sold his Austin (Page 137). But the new Opel GT supercharged cars impressed him so much that he had one built at Contemporary Fiberglass. John installed a 420" Chrysler that he had obtained from John Mazmanian. The beautiful Opel GT raced at the Southern California AA/GS meets, now often called Blown Gas Funny Car meets. Running in the BB/A class at NHRA events, the Herrera and Sons Opel set the NHRA E.T. record down to 8.37 sec. (1971). The speed that day was 170.45 mph. John Herrera again retired from racing in 1973. (Photo courtesy of Art Carr)

After racing his very successful BB/GS Prefect (Page 139) to a best of 9.11 sec., Steve Woods (No.Calif) switched to a Plymouth Cricket station wagon. The 2685 lbs. wagon had a 358" Chrysler and a B & J four-speed transmission. Steve set AA/GS records in 1975 (160.42 mph and 8.58 sec.) and the CC/A records in 1976 after the AA/GS class was eliminated. The Cricket's best times were 166.80 mph and 8.29 sec. (Photo courtesy of Steve Woods - Photo by Rich Carlson)

Ed Middlebrook (So.Calif.) built this Austin in 1971 for the BB/GS class competition. The "Myth" ran NHRA events and the last Southern California BB/GS circuit shows. The all steel Austin had a 365" Chrysler engine and a B&M Clutch-Flite transmission. The neat looking, 2750 lbs. Austin hit times of 145 mph and 9.58 sec. in 1972. Ed continued to run the car for seven years in the CC/A class to a best of 162 mph and 8.57 sec. It might have been the last all steel Austin among the top AA/GS competition in the last year of the class (1975). (Photo courtesy of Ed Middlebrook)

After running his Austin (Page 152) in the 1968 and 1969 seasons K. S. Pittman returned to Southern California and built a new car. The new Opel GT was actually the old Austin chassis, rebuilt by Steve Korney, with a Contemporary Fiberglass body on it. It is especially interesting to note that while others were building flip-top, single seat, Funny Car style AA/GS racers, K. S. built an NHRA legal, opening door, two seat car with no flip-top body. The Chrysler engine was bolted to a B&M Clutch-Flite and a Crower Glide clutch. The Opel GT set an NHRA record (8.54 sec.) in 1970 and recorded speeds up to 170 mph. K. S. continued to run the match race tours from 1970 to 1972 with the AA/GS Opel, racing "Ohio" George, Junior and others. But match racing was drying up for the AA/GS racers so he sold the Opel GT (1972) to Frank Harris (Virginia) who had purchased Chuck Stolze's S & S business. Interestingly the Opel GT was repainted blue that same year and campaigned as the Stone-Woods-Cook entry in BB/FC match races. (Photos courtesy of Harry Hall and K. S. Pittman - Burnout photo by John Kinker - At speed photo by Marcel Studios)

This neat little blue Anglia was owned by Chris Wheeler (So.Calif.). It ran in the Southern California BB/GS circuit meets in 1971 and 1972. The 2350 lbs. car was powered by a 292" Chevy engine. Performances of 137 mph and 10.0 sec. E.T.'s were recorded using a four-speed Muncie (manual) transmission. (Photo courtesy of Greg Castelli)

Fred Schirmer (No.Calif.) campaigned this fiberglass (but not Chevrolet fiberglass) Corvette at the California AA/GS shows in 1970 and 1971. Fred won the BB/A class at the 1971 NHRA Winternationals. The car was the former Warren Bros. car (Page 147). Unfortunately the car was destroyed in a towing accident late in 1971. The photo was taken in Northern California three months before the demise of the car. (Photo courtesy of Mike Bognod)

One of the Southern California BB/GS circuit's last events was an eight car show at Holtville, Calif. (Feb. 1972). Shown near the "Rockerhead" Willys, from left: Bill Montgomery, Don Montgomery, Larry Holt and Silas Pittman. The guys beside the Blair's Speed Shop Anglia were Pete Eastwood, Bud Fentress and Phil Lukens. The BB/GS circuit faded away with the recession in 1972. (Photos courtesy of the Author)

169

The AA/GS race cars had indeed become "high tech" by 1972. This is Gary and Jerry Mallicoat's Barracuda (Page 165). There was almost an indistinguishable difference between this AA/GS car and a Funny Car. The most interesting feature of this car was the turbo-charger setup. Although the turbo setup performed fantastically on the dyno, making it work on the drag strip was no easy task. The biggest problem was getting enough manifold pressure to strongly launch the car. Gary Mallicoat supplied the procedure that they developed with their driver, Tom Chambliss. It basically said to (1) stage last, (2) move into the pre-stage light, (3) lock brakes and apply full throttle, and (4) allow the car to creep into the staged light and hold. The engine is now at about 7400 rpm and the manifold pressure at 25 psi and the car is ready. The odds are 20% that you will red light, 10% that the brakes will burn out, 14% that your opponent will try to burn you down, and 50% that you will get a "super" run. The photo was at Fremont, 1972. (Photo courtesy of Gary Mallicoat)

170

- TECHNICAL -

A. Cars

The stampede to have a Willys for the blown gas classes had already started by 1960, the first year of the Supercharged Gas Coupe class competition. In fact by the end of the year both A/GS and B/GS were dominated by competitors running 1933 to 1942 vintage Willys'. The racers saw three main advantages in the what most still considered ugly Willys. They were light, cheap and available.

One look at the shipping weights in a used car guide was all it took to sell most racers on the Willys. The shipping weights for the early Willys coupe (1933-1936) were 1970 to 2034 pounds, while the late Willys (1937-1942) coupes were listed at 2137 to 2200 pounds. Previous to 1960 the early Ford coupes had been the most popular lightweight coupes. The weights of the 1932 to 1934 Ford V-8 coupes ranged from 2387 to 2448 pounds. Naturally when a competitor found that all his competitors had or were getting a Willys, he had to join the stampede.

Converting the Willys to a race car meant adding some weight. The supercharged Olds, Cad, Chevy or Chrysler engine added 300 to 500 pounds and the transmission, rear end and tires added some more. A little weight reduction was possible by tossing out the front bumper and a few other items but the NHRA street legal class rules limited what could be eliminated. So the majority of the Willys were race ready weighing about 2500 to 2800 pounds.

Most of the racers quickly learned that having the lightest car did not always win the race. If the car spun the tires too much at the starting line, the E.T. might not be good enough to win. And in 1960 the available horsepower was too much for the available traction. One of the solutions to this situation was to add weight on the rear tires. In practice from 200 to 700 pounds, or more, was added in an effort to get improved traction and in many cases move down a class.

The interesting part was the creative weight setups on the early gassers. The most effective place to put the weight was behind the rear wheels since this effectively transferred more weight to the rear. The NHRA rules allowed up to 100 pounds of removable ballast which had to be bolted in place. So in addition to the approved 100 pounds of weight, the racers often added two heavy truck batteries and perhaps steel or iron bars or lead weights into the frame sections. One popular weight was a four inch diameter water pipe rear bumper/push bar with end caps to hold lead weights in the pipe. There were many instances of cars with spare tires filled with concrete or doors and trunk lids filled with lead.

Since adding weight actually reduced acceleration, it is easy to see that the only reason to add weight to an A/GS car was strictly to improve traction or handling. Adding weights to a car in the B/GS or C/GS classes was generally done to meet the class weight breaks. One way to look at the A/GS traction situation is to compare the class records. In 1961 George Montgomery's A/GS record of 10.83 sec. E.T. was set with a Cadillac powered Willys running at approximately 5 lbs./cu.in. But the B/GS record of 10.99 sec. by Stone-Woods-Cook, at 8 lbs./cu.in., and even the C/GS record of 11.28 sec. by Pittman-Edwards at 10.6 lbs./cu.in. were only .16 and .45 sec. behind the A/GS record. Basically traction, or lack of it, seems to be the reason the Montgomery car was not able to get significantly better E.T.'s than the fastest B/GS cars. Proof of the traction problem in the A/GS ranks can be seen in the wide spread in E.T.'s (more than 1 sec.) in cars running in the same general speed area and even in the various runs of the same car. So the initial efforts to harness all the supercharged power were usually to add a little weight. It is impossible to say how much weight each car had but it can be said that a few of the B/GS Willys were bending the scales down to readings in the 3600 to 3800 lbs. area.

For the next few years the Willys dominated the Supercharged Gas Coupe classes. The only change was an increased interest in the lighter early, 1933, style Willys. But still the majority of the competitors were running 1937 to 1942 Willys. And almost all soon had fiberglass front fender assemblies that made them look like 1941 or 1942 models.

A major change to the Supercharged Gas Coupe classes came in the shape of foreign mini-cars. The most popular of the mini-cars were the 1950's English Ford Anglias and Austins. They were smaller and lighter. They even made the Willys look big. Although the Anglia was not a legal NHRA A/GS car growing numbers of them were racing the local A/GS shows. So many racers felt they had to build an Anglia or Austin just to remain competitive. So most of the top A/GS racers built mini-cars, including George Montgomery, John Mazmanian, Junior Thompson, Skip Hess, Gene Ciambella, the Lee Bros., Jim Oddy, the Kohler Bros., Steve Korney and many others. The mini-car invasion resulted in a few blown gasser competitors moving on to other classes or just dropping out of racing.

The next change in the race cars came only a couple of years later. The new trend was to late model cars. Developments in tires, chassis and engine power had made the larger cars competitive again. So new Mustangs, Barracudas, Corvettes and even mini Opel GT's were flooding the blown gasser ranks. The major difference now was that most of these new cars had

The references to blown engines in this book do not mean this! This is a real BLOWN engine. Although Jack Coonrod had a reputation for not breaking often, the 23rd run on this Chrysler was one too many. It is doubtful that Jack saved much from it. (Photo courtesy of Jack Coonrod)

23 RUNS

172

professionally built chassis' and fiberglass bodies. Also most of them were not legal NHRA AA/GS class cars. They were built for AA/GS shows and match races. Some of them also ran a few Funny Car shows.

One other change seemed of major importance to the blown gassers. That was the merging of the street roadsters into the blown gas coupe classes. However the effect was minimal as only a hand full of the roadsters ever ran in the AA/GS shows. For various reasons they were never very popular.

After 1971 most of the competitors were either moving to other classes, including BB/Funny Car, BB/Altered or Funny Car, or they were dropping out of drag racing. So only a few Supercharged Gassers were actually built in the last few years of the blown gas coupe era.

B.   Chassis

The early blown gas coupes were basically street type cars with "hot" engines. The Fords, Chevys and Willys coupes or sedans used stock frames and reinforced rear suspension systems. Efforts to improve weight transfer during acceleration soon resulted in the cars being raised higher and higher. This trend was quickly seen to be unsafe and a rule was made to limit the engine location (24" max.-ground to crank pulley).

Continued chassis development introduced coil spring suspensions and custom built front axle assemblies, replacing the stock axles. Various forms of rear radius rods, ladder bars or parallel rods were tried by most of the competitors. Most of the chassis work was aimed to make the car handle properly and to improve the traction. The combination of more horsepower, better tires, faster speeds and 25 year old economy car frames were often providing some exciting rides down the drag strips, both for the driver and the spectators. Handling and safety questions were increasingly raised about the short wheel-based Anglias and Austins.

A major improvement in safety was achieved with the change to custom built tube frames. Another development that came along about the same time was the lightweight fiberglass bodies. The combination of the custom frames and fiberglass bodies made the old street type race cars obsolete. Another factor in the chassis development was that most of the new chassis were being built by professional chassis builders. The new cars incorporated the experience from previous cars and usually included adjustments for weight distribution and rear suspension arm angle. And most of the professionally built cars looked "professional," not home built, as many of the older cars did.

The handling of the new custom chassis and bodied cars was much better than before. And the return of the new longer wheelbase cars, Mustangs and others, also aided making them go straighter. One result of improved handling was the ability to take better advantage of the available horsepower.

By the time the blown gassers faded out in the mid-1970's the cars resembled the early Supercharged Gassers in name only. The early blown coupes were almost 100% made of American automotive parts and components. The last of the AA/GS or BB/GS cars were built on custom tube frames with custom fiberglass bodies, many of them flip-top like a Funny Car. It appeared that even though the blown gassers made excellent technical progress, it did not prevent the loss of interest that led to the demise of the classes.

B.   Engines

The first year of the supercharged class was dominated by Olds and Chevy powered cars. Some excellent performances by competitors running Cadillac, Chrysler, Buick and Ford engines were recorded but they represented only a small number of competitors. In 1959 the Olds engine had been increased to 394 cu. inches. With a little boring and stroking as much as 460 cu. inches was achieveable. The Chevy was still at 283 cu. inches in 1960, so about 360 cu. inches was obtainable. This generally meant that the Olds engines ran in A/GS and B/GS while Chevys were usually competing in B/GS and C/GS. Typical horsepower ratings for the 1960's Olds were in the range of 450 to 575 hp while the Chevys were putting out around 350 to 470 hp.

Engine developments in the next few years was mostly in the blower area and the compression ratio-blower pressure combination. Many of the early Supercharged Gasser competitors started using a McCulloch or Latham supercharger or a S.C.O.T. or 4-71 GMC blower. As newly designed manifold and drive kits became available it was only a matter of time, and finances, before every competitor was using the 6-71 GMC blower. Incidently lots of these blowers were available in war surplus stocks. The 6-71 units displaced 50% more air than the 4-71 blowers. So it was easy to increase the manifold pressures up to the 18-20 psi. area from the 12 to 15 psi area previously used. But the increased blower pressure and intake temperatures could result in combustion chamber detonation and often burned pistons or other serious engine damage. Thus the engine builder had to develop a combination of blower pressure and compression ratio that the engine would tolerate. Generally most competitors built engines with compression ratios in the 8:1 to 9:1 area and manifold pressures from 15 to 18 psi.

The shift to Chrysler hemi power by 1965 resulted in power increases to over 800 hp. It also resulted in the disappearance of the Olds engines. The remainder of the years for the Supercharged Gassers would be dominated by the Chrysler "Hemis" and the small block Chevys. It should also be noted that numerous big block Chevys, a few late hemi Chryslers, and several SOHC Ford engines performed well in the Supercharged Gas Coupe class. Progress in the engine area continued especially with stronger components that allowed engine speeds to go over 9000 rpm with no problems. When the classes were initiated engine speeds of a just over 6000 rpm at the end of the quarter mile were typical. By the end of the 1960's even the big 450 cu. in., and up, engines were spinning up as high as 8500 to 9500 rpm. Naturally the cam grinders deserve some credit for the cams and springs that allowed the engines to continue to perform at speeds almost 50% faster than used a few years earlier.

The story of turbocharging in the Supercharged Gassers is interesting. Turbocharging was well known as a method of getting high performance from an aircraft engine or an Indy 500 engine. But the few efforts with turbochargers, or even centrifugal superchargers, at the drags had been less than inspiring. Then in late 1964 Jerry and Gary Mallicoat built up a dual turbo setup for their 6-71 blown 327 Chevy engine. The dyno indicated that the turbos jumped the power from 590 hp, with the 6-71, to 720 hp with the turbos. The 22% jump in horsepower helped the Mallicoats win their class at the Winternationals and later set the NHRA speed record (B/GS). The Mallicoat Bros. campaigned the car for one season and then sold it.

Although the Mallicoats had shown that a turbocharged car could be competitive there still was little interest in this complex and expensive technology. There were some efforts in both Dragsters and Funny Cars but still almost no one took notice. Suddenly in 1971 everyone in the Supercharged Gasser ranks took notice. The Mallicoats were back with a turbocharged 467 cu.in. Chrysler engine in their AA/GS Barracuda. Continuing on the work Hilborn and Gene Adams had been doing, the turbo engine hit 1131 hp. The 6-71 blown Chrysler it replaced had recorded 845 hp. The Barracuda broke George Montgomery's BB/A record by over 6 mph. Impressive, but still the other cars were competitive so there was no problem.

Then in 1972 George Montgomery used a turbocharged Boss 429 Ford engine in his Mustang to up the AA/GS record by over 3 mph. George estimated that the initial setup was yielding over 1100 hp.

In the meantime Paul Pittman had been fighting "teething" problems with his turbocharged 400 cu. in. Chrysler. Paul's BB/GS American Motors Gremlin made many poor runs while he worked with the injectors and turbo sizes. When Paul worked out the combination in 1972 he quickly lowered the E.T. record by .36 sec. and raised the speed record by over 4 mph.

Now all the Supercharged Gas Coupe competitors were alarmed. Suddenly their engines could be obsolete. Some of the Supercharged Gasser competitors apparently considered moving to another class and a few may have dropped out. After reviewing the situation, the NHRA decided to separate the turbocharged cars into their own classes with their own records. So Paul Pittman's 1972 records (9.02 sec., 158.45 mph) and then Panella-Miner's 8.98 sec. record in 1973 were the only BB/GS(T) records set and George Montgomery's 166.97 mph record set in 1972 were the only turbocharged records established in the Supercharged Gas Coupe classes. In addition George Montgomery reset the Mallicoats BB/A(T) record to 8.44 sec. and 167.59 mph.

When the turbochargers came in the classes were already fading away. Thus only a few of them ran in Supercharged Gas Coupe classes. In spite of the great performance potential, the turbocharged cars were difficult to stage and run consistently. This did not help their popularity. In fact after running in 1973 and 1974 with a turbocharged engine, the Panella-Miner Opel GT was back to a 6-71 style blower in 1975. So a few blown gasser competitors showed that the turbochargers had lots of potential but there were still a few problems to be solved to develop them to their full potential.

C. Transmissions

The Supercharged Gas Coupe competitors deserve much of the credit for the acceptance of the automatic transmissions in the fastest drag racing categories. By the late 1950's virtually all the automobiles were built with automatic transmissions. But on the drag strips the automatics were unpopular. Slippage and poor efficiency in the transmissions resulted in poorer performance than could be obtained with a manual transmission. The difference in performance resulted in rules by most drag strips and associations that set up separate classes for the automatic transmission stock cars and some gas class cars.

The Supercharged Gassers of the 1958 to 1960 period were generally using the prewar Cadillac floorshift transmissions. They were strong and readily available at the local junk yards, or recycling centers as we call them today. The three-speed gear ratios were 2.39:1, 1.53:1 and 1:1. Gear shifting, especially from first to second, was not particularly fast.

Traction was the main problem for the fastest Supercharged Gassers. If they started in low gear the tires would spin excessively. If the driver tried to reduce the tire spin by sliding the clutch, in most cases the clutch would "burn up" and slip all the way. The clutches could not take the heat like the new materials that are used today. So one alternative was to start in second gear. This reduced the tire spin but also reduced the acceleration and often could result in a slipping clutch. Adding weight helped reduce tire spin but also reduced the mid-range acceleration. This problem was mostly found in the high horsepower and low weight A/GS and B/GS cars. The small engined or heavy cars usually were able to solve their traction

The standard warm-up procedure for the supercharged cars after rolling them off their trailer is shown here. A floor jack was used to raise the rear wheels off the ground. Then the engine was started and allowed to warm up. After the engine started, the transmission was put in gear so that the transmission and rear end also were in operation. This photo shows the Willys of Brasher-Cummings-Rose and Del Rio-Carlson at OCIR (1970) for a 16-car Southern California AA/GS program. (Photo courtesy of John Chambliss)

Before burnouts were allowed various methods of cleaning the tires were used. Most teams wiped the tires off with rags. Here the Stone-Woods-Cook team was using brooms to clean the tires. Originally burning past the starting line to clear the tires of pebbles or dirt was grounds for disqualification. Finally it was discovered that the burnouts improved the show and manual tire cleaning was over. (Photo courtesy of Charles Strutt)

problems.

The Supercharged Gassers made a major "leap" forward with the introduction of racing versions of the General Motors, Four-Speed Hydramatic. Bob Spar, of B&M, worked initially with Supercharged Gasser racers like Dick Harryman and Pittman-Edwards to get the "hydros" working in the race cars. Continual developments to make the "Hydro-stick" hold up under the abuse of engines over 500 hp led to more and more racers running a "hydro". And naturally other transmission firms began to get racing hydros in the Supercharged Gassers too.

The racing Hydramatics were generally built using 1953 to 1956 model G.M. Hydramatics. The transmission had four speeds, 3.82:1, 2.63:1, 1.45:1 and 1:1. Instead of a clutch the unit used a fluid coupling (similar to the torque converters used in today's transmissions except the coupling does not multiply the torque like the torque converter does). The starting procedure was to run the engine up to about the stall speed (approximately 1800 to 3000 rpm in the early days) while holding the car with the brakes. At the green light the take-off was relatively smooth because all the gear train had been preloaded. A few racers wanted more rpm at the start so they sometimes wound up the engine and then put the transmission in gear. It was somewhat detrimental to the health of the transmission. The extremely low first gear allowed the car to make a quick jump but then it was time to shift. The typical Supercharged Gasser's engine was already past 6000 rpm at 30 mph. That first shift came up so fast that most competitors set the transmission gear selector in second gear, allowing the transmission to make the 1-2 shift automatically. A magazine writer commented about a Supercharged Gasser using a hydro transmission that the "Willys seems to jump straight up in the air, move forward 15 ft., put itself on the ground, change gear, and is gone".

Within a couple of years almost all of the Supercharged Gassers had hydro transmissions. Definite improvements in E.T.'s and handling were achieved. Naturally the successful use of the automatic transmission in the fastest stock bodied cars in drag racing encouraged others to develop the automatics in other classes.

Automatic transmission developments in the Factory Stock and Experimental classes led to the next step in Supercharged Gasser evolution. Although General Motors and Ford were working with their Experimental Stock racers in efforts to build transmissions that could hold up with the ever increasing horsepower being obtained, Chrysler already had a head start using their new Torqueflite transmission. The Torqueflite was introduced in 1962 and racing modifications were developed almost immediately for Chrysler Superstock racing programs. Developments continued as Chrysler moved up into the A/FX Experi-

mental Stock competition. Art Carr, of Arcadia Transmission, helped Chrysler with their racing program. At the same time Art was able to develop a strong, racing Torqueflite transmission. The first blown gassers to run Art Carr's Stick-Torqueflite were Shores-Hess and the Kohler Bros. Anglias. Although Art called it a Stick-Torqueflite most of them used Art's push-button "Nifty Shifter". The Kohler's Chevy powered Anglia quickly broke its AHRA class record and the rush was on. The Art Carr Torqueflites in the A/GS Anglias of the Kohler Bros. and Shores-Hess quickly pushed the E.T.'s down by .2 to .3 sec. Naturally competitive firms like B&M and C&O immediately worked with their racers and customers to update them into the latest 1966 developments.

The Torqueflite Model A-727 was a three-speed transmission (2.45:1, 1.45:1 and 1:1) with a torque converter. The torque converter could multiply torque up to 2.5 times at the start. Thus even though the first gear ratio of the Torqueflite was higher than the hydro, the total torque was greater by almost 40%. One of the best things about the Torqueflite was that the 1-2 shift was made at over 50 mph, instead of around 30 mph. The hydro 1-2 shift made many of the light cars break loose or jump around. So the Torqueflite offered only two shifts instead of three and better E.T.'s and improved handling.

It must be noted that almost immediately after the Torqueflite successes the transmission builders pushed their development of the racing G.M. Turbo-Hydramatics and Ford C-6 transmissions. All the transmissions were similar in design and operation, so the development was quickly accomplished. As a result Chrysler, G.M. and Ford automatic transmissions were all used in the blown gassers.

While the conversion to Torqueflites was proceeding well, there was still a problem for the heavier cars with smaller engines. They still didn't perform well enough at the lower engine rpm's required by the torque converter's stall speed. One solution was to machine the torque converter to increase the stall speeds up to as high as 5000 rpm. This could help but at a cost of slippage on the top end. Some hi-stall converters were slipping by as much as 500 to 800 rpm in the traps.

The next development helped to solve the small engine's problem with the low stall speed converters. The solution was to replace the converter with a clutch. In this manner the car could be launched with the engine up around 5000 rpm, or more, where it performs best. These conversions were called Clutch-Flites and Clutch-Turbos. They were very successful in CC/GS and BB/GS cars and as tires and cars improved many of the AA/GS competitors replaced their torque converters with clutches. Perhaps it is interesting to consider if anyone had an automatic transmission anymore, because they were using a clutch and manually shifting the gears. The only automatic function was that the clutch did not have to be used on the two shifts.

In the 1970's developments in the Dragsters spelled the end for most of the beefed-up stock automatic transmissions. Custom designed racing transmissions built by firms like Lenco and B & J were stronger, lighter and just better built for the job. Another development that some of the competitors tried was the multi-disc clutches. Some also worked with the centrifugally engaged Crower-glide. But the Super-charged Gassers were about dead and the continuing transmission developments were done in the Funny Car, and other, classes.

Although transmission development was spread over many classes it is fair to say that the Supercharged Gassers pioneered the use of the automatic transmis-

sions in the all-out racing classes. That is not to say that it would not have happened anyway, it is merely to say that the blown gassers were first.

D.   Tires - Slicks

Perhaps the biggest single technical improvement in drag racing during the 1960's was in tire traction. The first major step in tire development occurred in 1958 when M & H started selling their all new Racemaster Slicks. These custom built racing tires quickly replaced most of the recap slicks made by firms like Bruces, A-1, Inglewood and Moxley. Incidently M & H (Marvin and Harry Rifchin) had begun making circle track tires. Marvin did the design and development working with drag racers like Ernie

Here is an example of the weights added to an AA/GS chassis in 1969. This was Rod Barkers Corvette (Page 147). It had two 45 lb. batteries and 160 lbs. of lead bolted in the back of the frame. In addition 50 lb. weights were bolted to each side plus 35 lb. weights on each side of the front frame horn. Since the car only weighed 1970 lbs., weight had to be added to meet the 5.0 lbs./cu.in. rule with the 462" engine. Weight was often added to improve traction or handling. (Photo courtesy of John Chambliss)

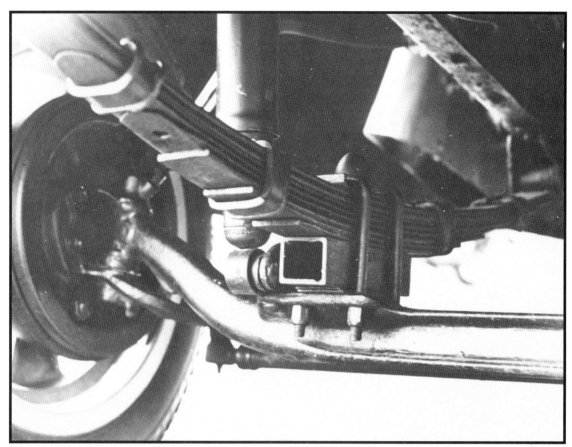

The quest for higher Willys in the 1960 to 1964 was only stopped by height rules. The front ends were initially raised with spacers. Then highly re-arched springs were used. The next step was a straight custom tube axle to replace the standard drop Willys axle. But the rule limits and then traction improvements eventually resulted in the cars dropping down instead of raising up. (Photos courtesy of Harry Hall and Mike Kuhl)

Hashim, Don Garlits and George Montgomery in the 1957 to 1960 era. He then contracted with Denman Tire Co. to assemble the slicks to the M & H specifications. M & H's success and the subsequent support of the factories in Super Stock racing soon resulted in production of drag racing tires by Firestone, Goodyear and Mickey Thompson. As usually happens when several companies compete for the same customers, improvements happen at a rapid pace.

It must be noted that the tire development work was really not done on or for the Supercharged Gassers. Basically the tire development work was aimed for the dragsters initially and the super and experimental stocks when the factory money became available. Competitors in the other classes, including the Supercharged Gassers, however were able to take advantage of the results of the continual development work in selecting tires for their race car.

The Supercharged Gassers initially had approximately 8" to 9" wide tires (8.20-15, 9.00-15). The manufacturer's recommended wheel width to make the tire lay flat was about 8". This required either widened steel wheels or custom wheels such as Halibrand's magnesium racing wheels. The next step in tire development was the larger, up to 10" wide, 16" tires. The recommended wheel widths moved up to about 10" for the huge (in 1962) tires. The basic tire design used essentially straight sidewalls with the wheel rim width equal to the tread width. The recommended tire pressure was from 24 (recommended minimum) to 30 psi.

Experiments in the Experimental Stock car ranks about 1964 led to the next step in tire development. In an effort to get more tread on the ground, the racers experimented with lower tire pressures. But lowering the pressure to 10 to 15 psi allowed the center of the tread to cave in and reduce the "foot print" of the tread on the ground. This problem was remedied by reducing the wheel rim width to about 5" or 6" which bowed in the sidewalls and pushed the center of the tread out. The tires designed to this concept soon were called "wrinkle-walls" because the sidewalls rippled as the wheel actually twisted the tire under hard acceleration.

These tires were good for about a .2 sec. improvement over the older high pressure designs. It wasn't long before racers had experimented with pressures as low as 2 to 3 psi. And some of the cars running low tire pressures had handling problems at the higher speeds.

The last half of the 1960's saw tires getting wider and wider. The widths of both 15" and 16" tires moved up from 10" to 11", to 12" and even 13" for the 16" diameter tires. The new tire designs allowed low pressures while using wide rims to help the car handle at speed. Naturally the tread compounds had improved also.

Although the tire developments in the 1960's were not done especially for the Supercharged Gas Coupes, the gassers did reap the benefits. From 1960 to 1970 the E.T.'s of the AA/GS cars dropped by almost 3.5 sec. At least 1.5 sec. of this improvement was due to tire technology improvements.

E.   Fiberglass Components

It appears that the first lightweight body parts to go on the Supercharged Gas Coupes were made by Curt Hamilton of Cal Automotive. Bob Spar of B&M called Curt about building a fiberglass hood and fenders for the Pittman-Edwards Willys. This quickly led to components for the cars of Chuck Finders, Stone-Woods-Cook, John Mazmanian and others.

Soon numerous firms like Hill and Zartman, Fiberglass Trends and Anderson (A-1) were making fiberglass body components. Funny Car developments soon resulted in many of the firms supplying complete fiberglass bodies. Thus the new professionally built Supercharged Gassers in the late 1960's usually had complete fiberglass bodies by firms like Competition Fiberglass, Contemporary Fiberglass or B & N Fiberglass.

The Supercharged Gas Coupes were merely three classes among the many classes of drag racing. Technical improvements in drag racing were not totally class oriented. That is most improvements could be adapted to several or many other class racers. So it is impossible to credit the Supercharged Gassers with too many specific technical break-throughs. But it can be said that the strong blown gasser competition did help drag racing's technical progress.

The guy with the welder's helmet was strongly involved with the Supercharged Gas Coupes throughout the 1960's. Chuck Finders lived near Junior Thompson and Doug Cook in Southern California. He built blown gassers to race for himself and for other people. He drove numerous cars. After moving to Ohio he continued to build and race blown gas coupes. A careful look at the cars in this book will show many of his customers including Junior Thompson, K. S. Pittman, Jack Coonrod, etc. The photo was taken while Chuck and Junior Thompson were building Junior's Austin in 1965. (Photo courtesy of Junior Thompson)

Norm Paddack decided to build an Opel GT for the AA/GS class. Unfortunately the new Opels were not out yet and the local Buick dealer was no help. So Norm called Adam Opel personally and got a body shipped from Germany. The body price was $497 while the freight charges were $534. The photo on Page 146 shows how it looked when Norm was done building it. (Photo courtesy of Vicki Paddack)

Chassis developments had not progressed very far when the Anglias came into the blown gas coupe classes. The emphasis was on light weight as indicated by the many holes cut in the frame of Steve Korney's "Goldfinger" Anglia. Many of the early mini-cars had problems with frame flexing which often resulted in lifting one wheel, poor traction or evil handling. After running the Anglia with the Chrysler engine, Steve built a new and stronger frame than the one shown here. (Photos courtesy of Steve Korney)

Harold Doolin and Bob Stroup (So.Calif.) built this Anglia in 1969. It had a metal body and had just been chopped in this photo. The team installed a neat aluminum interior and when finished with a 440" Chevy engine it weighed only 1900 lbs. The team even toured the "Super Satan" in the East racing UDRA and match races. (Photo courtesy of Bob Stroup)

This chassis was built for Jack Coonrod's '33 Willys (1966). Note the torsion bar front suspension setup. The left side driver location was required by rules (two seats required). Roll bar arrangements like this were typical then but in a few years full roll cages were the correct thing. Chuck Finders did some of the chassis work for Jack (and also drove on occasion). (Photo courtesy of Jack Coonrod)

The most popular front axle assembly for the blown Willys coupes in the early 1960's was the one built by Don Long. It was strong and light. The class rules said brakes were required so Don supplied spot brakes. The units sold for about $400. Don went into the chassis business and his firm, De Long Manufacturing, builds dragster components today. The Pomona race photo shows Don Long (Fiat BB/A) racing the Stone-Woods-Cook Willys for Middle Eliminator at the NHRA Winternationals. (Photos courtesy of Don Long)

This rear suspension had quarter-elliptic springs and long "ladder bar" style radius arms. It was built by Don Long for the Shores-Hess Anglia in 1965. Quarter elliptic springs were used to free the axle from the original, stock semi-elliptic arrangements. By the late 1960's most of the chassis builders were using coil spring suspensions. (Photo courtesy of Skip Hess)

The first really popular supercharger at the drags in the 1950's was the Mc Culloch centrifugal blower. They were produced to fit many different engines. Lots of racers "got their feet wet" in supercharging with a Mc Culloch. The normal boost pressure of 7 psi was actually too low for all-out racing so only a few of them were competitive in the Supercharged Gas Coupe classes in the 1960's. (Photo courtesy of Mike Kuhl)

The first successful turbocharged gas coupe was the Mallicoat Bros. Willys (1965). This was the 327" Chevy engine on Isky's dyno. Bob "Bones" Balogh did the dyno work that recorded 720 HP, which was 140 HP more than the 6-71 blower version. One of the engineers who helped the Mallicoats was Duke Hallock, a top Southern California dry lakes racer in the 1930's and 1940's. (Photo courtesy of Gary Mallicoat)

In the late 1960's the "standard" A/GS engine was the 1956 to 1958 Chrysler Hemi. The '56 model displaced 354" which could be easily enlarged to 420" while the '57 - '58 engines (392") were usually increased to 467". Although the 354" engine had a smaller displacement than the 392" Chrysler, it was often preferred because it was about 50 lbs. lighter. Also after cylinder head port flow benches came into common use most of the racers found that the 1955 and 1956 Chrysler heads flowed better than the 1957 and 1958 heads. So the earlier heads became the proper heads to use. The 1954 - 1955 Hemi engines were smaller (331") and were found in the B/GS and C/GS class cars. This engine was in Brad Anderson's Prefect. (Photo courtesy of Brad Anderson - Photo by Lou Klamm)

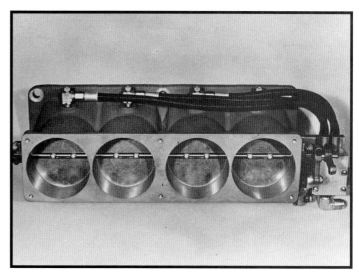

Many of the competitors would have probably enjoyed the opportunity to do the work Bob Balogh did on Isky's dyno. It would have helped most of them work out engine combinations without much of the trial and error trips down the strip. The dyno did not solve all the problems but is certainly helped develop good design parameters. Many blown gas competitors including Bob Balogh, George Montgomery, the Mallicoat Bros. and Bob Panella used dyno testing to reduce their testing times at the drag strip. (Photo courtesy of Bob Balogh)

The most popular injector in the Supercharged Gas Coupe classes was the Hilborn "four-holer" (shown here). Hilborn's first injectors for the GMC blowers were smaller "two-hole" models. The "conventional wisdom" in the early 1960's was that the "four-holer" was too big for all except the biggest engines. The "wisdom" considered that the big injector would not give good throttle response or low end power. The thinking was compared to an engine with carburetors that were too big. But the racers soon proved all the "wisdom" was not correct. Most of the competitors switched to the four-holer, or forward facing "bug catcher" model, and were happy to find that the bigger injector added almost one pound of boost. This was worth about 20 horsepower. (Photo courtesy of Verne Tomlinson of Hilborn)

Beginning around 1960 the 6-71 GMC blower was the "standard" supercharger in drag racing. By 1962 the blown cars had become so dominate, particularly dragsters, that Drag News was printing a few articles by people who said that blowers should be banned because they were ruining drag racing. Obviously blowers were not banned. Initially most of the blowers had their clearances opened up so the rotors wouldn't rub on the case at the high speeds. Continual developments by supercharger builders resulted in improvements like anodized cases and rotors, Teflon strips to reduce leakage and new magnesium cases. A number of racers went into the business of building blowers. In the early days of his business Don Hampton's blower rebuild business was in a shop behind his house (So.Calif.). He is shown here with a GMC blower case. Don's products were on many of the blown gas coupes. (Photo courtesy of Don Hampton)

Only a few competitors tried the turbocharger route. The rewards were good for Bob Panella-Fred Miner (shown here), George Montgomery, Jerry and Gary Mallicoat and Paul Pittman. But it didn't come cheap. All of them spent heavily for the technology and hardware, then worked out the "bugs" and developed run methods to get record performances. Then they all endured the protests, complaints and comments from many of their competitors. The Panella-Miner team was fortunate to have the Mallicoat twins' turbocharged Barracuda experiences to draw against. Tom Chambliss (the Mallicoat's driver) built the Panella chassis and helped "wring it out" and set up the driving procedure (1973). (Photo courtesy of John Chambliss)

The most popular manual transmission for early blown gassers was the Cadillac, or La Salle, three-speed model. The 1937-38 transmissions were stronger than any of the car transmissions, excluding the equally stout Buick and Packard models. Most Olds, Cad and Chrysler engined gassers used the Cad trans because it was the best available alternative. The Hydramatic transmission was a four-speed automatic transmission. It used a fluid coupling instead of a torque convertor or clutch. The initial success of B&M's racing "Hydro-Stick" model pushed the Cadillac transmissions out of almost all the blown gas coupes. The Hydro ruled supreme until the next development, the Torque-flite. (Photos courtesy of Gene Adams and Bob Spar)

Bob and Don Spar (B&M Industries) developed the General Motors Hydramatic to be the first automatic transmission capable of improving the performance of the fastest gas coupes. Their work with Dick Harryman, K. S. Pittman-John Edwards and others quickly led to a rapidly expanding business. In a few years the majority of fast Supercharged Gas Coupes were using B&M Hydros. B&M was actively involved in many racing projects, such as the Hemi-Cuda. Continual development work put B&M into the manufacturing area, producing stronger and improved components. B&M continues today as one of the most successful firms to grow from a drag racing oriented product. Bob and Don are shown here running a test in their transmission test cell. (Photo courtesy of Jim Davis of B&M)

The second automatic transmission revolution in the blown gas classes was caused by the Chrysler Torqueflite. Art Carr (his firm was called Arcadia Transmission) had been developing stronger Torqueflites for the Super Stock cars and Factory Experimental racers. The red, white and blue Dodge Charger is shown in front of Art's shop. The two Dodge Chargers were factory supercharged exhibition cars and helped start the development of the Funny Cars. Immediate success came with impressive performances in the Shores-Hess and Kohler Bros. Anglias. Art Carr, who was a racer also and even occasionally drove the Kohler's A/GS Anglia, continued to develop racing transmissions. His business was successful and today the Art Carr Co. is still manufacturing performance transmissions and components. (Photos courtesy of Art Carr)

185

The front suspension in this Austin (Cottrell-Reichard, Page 131) was typical of many of the mid-1960's blown gassers. It had a cross spring, early Ford style. This setup was fairly light, the spring centered the axle so no other locating bar was required and the frame could be cut off at the axle. (Photo courtesy of Len Cottrell - Photo by R. F. Bissell)

The AA/GS class Roadsters almost looked like a big blown Chrysler engine with a fiberglass roadster body behind it and a front axle assembly mounted on the front of it. This was Gary Burgins' (So.Calif.) red '27 T Roadster. Note the weight strapped to the front axle. The front wheels were Halibrand spindle mount (no hub) wheels. This photo was at OCIR (10-68). (Photo courtesy of Ron Arcangeli)

The stock frames were not strong or rigid enough for the horsepower of the supercharged engines. So the frames were strengthened by welding plates over the open side of the frame channel. This made the frame essentially rectangular tubing and it was called a boxed frame. Usually new cross members were added also. This frame is the boxed frame for Ed Middlebrook's Austin (Page 167). (Photo courtesy of Ed Middlebrook)

This Austin chassis was built during the first year of the NHRA's acceptance of custom frames in the Supercharged Gas Coupe classes (1968). The frame rails were 3" x 2" rectangular tubing. The front suspension used Koni coil-over-shocks. These spring units were light and the spring rates could be adjusted. The chassis is shown as it was ready for final assembly, with a mock-up late Hemi engine. It was built by Tom Chambliss for Mike Steinberg (No.Calif.) and the completed car is on Page 158. (Photo courtesy of Rod Barker)

The Corvette chassis that Tom Chambliss built for Larry and Gary Warren (No.Calif.) looked like this when they rolled it out of the garage (it even had "trick" tires). The Corvette had 3" x 2" rails and a full cage roll bar. This Corvette (Page 147) was not a topless car. Note the welded gussets on the rear end housing, like the dragsters all have today. Experience had taught Tom that the tremendous drive forces were actually bending the stock 8 3/4" Chrysler housings. Note that the springs had not been installed over the shocks yet. (Photo courtesy of Brooke Clark)

The Storck Bros. (So.Calif.) Opel GT had full roll cage roll bar and polished aluminum interior paneling. The flip-top body was easily removed for maintenance of the chassis or engine. Although most of the professionally built, often flip-top, chassis were for the AA/GS class cars, a number of them were built for the BB/GS class cars beginning about 1969. The Storck Bros. Opel GT is shown on Page 162. (Photo courtesy of Jeff Storck)

187

The chassis Jim Kirby built for Skip Hess' Mustang used a cross spring front suspension and coil springs with separate shocks in the rear. It was made for the SOHC Ford engine that Skip was building and was one of the first late model AA/GS in Southern California. The SOHC Ford engine was probably the widest engine that was used in the blown gas coupe classes. The completed car is shown on Page 132. (Photo courtesy of Skip Hess)

The professionally built chassis, built for AA/GS competition in the last years of the class, looked like a Funny Car chassis with the engine not as far back (10% rule). These AA/GS cars all had fuel and water tanks in front. The interesting independent front suspension was on the Miller-Nicholson flip-top Dodge (1970). The chassis with the 392 Chrysler and triangular tanks was Ron Rinauro's 1970 Dodge. The turbocharged car was the Mallicoat Bros. Barracuda with its impressive manifolding. (Photos courtesy of Brooke Clark, John Chambliss and Gary Mallicoat)

NHRA AA/GS NATIONAL RECORDS

CLASS	DATE	ET	MPH	NAME	P.P.C.I.
A/GS	9/59		124.65	George Montgomery	0
A/GS	5/60	12.02		Burt Looney	0
A/GS	6/60	11.84	124.83	Butler & Day	0
A/GS	7/60	11.67		Burt Looney	0
A/GS	7/60	11.67	126.58	Butler & Day	0
A/GS	7/60		126.58	Parker Construction	0
A/GS	7/60		130.05	George Montgomery	0
A/GS	9/60	11.53	131.57	George Montgomery	0
A/GS	10/60	11.40		Jim Butler	0
			1960 RECORDS CLOSED OUT		
A/GS	2/61	11.98	118.40	Pisano Brothers	4.00
A/GS	5/61	11.57	123.11	Jim Butler	4.00
A/GS	5/61	11.55	126.76	Cook & Howard	4.00
A/GS	5/61		128.02	George Montgomery	4.00
A/GS	6/61	11.28		Jim Butler	4.00
A/GS	6/61		128.02	George Montgomery	4.00
A/GS	7/61		129.12	Jim Butler	4.00
A/GS	9/61	10.83	131.77	George Montgomery	4.00
			1961 RECORDS CLOSED OUT		
A/GS	5/62	10.87	132.93	Hishfield, Finder	5.00
A/GS	6/62	10.55	135.56	Pittman, Edwards, Cizar	5.00
A/GS	6/62		137.61	Eddie Schartman	5.00
A/GS	7/62	10.25	140.84	Stone, Woods, Cook	5.00
A/GS	9/63	10.04		George Montgomery	6.00
A/GS	6/64		143.54	John Mazmanian	6.00
A/GS	9/64	9.99	146.10	K.S. Pittman	6.00
A/GS	7/65		147.54	Stone, Woods, Cook	6.00
A/GS	7/65	9.91		George Montgomery	6.00
A/GS	10/65	9.71	152.28	John Mazmanian	6.00
AA/G	5/66	9.71		George Montgomery	6.00
AA/G	7/66	9.64		Jack Merkel	6.00
AA/G	7/66	9.53		Jack Merkel	6.00
AA/G	8/66		154.10	George Montgomery	6.00
AA/G	9/66	9.34	155.97	George Montgomery	6.00
AA/G	6/67	8.93	162.16	George Montgomery	5.00
AA/GS	6/68	8.77	163.04	George Montgomery	5.00
AA/GS	9/68	8.72		George Montgomery	5.00
AA/GS	9/69	8.59		George Montgomery	5.00
AA/GS	5/70		165.44	George Montgomery	5.00
AA/GS	9/70	8.54		K.S. Pittman	5.00
AA/GS	5/72		163.50	Minimum	
AA/GS	6/72		166.97	George Montgomery	5.00
AA/GS	7/72	8.46		Brad Anderson	5.00
AA/GS	10/72		163.63	Minimum - 166.97 Record put in new AA/GST class.	
AA/GS(T)	6/72		166.97	George Montgomery	5.00
AA/GS	*5/73		158.17	Jim & Kathleen Oddy	8.00
AA/GS	*12/73	9.26		Tommy & Joanna Shinholster	8.00
AA/GS	2/74	8.92		Panella, Miner	8.00
AA/GS	9/74	8.88		Panella, Miner	8.00
AA/GS(T)	3/75	8.58		Minimum	
AA/GS	5/75	8.69	157.61	Steve Woods	7.00
AA/GS	6/75	8.58	160.42	Steve Woods	7.00
AA/GS	7/75	8.44	163.33	Panella, Miner	7.00

*BB/GS records put in at the start of 1974 because of the new 8 pound weight break.

NHRA BB/GS NATIONAL RECORDS

CLASS	DATE	ET	MPH	NAME	P.P.C.I.
B/GS	9/59		109.89	Junior Thompson	8.60
B/GS	5/60	12.05	119.04	Hirshfield, Howard, Cams	8.60
B/GS	7/60		119.40	Don Montgomery	8.60
B/GS	7/60	11.51	122.61	Wilton Zaiser	8.60
B/GS	11/60		125.87	Wilton Zaiser	8.60
			1960 RECORDS CLOSED OUT		
B/GS	2/61	11.11	127.04	Stone & Woods	8.60
B/GS	11/61	10.99	128.57	Stone, Woods, Cook	8.60
			1961 RECORDS CLOSED OUT		
B/GS	2/62		126.31	Stone, Woods, Cook	9.00
B/GS	4/62	12.01		Airoso Brothers	9.00
B/GS	5/62	11.20		Thompson, Cornelius, Pisano	9.00
B/GS	6/62	11.15	127.77	Thompson, Cornelius, Pisano	9.00
B/GS	8/62	11.03	129.68	Mike Marinoff	9.00
B/GS	2/63	10.60	130.97	Stone, Woods, Cook	9.00
B/GS	9/63		131.77	Jack Merkel	9.00
B/GS	8/64	10.42	135.13	Jack Merkel	9.00
B/GS	10/65		136.36	Mallicoat Brothers	9.00
B/GS	10/65	9.94		Ron Nunes	9.00
BB/G	9/67		137.61	Airoso Brothers	8.00
BB/G	9/67		139.96	Pittman & Edwards	8.00
BB/G	10/67	10.44		Minimum	8.00
BB/G	10/67	10.43		Marrs Boys	8.00
BB/GS	5/68	10.25		Eastern Automotive	8.00
BB/GS	5/68		142.85	Paul Day & Jerry Baird	8.00
BB/GS	6/68		143.31	Paul Day & Jerry Baird	8.00
BB/GS	8/68	9.96		Marrs Boys	8.00
BB/GS	9/68	9.89		Billy Holt & Fowler	8.00
BB/GS	9/68		143.76	Marrs Boys	8.00
BB/GS	6/69	9.79		Panella Trucking	8.00
BB/GS	6/69		144.92	Bob Chipper	8.00
BB/GS	7/69	9.76		Bob Chipper	8.00
BB/GS	9/69	9.74		Panella Trucking	8.00
BB/GS	9/69	9.58	146.81	Holt, Suski, Fowler	8.00
BB/GS	6/70	9.39		Mell Marrs & Phil Lukens	8.00
BB/GS	6/70		151.00	Steve Woods	8.00
BB/GS	9/71	9.38		Page, Vitar, Dyno Tech.	8.00
BB/GS	4/72		154.10	Shinholster, Lehmann, Holt	8.00
BB/GS(T)	9/72	9.02	158.45	Paul Pittman	8.00
BB/GS	5/73	9.27		Storck Brothers	8.00
BB/GS	5/73		158.17	Jim Oddy	8.00
BB/GS(T)	7/73	8.98		Panella, Miner	8.00
BB/GS	12/73	9.26		Tom Shinholster	8.00

NHRA CC/GS NATIONAL RECORDS

CLASS	DATE	ET	MPH	NAME	P.P.C.I.
C/GS	9/59		105.88	Doug Cook 10.60	
C/GS	7/60	12.08	116.73	Cook & Howard	10.60
C/GS	9/60		120.16	Cook & Howard	10.60
C/GS	11/60	11.84		Junior Thompson	10.60
			1960 RECORDS CLOSED OUT		
C/GS	2/61	11.28	123.68	Pittman & Edwards	10.60
C/GS	9/61		126.22	Pittman & Edwards	10.60
			1961 RECORDS CLOSED OUT		
C/GS	2/62	12.66	107.76	Pittman & Edwards	12.60
C/GS	6/62	12.10	114.94	Moody & Jones	12.60
C/GS	8/62	12.05		Moody & Jones	12.60
C/GS	9/62		115.08	Moody & Jones	12.60
C/GS	2/63		124.37	Brown Brothers	12.60
C/GS	6/63	11.99		Moody & Jones	12.60
C/GS	9/63	11.74		Tarantola & Cruciata	12.60
C/GS	8/64	11.62		Tarantola & Cruciata	12.60
C/GS	4/65	11.62		Levy, McLorn, Covas	12.00
C/GS	6/65	11.59		Leibham & Strine	12.00
C/GS	7/65	11.56		Tarantola & Cruciata	12.00
C/GS	9/65	11.52		Tarantola & Cruciata	12.00
CC/G	4/66		126.58	Marrs Boys 12.00	*
CC/G	7/66	11.25		Marrs Boys 12.00	
CC/G	7/66	11.17		Tarantola & Cruciata	12.00
CC/G	5/67	10.75	130.43	Marrs Boys	11.00
CC/GS	5/68	10.69		Bill Lindner	11.00
CC/GS	2/69	10.30		Minimum	10.00
CC/GS	5/69		136.15	Shinholster & Lehman	10.00
CC/GS	10/69	10.26		Shinholster & Lehman	10.00
CC/GS	6/70	10.00		Eddie Flora	10.00

Early and late views of the Author's 1941 BB/GS Willys. The early photo was a 1959 photo taken at the Santa Ana drag strip. The 342" Chrysler engine had a chain driven SCOT blower and six carburetor manifold that Phil Weiand made for me. The car was all steel, street legal, with mufflers and a Cadillac transmission. It had Moon discs on the front wheels and 8" wide Bruce's slicks (recaps) on the rear wheels. Like most of the cars there was no identification on the car. In 1970 the black Willys had changed. It had a 365" Chrysler engine and a B&M Torqueflite transmission. "Rockerhead" was a nickname given to me by a fellow member of our Lakes racing club (Glendale Coupe and Roadster Club) because in 1949 I was running an overhead valve (with Rocker arms) Buick straight eight when almost everyone else was racing with flatheads. The Willys ran B/GS, BB/G and BB/GS from 1960 to 1972. (Photos courtesy of Greg Sharp and the Author)

THE AUTHOR

I ran a Supercharged Gas Coupe for a period of thirteen years beginning in 1959. Like all drag racers I had some good times and a few unpleasant experiences. But overall I enjoyed it.

In the beginning, most of the Supercharged Gas Coupe competitors advanced up from the unblown gas classes. Usually a blower or complete blown engine was installed in the gas class car they had. The results ranged from good to expensive. Some of the guys competed in the Supercharged Coupe classes for a long time while others competed in them for only a brief period. A few competitors successfully earned a living running Supercharged Gassers.

My situation was different in that I had started with Lakes and Drag racing in 1948 and by 1957 was running one of the fastest full fendered, stock bodied A/Fuel coupes in the country. Then came the fuel ban and my car was instantly obsolete. Although it could have been switched to gas, the Altered class in which it would have to run was dominated by much smaller Fiats and Crosleys. So my S.C.O.T. blown 1951 Chrysler was removed and the '32 Ford 3-window coupe was sold (dumbest thing I ever did).

My new car turned out to be a 1941 Willys American coupe. I rescued it from a San Fernando Valley junk yard for $40. I had always considered the Willys to be an ugly and pregnant version of the 1940 Ford. But the light weight of the Willys and the excellent performances that K. S. Pittman was getting with his recently completed '41 Willys convinced me that the Willys was the way to go, ugly or not.

The Willys was ready to run in 1959 with my 331" Chrysler. In 1960 the NHRA set up the Supercharged Gas Coupe classes and my Willys fit into B/GS. So for the next twelve years my Willys competed in the B/GS class, also known as BB/G and BB/GS.

Drag racing was a hobby for me. I enjoyed building the engines and running the car. And it was a wonderful way to put aside the daily problems of my job. But like many guys over thirty I had a family, including three great kids, and so was limited on how much money could be spent on the car. As a result the Willys was usually a little behind on technology, especially in the chassis and transmission areas. In spite of this the engine was usually strong and the Willys usually hit excellent speeds. Naturally after about 1968 the Willys was obsolete.

In 1968 I was able to get the local strips to give us an opportunity to put on BB/G shows. With the help

of the Pittman Bros., the Marrs Boys, Dave Fentress, Jack Carlson and several others, the Southern California BB/G circuit was up and running. We tried to offer an inexpensive show for drag strip managers to use in addition to the primary show. Usually the BB/G shows, which soon became eight-car shows, were booked to run with a AA/Fuel Altered, AA/GS or Injected Funny Car show.

The Southern California BB/GS circuit ran meets from 1968 to 1972. Most of the meets were held at the three major Los Angeles area strips (Long Beach, Orange County and Irwindale). However we did get a few "away from home" meets at Las Vegas, Sacramento and Holtville. But by 1972 changes in drag racing and the economy caused the drag strip managers to cut their expenses way back. The result was the end of the mini-shows for us and almost everyone else except for the Professional class cars.

The BB/GS circuit was great. We had heads-up racing, won some money (no one got rich in BB/GS) and even ran some round-robin races so that everyone could run three races. There was a points competition with a banquet, trophies and awards at the end of the season. In addition the drag strips gave us professional status treatment.

When our racing dried up in 1972 my Willys was set aside with the idea that eventually it would become a street rod. It is still buried in the corner of the garage as other street rod projects have been done (No, it is not for sale).

One of the interesting things about doing the research for this book has been that I can now see very clearly what I should have done to the engine and chassis back in the '60's to have a winner.

It has been fun reviewing all the events and activities of the old gasser days. I have really enjoyed talking with so many of the blown gas coupe competitors, many of whom I knew back then and others who I had never met. Also I have enjoyed talking to many drag racing enthusiasts who still today think the Supercharged Gas Coupes were "special".

My previous three books were on the earlier days of hot rodding, so this book is about almost the next generation of hot rodders. This book is meant to tell what happened in the interesting and usually exciting blown gas coupe classes during the time period when drag racing was changing from a hobby to a professional operation. I hope it brings back memories for the guys who were there and gives others a real look at the Supercharged Gas era.

The Southern California BB/GS circuit conducted races from 1968 to 1972. These photos were taken at Lions, where C. J. Hart was the Manager. The race photo shows my Willys and the Mel Marrs-Phil Lukens Corvette. The Corvette said CC/GS because it had recently run at an NHRA meet with Paul Pittman's small Chrysler but was now back in the BB/GS class. The car in the background was Milt Stewart and Bill Cook's Chevy panel truck ("Blue Power"). (Photos taken by John Ewald)

The Authors' Willys looked like this just prior to its retirement in 1972. The best times were 144 mph and 9.85 sec. It was all steel except for the one-piece fiberglass front fender-hood assembly. (Photo courtesy of the Author)